The Postcolonial Short Story

Also by Paul March-Russell:

LEGACIES OF ROMANTICISM: Literature, Culture, Aesthetics (*Ed. with Carmen Casaliggi*) forthcoming

MODERNISM AND SCIENCE FICTION forthcoming

RUSKIN IN PERSPECTIVE: Contemporary Essays (*Ed. with Carmen Casaliggi*)

THE SHORT STORY: An Introduction

UNCANNY STORIES by May Sinclair (*Ed.*)

THE WHEEL OF GOD by George Egerton (*Ed.*)

The Postcolonial Short Story

Contemporary Essays

Edited by

Maggie Awadalla and Paul March-Russell

First published 2013 by
PALGRAVE MACMILLAN

Palgrave Macmillan in the UK is an imprint of Macmillan Publishers Limited,
registered in England, company number 785998, of Houndmills, Basingstoke,
Hampshire RG21 6XS.

Palgrave Macmillan in the US is a division of St Martin's Press LLC,
175 Fifth Avenue, New York, NY 10010.

Palgrave Macmillan is the global academic imprint of the above companies
and has companies and representatives throughout the world.

Palgrave® and Macmillan® are registered trademarks in the United States,
the United Kingdom, Europe and other countries.

ISBN 978–0–230–31338–5

This book is printed on paper suitable for recycling and made from fully
managed and sustained forest sources. Logging, pulping and manufacturing
processes are expected to conform to the environmental regulations of the
country of origin.

A catalogue record for this book is available from the British Library.

A catalog record for this book is available from the Library of Congress.

10 9 8 7 6 5 4 3 2 1
22 21 20 19 18 17 16 15 14 13

Printed and bound in Great Britain by
CPI Antony Rowe, Chippenham and Eastbourne

Contents

Acknowledgements

We would like to thank Paula Kennedy and her assistant, Benjamin Doyle, at Palgrave Macmillan for their patience and encouragement in bringing this project to fruition. We would also like to thank our contributors without whom there simply would not have been a book. Lastly, we would like to thank our respective families in Kent, in Cairo and elsewhere.

Notes on Contributors

Shola Adenekan recently completed a PhD on African literature in the digital age at the Centre of West African Studies, University of Birmingham. He is also a freelance journalist for BBC News Online, jobs.ac.uk and *The Guardian*, and editor of the online journal thenew blackmagazine.com. With Helen Cousins, he convened a roundtable discussion for the 2009 Cadbury Conference *OHUN TITUN: New Directions in African and Caribbean Writing* on 'The Internet and New Writers from Africa'.

Maggie Awadalla is Coordinator of Arabic at Imperial College, London and also teaches Comparative Literature at the University of Kent. She was previously a Research Fellow for the project, *Europe in the Middle East: The Middle East in Europe*, at Wissenschaft College, Berlin. She has published widely on Arabic literature and culture and, with Rana Dayoub, co-edited the journal *Postcolonial Forum*. Her main research interest focuses upon women's writing in the Arab world.

Lee Skallerup Bessette is an Instructor of English at Morehead State University. She has previously published on Nalo Hopkinson and the Haitian writer Dany Laferrière. She is currently working on a project that explores Hopkinson's challenges to the dilemmas of colonialism and postcolonialism through speculative and fantastic fiction.

Antara Chatterjee is a lecturer at an undergraduate college in Calcutta, affiliated to the State University, West Bengal, and has recently completed her PhD at the University of Leeds. Her thesis examines home and identity in Bengali diasporic fiction and analyses their relationship to the space of Bengal.

Barbara Cooke is a PhD candidate at the University of East Anglia. Her interdisciplinary project, *Oil Men: The Twinned Lives of Arnold Wilson and Morris Young*, combines archival research with historiographical and biographical techniques. She has organized a conference on biography, history and myth (November 2009) and has presented a paper at the *Narrative 2009* conference at the University of Birmingham.

Helen Cousins is Senior Lecturer in Literature at Newman University College, Birmingham. Her research interests include women's literature of the African Diaspora, black feminism and popular practices of reading. Recent publications include *Emerging Perspectives on Yvonne Vera* (2012), co-edited with Pauline Dodgson-Katiyo, and *The Richard and Judy Book Club Reader* (2012), co-edited with Jenni Ramone.

Ailsa Cox is Reader in English and Writing at Edge Hill University, and the author of *Alice Munro* (2004) and *Writing Short Stories* (2005). She is the editor of *The Short Story* (2009), *Teaching the Short Story* (Palgrave, 2011), the journal *Short Fiction in Theory and Practice* and co-editor of the online journal *21*. Her short story collection, *The Real Louise and Other Stories*, was published in 2009.

Philip Holden is Associate Professor in the Department of English Language and Literature, National University of Singapore. Recent publications include *Autobiography and Decolonization* (2008), *The Routledge History of Southeast Asian Writing in English* (2009), co-authored with Rajeev Patke, *Race and Multiculturalism in Malaysia and Singapore* (2009), co-edited with Daniel P.S. Goh, Matilda Gabrielpillai and Khoo Gaik Cheng, and *Writing Singapore: An Historical Anthology of Singapore Literature in English* (2009), co-edited with Angelia Poon and Shirley Geok-Lin. He is also a practising short story writer and vice-president of Singapore Heritage Society, an independent NGO that works on heritage-related education, advocacy and publication.

M. Catherine Jonet is Assistant Professor of Women's Studies at New Mexico State University. Her research focuses upon the representation of women in literature, film and visual/digital media as well as women's own cultural productions. She is also a translator and conceptual artist.

Michelle Keown is Lecturer in English Literature at the University of Edinburgh. She is a member of the Academic Council for the

Centre for New Zealand Studies (Birkbeck College, London), the Publications and Online Journal committees for the UK Postcolonial Studies Association, and editorial and advisory boards for the *Journal of Postcolonial Writing, Ka Mate Ka Ora* (journal of the New Zealand Electronic Poetry Centre), the *CNZS Bulletin of New Zealand Studies* and *Dreadlocks* (a journal of Pacific studies). Her publications include *Postcolonial Pacific Writing: Representations of the Body* (2005), *Pacific Islands Writing: The Postcolonial Literatures of Aotearoa/New Zealand and Oceania* (2007) and *Comparing Postcolonial Diasporas* (Palgrave, 2009), co-edited with David Murray and James Proctor. She is also one of the editors of *The Edinburgh Introduction to Studying English Literature* (2010).

Paul March-Russell teaches Comparative Literature at the University of Kent. He is the author of *The Short Story: An Introduction* (2009) and co-editor, with Carmen Casaliggi, of *Ruskin in Perspective* (2007) and *Legacies of Romanticism* (2012). He edits the SF Storyworlds series published by Gylphi.

Alex Padamsee is Lecturer in English and American Literature at the University of Kent. His previous publications include *Representations of Indian Muslims in British Colonial Discourse* (Palgrave, 2005). In 2010, he organized a conference at Kent on the South Asian short story. His current research focuses upon the idea of community in postcolonial Indian literature, ranging from the rhetoric of Hindu nationalist writers in the 1930s and 1940s to the fictions of Anita Desai and the films of Satyajit Ray.

Caroline Rooney is Professor in English and American Literature at the University of Kent. She is currently a Fellow of the ESRC Global Uncertainties scheme leading a major research project on 'Radical Distrust'. She serves on the editorial boards of *Atlantis*, *The Oxford Literary Review* and *Postgraduate English*, and is consultant editor for the Routledge Research in Postcolonial Literatures series. Her publications include *African Literature, Animism and Politics* (2000), *Book Unbinding* (2005), co-written with the visual artist Vera Dieterich, and *Decolonising Gender* (2007).

Introduction: The Short Story and the Postcolonial

Maggie Awadalla and Paul March-Russell

In 'The Storyteller' (1936), his meditation upon the death of orality, Walter Benjamin writes:

> We have witnessed the evolution of the 'short story', which has removed itself from oral tradition and no longer permits that slow piling one on top of the other of thin, transparent layers which constitutes the most appropriate picture of the way in which the perfect narrative is revealed through the layers of a variety of retellings. (92)

For Benjamin, the short story exemplifies the cultural tendency for abbreviation, a symptom of the economic, bureaucratic and technological organization of society that 'quite gradually' has 'removed narrative from the realm of living speech and at the same time is making it possible to see a new beauty in what is vanishing' (86). Benjamin's melancholic diagnosis, 'Death is the sanction of everything that the storyteller can tell' (93), seeks to recover those trace elements of the oral tradition that he finds, especially, in the work of Nikolai Leskov but also J.P. Hebel, Rudyard Kipling and Edgar Allan Poe. Benjamin is unclear as to exactly when the oral tradition began to disappear – although its demise seems to coincide with the development of print culture – and he tends to mythologize the figure of the storyteller as an epic bard for whom 'counsel woven into the fabric of real life is wisdom' (86). He is equally unclear on the figure of the short story writer, the diminished counterpart of the storyteller, although Benjamin might have been thinking of someone like O. Henry, a hugely popular writer yet increasingly criticized for his allegedly mechanical and formulaic fiction (O'Brien, Pattee; a more positive response is offered by Éjxenbaum). These omissions indicate, however, the poetic quality of Benjamin's analysis. He is not attempting to construct a history for the decline of orality: 'nothing would be more fatuous than to want to see in it merely a "symptom of decay", let alone a "modern" symptom' (86). Instead, in concert with Benjamin's philosophic method, he is seeking to freeze the momentum of history since 'thinking involves not only the flow of thoughts, but their arrest as well': 'in this structure [one] recognizes the sign of a Messianic cessation of happening, or, put differently, a revolutionary chance in the fight for the oppressed past' (254). By compelling myth and history into a dialectic, in which the condition of storytelling acts as the focus, Benjamin mounts a defence against the forces of instrumental reason that would not only abbreviate critical thinking but also imaginative wisdom.

Despite its disregard for empirical analysis, Benjamin's essay is a valuable starting-point for the consideration of storytelling and, more particular, the relationship between the short story and modernity. Whereas Benjamin is dismissive of the short story form, the writers that he cites (to whom could be added Joseph Conrad, Guy de Maupassant or Ivan Turgenev) can retrospectively be seen as pioneers of the medium. Yet, the short story has a much more troubled – and troubling – relationship to modernity than Benjamin necessarily suggests. The form is shadowed by its oral past, partially because of its fusion of the folktale with the sketch, the latter tending towards realism whereas the former tends towards fantasy. Postmodern collections, such as Angela Carter's *The Bloody Chamber* (1979), are a bricolage of folktale remnants mediated through other cultural debris. Postmodernists (John Barth, Italo Calvino), feminists (Emma Donoghue, Ali Smith) and urban fantasists (Neil Gaiman, China Miéville) frequently turn to the language, content and imagery of the folkloric tradition as part of their individual practice. Their formal experiments disrupt the composed authority of the printed page, and by so doing, connect with the early modern storytellers (Giambattista Basile, Giovanni Boccaccio, Geoffrey Chaucer) whose tales are marked by the use of accent, idiom, register and pastiche that foreground the ways in which their narratives are framed. By breaking frame and drawing attention to the writerliness of the text, these same literary techniques invoke their oral roots: the pauses, hesitancies and digressions of living speech. It is in this respect that, contra Benjamin, a tradition can be observed to run from the folktale to the contemporary short story.

A similar assumption can be made in terms of the relationship between orality and the postcolonial short story. In the case, for example, of modern African storytelling, the use of folklore and the emulation of living speech draw upon the formal properties of oral tales and the conventions of their performance. Both the presence and continuing development of Africa's verbal traditions forge a link between oral and print cultures. Harold Scheub argues that Africa's close proximity to Egypt, with its artistic combination of the oral and the literary, offered the necessary continuation and homogeneity of Africa's oral panegyric and lyric tradition (1–72). With the introduction of Arab culture via Egypt in the seventh century, the close ties between the oral and written word continued to develop. Most revealing is that, in the Arabic tradition, the word *adab* (literature) refers to both the oral and the written word. With the spread of the Arabic language a semi-popular literature appeared in which 'the history and legends were worked into connected romances in interspersed prose and verse, suitable for public recitation' (Lewis 9–10). The stories of Antar (Antarah Ibn Shaddād al-ʿAbsī) or *The Thousand and One Nights* exemplify narratives that have become the genesis of a long literary tradition.

A focus, however, on the sustained presence of orality in postcolonial short stories is problematic since the oral practice of the performed tale evokes a communal setting of participatory taletelling (Daymond 331–46). In contrast to the face-to-face communication between narrator and audience, the postcolonial short story often occurs in isolation from its readers. This sense of alienation is complemented by the postcolonial short story's emergence, as many of the authors in this collection note, as an expressive medium for themes of fragmentation, displacement, diaspora and identity.

A discussion of orality and postcolonial short stories raises at least two questions. First, how did the oral forms respond to the cultural effects of both colonialism and foreign influences? Second, to what extent do the multiple cultural resources affect the form of the postcolonial short story? Orality either could be seen as a disruptive element within the short story or, as Mary Louise Pratt suggests, could be regarded as a trope to which the short story is drawn (107–8). In the postcolonial short story, orality could be seen as evidence of cultural survival, acting as one of the contrary means by which the onslaught of colonization and the eradication of indigenous cultures are challenged. Frantz Fanon, in *The Wretched of the Earth* (1961), calls for the involvement of the entire population in the process of nation-building, especially at a grass-roots level, and argues that it is one of the crucial elements for the success of national representation. In this instance, the short story's association with the oral roots of folk culture raises further issues upon the political process of nation-hood. In passing, though, it might explain why the short story has been keenly used by postcolonial writers and critically endorsed by literary awards such as the Caine Prize, established in 2000, whereas in the West there remains a sense that the short story is marked by critical and popular neglect (May 14–25).

This tendency most probably arises from the development of the short story in the Western context as the mirror image to the realist novel. Whereas nineteenth-century realism tends towards a hierarchy of discourses, in which the voices of the narrator and the central characters are given priority over the supporting characters (Belsey 70–2), this hierarchy is inverted in the short story. The lack of space, so that language is distilled and both character and plot development are subordinated to the needs of the situation, encourages writers to concentrate upon the characters – and the voices – more often relegated to a minor role in the novel. Mark Twain's monologue, 'A True Story Repeated Word for Word as I Heard It' (1874), delivered by a freed African-American slave, is a pertinent example. Yet, as this instance suggests, orality and agency – who gets to speak of what and how – are bound up with political, historical and cultural distinctions that imprint the text. The short story's inversion of discursive hierarchies is not, of itself, dissident: dissidence arises from who and what the short story focuses upon. The form's potential capacity for dissidence is magnified by its ambiguous cultural position: on the one hand, a visibly commercial product residing in popular magazines and sub-literary genres, and on the other hand, an artistic medium praised by writers for its technical difficulty and associated with small-press, avant-garde or counter-cultural titles. Simultaneously a product of mass and minority culture, the short story defies categorization.

In a society that Benjamin correctly sees as driven by 'the secular productive forces of history' (86), this resistance to being either high or low culture has determined the short story's relatively marginal position to that of the novel. Marginality could, following Benjamin's associate Theodor Adorno, be recuperated in the form of a negative dialectic – the value of the short story arises from what it is not – but this move would only privilege those short stories that most appropriately fit with Adorno's conception of the avant-garde (Baudelaire, Beckett, Kafka). The short story, instead, exists within the 'torn halves' of art and culture (Adorno and Benjamin 130), and it is this liminal position that produces a form rich in both tension and possibility. Nadine Gordimer hints at something of its measure when she describes the short story as 'a fragmented and restless form' (Gordimer 265). Not a fragment of something larger but complete in itself: striven with its own fault-lines.

Adrian Hunter has recently proposed the possibility of reading the short story in terms of, what Gilles Deleuze and Félix Guattari have called, 'minor literature' (Hunter 219–38). They define minor literature as 'that which a minority constructs within a major language'. It consists of three elements: 'deterritorialization', whereby language is displaced and contorted by the pressure of colonization; politicization, whereby the limited spaces in which language can operate means that it connects 'immediately to politics'; and lastly, 'collective value', whereby, since 'the political domain has contaminated every statement', all expressions of the minor culture 'already constitutes a common action' that permits 'the conception of something other than a literature of masters'. In emphasizing the 'strange and minor uses' to which the major language is put, Deleuze and Guattari propose minor literature as a type of bricolage that works upon the remains of the dominant culture (16–17). De- and reterritorialization are consequently simultaneous processes in which their very parameters are constantly being rethought.

Although derived from postmodern theory, the concept of minor literature is highly suggestive for rethinking the liminal, open-ended and fragmented form of the short story. Until now, though, it has had more application within postcolonial studies. Consequently, minor literature is one of the frameworks by which the short story and the postcolonial could be read together. (There are other possible approaches and these are discussed elsewhere in the collection.)

For example, the emphasis upon orality that Pratt sees in the work of Mexican, African-American and Afro-Caribbean short story writers can, at least partially, be explained in terms of minor literature (108). Benjamin's Eurocentric account, accentuated by its historical and ideological contexts, tends towards pathos by presenting as universal the displacement of traditional communal structures, which supported the rituals of storytelling, by the economic forces of industralization, urbanization and secularization. In developing and postcolonial nations, patterns of economic and technological development have been far less clear (even) than in the Western capitalist model. The sharp divides between rich and poor, between the city and the country, and in literacy and mortality, which have undercut the independence movements since 1945, have also meant that oral and performance cultures have endured within the making of postcolonial literature. Orality becomes a resource for North African and Afro-Caribbean writers (see, for example, the respective chapters by Caroline Rooney and Lee Bessette) to shadow the importation of Western modernity into indigenous cultures: to counter the demise that Benjamin tends to see as inevitable. The short story becomes a site in which these tensions can be played out rather than subsumed or hypothetically resolved as melancholic pathos.

Orality plays a part, too, in the form of memory and anecdote within the exiled imagination. The disappearance of communal and intergenerational ties, which Benjamin regards as melancholically beautiful, is for the former colonial subject, whose social condition has often been represented as grotesque or sublime, intensely political. The fact of diaspora, to which can also be added the fact of globalization, mean that memory inexorably becomes a political act as seen, for instance, in the chapters by Antara Chatterjee, M. Catherine Jonet and Paul March-Russell. The displacement of communities, either by enforced or by voluntary migration, complicates Frank O'Connor's thesis in *The Lonely Voice* (1963) that the short story thrives in transitional societies, whose foundations are not yet established, so that the voices of submerged populations have an opportunity in which to be heard. O'Connor's study, which is imbued with a melancholy similar to that of Benjamin's essay, turns upon a relatively unsophisticated account of community and historical development that Michelle Keown takes to task in her reading of the New Zealand writer Patricia Grace and her successors. Like

Keown, Alex Padamsee registers language (in this instance Urdu) as a key factor to which O'Connor fails to give due emphasis, but which Padamsee shows to be integral to the undecidability of Partition and its historical aftermath for India and Pakistan. At the same time, the comparative studies by Keown, Ailsa Cox and Philip Holden suggest communities of writers, who not only celebrate the particularities of geographical space, but whose intergenerational dialogue also overlaps the borders of history, language and location.

A dialectic that emerges around the notion of community may help to explain the current collection's emphasis upon women's writing as opposed to Benjamin's exclusively male account or O'Connor's misguided critique of Katherine Mansfield. Women are central, even as they are marginalized, to the independence movements due to their biological and social functions. Their paradoxical and ambiguous place within colonial and postcolonial society renders their lives suitable subject matter for the short story. Furthermore, their stories complement Sabry Hafez's observation that the short story concentrates upon 'the small fragments of the large fresco' (38) rather than the panoramic view that tends to be the proper business of the novel. Women's writing sits awkwardly in relation to the political act of nation-building and postcolonial literature's attempt to describe, what Fredric Jameson once controversially termed, the national allegory (65–88). The tendency instead, as Jonet's study of lesbian short fiction from the Caribbean argues, is towards the interstitial. Yet, it is here that the short story is also found to be at its most political, and most open to the needs of men *and* women, for example in Barbara Cooke's emphasis upon the distressed body in South African fiction.

It is surprising then that, until recently, there has been little critical attention paid to the postcolonial short story, with only one previous major collection: *Telling Stories: Postcolonial Short Fiction in English* (2001), which was marred by the death of its principal editor, Jacqueline Bardolph. Part of the reason may be due to the fact that the short story tends to appear in ephemeral publications: either the mass circulation or little magazine. Yet, these titles have played a substantial role in the development of postcolonial cultures while a number of them have received academic support: for example, *Okike* following its founder's, Chinua Achebe, relocation to Massachusetts; *Kunapipi*, launched by Anne Rutherford, an Australian academic then working in the Netherlands; and *Wasafiri*, which was founded at the University of Kent in 1984 and continues to be edited from within the Open University although published by Routledge. *Okike*, possibly the most celebrated and certainly one of the most enduring little magazines, was founded in the aftermath of the Biafran War with the intention of sustaining Igbo culture in Nigeria but quickly added to that a Pan-African dimension. In its range and quality of writing, and in its readiness for controversy, *Okike* is a central text in the history of postcolonial writing from Africa. South African titles by contrast, such as *Drum* (especially in the second half of the 1950s) and *Staffrider* in the 1970s and 1980s, are intriguing because of their popular base. Whereas *Okike* was, to some extent, a product of elite culture, *Drum* especially was a general interest magazine which, as a consequence, provided an outlet for short fiction. The broad appeal of *Drum* and *Staffrider*, itself a riposte to the segregated policies of the apartheid regime, was key to their survival. By comparing the publishing history of all three African magazines, it is possible to describe how the short story survives within the spaces of elite and popular culture, and that this ambiguous existence attests to its political potential. Similarly, magazines such as *Bim*, *Kyk-over-Al*, *Savacou* and *Voices* are integral to the history of Caribbean literature; both within the region itself and as part of the post-war diaspora (see Donnell). During the past decade, the Caine Prize, which awards African short story writers published in English, has further played an important role in promoting and supporting the genre. Its influential patrons include Wole Soyinka, Nadine Gordimer, J.M. Coetzee and Chinua Achebe. Elsewhere, there exist numerous samizdat publications and increasingly, as Shola Adenekan and Helen Cousins discuss in their chapter, writing on the internet. Yet, what is seriously needed, and which the present volume can only register, is a detailed analysis of the role that magazine culture has played within the development of postcolonial literatures.

In taking what might be deemed to be of marginal interest – the short story – and placing it centre-stage, we hope to have extended the postcolonial critique of centres and margins that underwrites the hierarchical practice of Empire but which, arguably, has been sustained by the neo-colonial activities of globalization. In this scenario, the restless fragmentation of the short story has a vital role to play. Although the short story form has been of significance to

older writers, such as Achebe, Gordimer, Bessie Head, Doris Lessing
and Samuel Selvon (and some of these writers are addressed in the
earlier Bardolph collection), for this anthology we have focused
upon the work of writers from the mid-1970s to the present day.
Although, again, the roots of postcolonial criticism lie in the period
of the independence movements – in the work of intellectuals such
as Aimé Césaire, Frantz Fanon and C.L.R. James – postcolonial studies
(as they are currently conceived) have their origin in the late 1970s
when, as Robert Young describes, the political concerns of postcolonialism and the intellectual interests of post-structuralism converged
in texts such as Edward Said's *Orientalism* (1978). This convergence
continued to be refined during the 1980s and 1990s, in the work of
principal theorists such as Homi Bhabha and Gayatri Chakravorty
Spivak, often in correspondence with the interests of postmodern
theory and identity politics. Yet, at the same time as these intellectual developments, new and continuing patterns in migration,
diaspora and globalization were radically affecting the postcolonial
experience. At the start of a new decade, after an already turbulent
start to the new millennium, it is time to re-examine the current state
of postcolonial studies through reference not only to contemporary
writing but also to the media through which writers have chosen
to express themselves. A re-evaluation of forms such as the short
story, we argue, is integral to a wider reconsideration of postcolonial
studies as a whole.

One consequence that we see of questioning the borders through
which postcolonial criticism has operated is a renewed appreciation
of eclecticism. During the same period that postcolonial studies rose
to prominence, notions of the eclectic became intermingled with
postmodern thought, for example in the wake of pioneering studies such as *Learning from Las Vegas* (Venturi et al. 1972) where the
architecture of the Strip is regarded as a wilful abandonment of taste
and a celebratory elision of high and low art. Similar senses, where
the eclectic is symptomatic of postmodern surface, runs throughout
the influential work of postmodern theorists such as Jean Baudrillard
and Fredric Jameson. This emptying of content, which the eclectic
appears to signify, runs contrary to the tenor of postcolonial studies
where the physical and historical embodiment of pain and oppression has been of central importance. Yet, in exploring contemporary postcolonial short fiction, eclecticism becomes one of its chief

characteristics as an indicator both of the short story's technical
flexibility and cultural marginality as well as a symptom of globalization. In a global culture that, as David Punter suggests, is saturated
by the effects of postcolonialism, eclecticism emerges not as a sign of
historical evacuation but as an entry-point into the messy complexity of the postcolonial world. Consequently, the following essays
are eclectic in their content and approach although themes emerge
that interlace them, such as cultural memory, the city, diaspora,
community, gender, sexuality and embodiment.

The first three chapters tackle the notion of legacy in contemporary
postcolonial writing, thereby rooting current literature within the
recent historical past. In particular, Alex Padamsee focuses upon the
Urdu short story in order to explore the cultural memory of Partition,
one of the decisive events within the shaping of the postcolonial
world. Padamsee argues, following the work of trauma theorists
such as Cathy Caruth, that the agonistic structures of these stories
not only mediate the horrors of Partition but that a resulting aesthetic of repetition also disturbs the possibilities of communicable
experience. By contrast, in tracing the influence of Patricia Grace
upon contemporary Māori short fiction, Michelle Keown describes
how indigenous writers have reclaimed the right to communicate
their experience often through such key areas as the politics of
representation, bilingualism and the relationship between politics
and aesthetics. Lastly, Philip Holden sets into context contemporary
Singaporean short fiction and shows how Singaporean writers have
rethought their imaginary community. In particular, by emphasizing the short story's commercial roots, Holden argues that instead
of producing a dependent and instrumental form of literature these
links connect the short story to larger narratives of commerce, politics, tradition and family: constituent elements in the Singaporean
social imaginary. Holden, Keown and Padamsee insist upon the
particularities of historical experience, specificities that are often lost
within – as Holden suggests – rhetorically persuasive accounts such
as Benedict Anderson's notion of imagined communities.

Following Holden's analysis of Singaporean writing, the next three
chapters consider the roles of urban and diasporic experience. The
city operates paradoxically in postcolonial writing both as a symbol
of modernity, imbued with a Western teleology, and as a repository

of memory that works against that same historical schema. Ailsa Cox compares Alice Munro's *Runaway* (2004) with Nancy Lee's debut collection, *Dead Girls* (2002), in the context of Vancouver and its representation as a postmodern landscape. Cox's consideration of place, though, is mediated through the motifs of severance and dismemberment that exist as graphic markers for the dislocation of Vancouver society, especially for its female inhabitants. Another postmodern trope for exploring urban space – psychogeography – is reassessed by Paul March-Russell through a comparative analysis of the work of Iain Sinclair, looking especially at the colonial subtexts of his composite novel *Downriver* (1991), and Syed Manzurul (Manzu) Islam's collection, *The Mapmakers of Spitalfields* (1997). March-Russell examines the Situationist rhetoric of the concept, traces of which can be found in the work of later theorists such as Michel de Certeau and Deleuze and Guattari, to argue that Islam performs his own *détournement* upon critical theory and upon Sinclair's latter-day Romanticism in order to describe the condition of the émigré. Lastly, Antara Chatterjee examines the notion of home in relation to the work of Jhumpa Lahiri and the experience of Bengalis and their children in North America. Drawing upon theorists such as Bhabha, Chatterjee grounds theoretical notions of hybridity within domestic activities such as cooking that afford a provisional sense of inherited identity. Chatterjee relates the contestation of identities to the short story form as a type of photomontage that exposes the operation of culture and history.

Political events since 2001, including the recent wave of revolutions in the Middle East, have demanded greater understanding between East and West. The next two chapters concentrate upon writing from the Arab world. Following Chatterjee, formal issues are also explored by Caroline Rooney in her reading of the Egyptian writers Ahmed Alaidy and Khaled Al Khamissi. In rejecting the Western terminology of short story cycles, sequences and composite novels, Rooney proposes the notion of the *maqāma* (meaning literally 'assembly') in order to explore the interaction between the novel and the short story. Rooney's choice of nomenclature for her chosen texts allows her to relate the shifting borders of genre to the interstitial spaces between the public and the private, the individual and the nation-state, notions of ethical, democratic and civic space that have been sharply foregrounded by the recent events of the Arab Spring.

Maggie Awadalla complements Rooney's analysis of literary form and democratic expression by examining how Arab women's short stories have challenged earlier encodings of the gendered body to address the dilemma of gender and confinement. These stories, too, explore the possibilities of reclaiming both public and private space but in a predominantly patriarchal society.

In starting the final quartet of chapters that focus upon short story writing from Africa and the Caribbean, M. Catherine Jonet follows the consideration of liminal spaces in Awadalla and Rooney by exploring the place of lesbian short fiction within the Caribbean. Whilst debating the advantages of the short story form for the expression of a sexual minority that has been discriminated against within its own culture, Jonet argues that the fiction produced by lesbian women acts as a commentary upon the process of diaspora into and out of the Caribbean. Themes of expression and transcendence are also investigated by Lee Skallerup Bessette in the work of another Caribbean author, the fantasy writer Nalo Hopkinson. Bessette explores Hopkinson's use of fantastic techniques in her collection *Skin Folk* (2001) as a means of problematizing the relationship of black women to their bodies. An important characteristic of Hopkinson's work, which also stems from her role as a genre writer, is her belief in utopia as both political aspiration and instrument of change. In contrast, Barbara Cooke concentrates upon depictions of the distressed body in fictions by J.M. Coetzee, Nadine Gordimer and Etienne van Heerden to dramatize the political condition of apartheid South Africa. Drawing upon Marxist and psychoanalytic critiques from John Berger, Julia Kristeva and Elaine Scarry, Cooke asks what analogies can be drawn from descriptions of the body in an animalistic or abject state. The final chapter, by Shola Adenekan and Helen Cousins, turns instead to the disembodiment of cyberspace and explores the uses to which the internet is being put by young African writers, especially in relation to questions of national identity in the seemingly stateless arena of digital communication.

In concluding with contemporary modes of self-publication, the collection has effectively come full circle. If the trauma of Partition was profoundly undecidable, so that this sense of the indefinite has succeeded to haunt postcolonial literature, then we also exist on the cusp of some indefinable future that, nevertheless, will be determined by the interaction of new technologies, unpredictable

patterns of economic development and cultures imbued with the
vestiges of tradition, especially those of orality and the folkloric. In
our cross-section of writing from the past 35 years, we hope to have
displayed the vital role that the short story has had – and will have –
in the transformations of postcolonial literature then, now and into
the future.

Works cited

Adorno, Theodor W. and Walter Benjamin. *The Complete Correspondence,
1928–1940*. Trans. Nicholas Walker, ed. Henri Lonitz. Cambridge: Polity
Press, 1999.
Belsey, Catherine. *Critical Practice*. London: Methuen, 1980.
Benjamin, Walter. *Illuminations*. Trans. Harry Zohn, ed. Hannah Arendt.
London: Fontana, 1992.
Daymond, Margaret J. 'Complementary Oral and Written Narrative
Conventions: Sindiwe Magona's Autobiography and Short Story Sequence.'
Journal of Southern African Studies 28.2 (2002): 331–46.
Deleuze, Gilles and Félix Guattari. *Kafka: Toward a Minor Literature*. Trans.
Dana Polan. Minneapolis: University of Minnesota Press, 1986.
Donnell, Alison. *Twentieth-Century Caribbean Literature*. London: Routledge,
2006.
Éjxenbaum, B.M. 'O. Henry and the Theory of the Short Story.' *The New Short
Story Theories*. Ed. Charles E. May. Athens OH: Ohio University Press, 1994.
81–8.
Fanon, Frantz. *The Wretched of the Earth*. Trans. Constance Farrington.
London: Penguin, 2001.
Gordimer, Nadine. 'The Flash of Fireflies.' *The New Short Story Theories*. Ed.
Charles E. May. Athens OH: Ohio University Press, 1994. 263–7.
Hafez, Sabry. *The Quest for Identities: The Development of the Modern Arabic Short
Story*. London: Saqi, 2008.
Hunter, Adrian. 'Story into History: Alice Munro's Minor Literature.' *English*
207 (2004): 219–38.
Jameson, Fredric. 'Third-World Literature in the Era of Multinational
Capitalism.' *Social Text* 15 (1986): 65–88.
Lewis, Bernard. *Land of Enchanters: Egyptian Short Stories from the Earliest Times
to the Present Day*. London: Harvill, 1948.
May, Charles E. 'Why Short Stories are Essential and Why They are Seldom
Read.' *The Art of Brevity: Excursions in Short Fiction Theory and Analysis*. Ed.
Pers Winther et al. Columbia: University of South Carolina Press, 2004.
14–25.
O'Brien, Edward J. *The Advance of the American Short Story*. New York: Dodd,
Meal, 1931.
Pattee, F.L. *The Development of the American Short Story*. New York: Biblo and
Tannen, 1975.

Pratt, Mary Louise. 'The Short Story: The Long and the Short of It.' *The New Short Story Theories*. Ed. Charles E. May. Athens OH: Ohio University Press, 1994. 91–113.

Punter, David. *Postcolonial Imaginings: Fictions of a New World Order*. Edinburgh University Press, 2000.

Scheub, Harold. 'A Review of African Oral Traditions and Literature.' *African Studies Review* 28.2/3 (1985): 1–72.

Venturi, Robert et al. *Learning from Las Vegas: The Forgotten Symbolism of Architectural Form*. Cambridge MA: MIT Press, 1978.

Young, Robert. *White Mythologies: Writing History and the West*. London: Routledge, 1990.

1

'Times are different now': The Ends of Partition in the Contemporary Urdu Short Story

Alex Padamsee

Violence is a total phenomenon, but it comes to us as a total fragment. Something terrible has happened and there is no plot, no narrative, only traces that lead nowhere. (Van der Veer 269)

When I now read descriptions of troubled parts of the world, in which violence appears primordial and inevitable [...] I find myself asking, Is that all there was to it? Or is it possible that the authors of these descriptions failed to find a form – or a style or a voice or a plot – that could accommodate both violence and the civilized willed response to it? (Ghosh 62)

Introduction

If collective violence arrives without a narrative, what then might constitute a 'civilized willed response' in writing out its trauma? Almost half a century had elapsed before historians began to excavate the experiences of physical and emotional violence that accompanied, and long survived, the partitioning of India in 1947.[1] While they have established at least some of the contours of what was lost to official nationalist histories, there is a general agreement that the experience itself, the complex effects of Partition violence and its elusive language of trauma, have yet to find an appropriate mode of critical analysis (see Das; Pandey 'In Defense'; Van der Veer). The recent rhetoric of disciplinary failure, however, has been marked by a common recuperative gesture. At the moment in which hermeneutic frameworks for witnessing seem either to fail or to require further

15

interrogation, the social scientist and the historian of Partition often turn to the fictitious testimony of literature – and frequently to the Urdu short story (Das 47; Pandey *Remembering Partition* 200–3). More than any other literary genre in the subcontinent, it is this medium that has been called on to supply the missing words in the reconstruction of the effects of Partition.

The turn to fictional testimony is striking given that the recording of accounts by survivors of Partition drew directly on the example set by the recovery of memories of the Holocaust, a subject in which fiction as a whole had for so long seemed to be placed in doubt as a form of witnessing (Eaglestone; Franklin 1–19). At least some of the criteria that have marked out the Urdu short story as an irreplaceable medium for encountering the trauma of Partition stem from the mediating role of the language, spoken across religious and regional divides in North India. Indeed, the ability of the genre to stage continued dialogues not just across sectarian or nationalist borders, but across disparate linguistic regions, has made it a unique archive for interrogating the ideologies that underpinned Partition. Aijaz Ahmad has argued that it was through the 'mirror of Urdu', and primarily through the short story, that a sense of South Asian community and communication was held open across the political borders long after the last refugees were admitted to both countries (Ahmad 103–25). In Partition, the Urdu short story had found its most enduring and obsessively rewritten subject (see Memon 'Partition Literature'). Perhaps unsurprisingly, then, it is the increasing self-reflexivity – and at times, opacity – of the Urdu short story from the 1950s onwards that most distinguishes its treatment of Partition among South Asian literatures (Palakeel 330; Saint 242). This textual difficulty constitutes a uniquely intensive reworking of the affective inheritance of Partition: in problematizing the form of the Partition story, Urdu writers anticipated the later emphasis in trauma studies on the importance of narrative and indeed its very possibility, in attempting to reflect, work through and understand the elusive effects of collective violence. Decades before historians had noticed the missing lexis of Partition in the founding narrative of the nation, the Urdu Partition short story had begun to articulate the traumatized absent spaces where those words might have been. Absence, in a sense, was its necessary subject, the paradoxically 'willed' narrative response that Ghosh could not find in other troubled parts of the world.

The shift from realism towards interrogating the medium itself is marked just a few years after Partition by Intizar Husain's 'An Unwritten Epic' (*Ek bin-likhi razmiya* 1952). Husain turns the focus of his short story on to the act of writing itself, suggesting that any reliance on established forms – here, the epic novel – obscured, and so risked complicity with, the unprecedented violence of its subject. At the same time, the story illustrates the growing realization that a mode of address directed exclusively towards rendering a static, spectacular history of trauma missed the crucial ongoing experience of violence in the present. Recent critical studies have emphasized that it is never at the time of its event that the experience of traumatic violence is registered. Trauma, in this respect, has no past; it can only be felt in the present (see Caruth). In the middle of an initially graphic narrative, the writer-narrator of Husain's story thus turns on his surviving warrior protagonist, now a poor migrant in Pakistan, and wishes him back to the scene of violence so that a coherent story can be told about him in his absence. The violence is at once ongoing, displaced and reconceived: 'If novels and short stories got written this way,' the narrator admits, 'writers would be tried for murder every day' (177). In the fragmented diary entries of the narrative that follow – standing in for the epic that fails to arrive – the absent experience of collective violence in South Asia had found its first fully self-reflexive form (see Padamsee). The achievement of Husain, Saadat Hasan Manto, Rajinder Bedi and others from this generation has, for scholars at least, been an overpowering one. For these critics, witnessing Partition in the Urdu short story both opens up and ends in a single post-Independence generation. But if, as Veena Das and others insist, Partition is a continually re-evoked, changing and intertwined moment in the experience of contemporary collective violence in South Asia, the question of absent experience first posed by these Urdu writers may preface a linked and ongoing written history of the South Asian present that cannot otherwise be registered (see Das 10–17; Datta; Pandey 'In Defense' 41–3). While historians reflecting on writing violence turn readily to the fictive testimony of the immediate post-Partition stories, it is this still evolving legacy in more contemporary Urdu short stories that has gone missing.

In particular, a renewed language of representation, steeped in the accents of Partition, begins to speak to a rapidly changing context of collective violence in the work of Urdu short story writers in the 1980s and 1990s. These stories point to a continuing trans-generational history of trauma whose evolution begins where most studies of the genre end (see Chughtai; Kumar *Narrating Partition*; Saint). One of the most striking formal and affective innovations of these contemporary narratives lies in their reconfiguration of the trope of absent address. Cathy Caruth argues that if we are to hear their testimony we need to listen to the repetitions in narratives of trauma less as a stranded monologue than as two distinct and mutually incomprehensible voices staging a 'double-telling' of an intimately shared history (7). The telling of trauma is in this respect intensely transactional, not just between victim and listener, but between the survivor and those absent others implicated in the original event. It is this restaged original dialogue, evoking an absent presence in its forms of address, which theorists of trauma had too often translated as a single traumatized self compulsively repeating an original wound (Caruth 4). Caruth, along with other founding figures in trauma studies such as Shoshana Felman and Dominic LaCapra, has been attacked for the potential of this insight to shrive the individual of wider (and especially, postcolonial) historical contexts and focus instead on an individualized linguistic confrontation with trauma (Craps 51–6; Craps and Buelens 1–11; Herrero and Baelo-Allue xix). Yet 40 years after Partition, this form of absent address is redirected in Urdu writing precisely to evoke its structural situation, its own founding circumstances in a South Asian continuum of historical rupture (see also Kabir). In Surendra Prakash's 'Wood Chopped in the Jungle' (*Jangal se kati hui lakriyan* 1989), the narrator and his exiled community of woodcutters open yet another coffin by the riverside, only to find that what they saw 'was no illusion – it was quite the right thing. It was my own corpse that lay in the coffin' (163). Burying the South Asian past is no longer possible. The original traumatic event has been reconstructed as the absence of its narrator, compulsively chopping the wood by which he will be – has already been – crucified. Unmaking the past in the present, the 'double-telling' of the story enacts not just the impossibility of the original survivor's history (Caruth 39), but the incomprehensible collective legacy of its inheritance.

    As collective violence entered a new era of 'routinisation' in the 1980s (Pandey 'In Defense' 46), the narration of trauma in the Urdu short story begins to shuttle even more self-consciously between its past and present locations, its present and absent interlocutors. It is as if the polarities of experience between a wounded past and an amnesiac present had been rediscovered and recharged. The absent address, so crucial to understanding the testimony of violence, now becomes an important form of expression passed between the generation who had experienced Partition and those second-generation witnesses to whom its affects, and socio-political after-effects, were bequeathed. The crucified corpse in the coffin in Surendra Prakash's story exemplifies not only an ongoing sectarian violence that must now at some level be 'owned', but the absent presence of an original traumatic loss that can no longer possibly be witnessed. That a second-generation, non-Muslim Indian writer chose to convey this traumatized experience in a language by then associated exclusively with Muslims, makes the relevance of absent address only the more urgent. That he chose to tell it through a Christian motif points us forward to the mutually incomprehensible 'double-telling' of the story he has inherited.

Passing it on

Comprising some of the first printed texts in South Asia in the early nineteenth century, the Hindustani (Urdu) short story had from the start appealed to a cross-communal audience, read alike by educated Hindus, Sikhs and Muslims across North India (see King; Metcalf; Pollock 805–911; Pritchett). These texts were often composite intertwining tales (*qissa*) that foregrounded the role of the storyteller. Though populist in orientation, they maintained a vital contemporary relevance, and at times dissidence, to the social contexts out of which they arose (see Oesterheld). In the late nineteenth century, politicized language movements began to divide Hindustani as a written form into the separate scripts of nagri and nastaliq, associated respectively with Hindi and Urdu, attempting at the same time to purify Hindi of its Perso-Arabic roots (see Dalmia).[2] The modernist twentieth-century Urdu short story was in part a direct critical response to these divisive energies.[3] In Pakistan in particular, where from 1952 Urdu was problematically imposed by the state as the national language (see Ayres), Urdu writing has taken on the oppositional work of a dissenting minor literature. In India, it remains a marginalized forum for speaking within and beyond the nation (see Hansen and Lelyveld; Memon 'Urdu Fiction'). In both countries, the long evolved role of the genre as a dissenting form critiquing social coercion and rupture has re-emerged in recent years alongside an urgently renewed appeal to its storytelling past.

The psychoanalyst Dori Laub has described a process of eliciting Holocaust memories in which testimony is less the retrieval of facts than 'a genuine event, an event in its own right', and one that neither witness nor listener 'yet knows' (Laub 67). In many contemporary Urdu Partition stories, rather than abandoning the story form altogether, it is the repeated performative action of telling and listening to incoherent stories that produces the unknown event. By telling these stories to an intimate but uncomprehending listener, and so restaging the absent address of the original trauma, the witness opens up their repetitive history to something new, an unprecedented knowledge. In part, this is a knowledge of its relevance to, indeed its alteration within, a changing history of others – and therefore its own dependence and vulnerability to change (Caruth 18–24, 37–9). At the start of his short story 'The Refugees' (*Muhajirin* 1987), Abdullah Hussein's narrator states that 'events don't occur in a void, but are related to the great unknowns that flank them on either side' (50). As with so many Urdu stories of the period, the one about to be told makes no sense on its own; it is the event of its retelling, emerging from between these flanking and absent 'unknowns', which creates its present meaning.

The story crosses between two moments of personal history, both of which are at once familiar and unprecedented. The first occurs one afternoon in 1940, when Aftab's father, without warning or apparent reason, retires alone to his room and shoots himself; the second, 30 years later, when the son returns to the scene of suicide in his natal town, a place as remote and inaccessible to him as those left by the original 'Muhajirs', the designation inextricably associated in Pakistan with Partition refugees from India (68). Written at a time when General Zia-ul Haq's 'Islamization' programme in Pakistan had exacerbated rather than contained the fissiparous tendencies of the state (see Jalal *Democracy and Authoritarianism* 61–2; Shaikh), the story situates itself between two prior moments of historical division: the political demand for Pakistan by the Muslim League in 1940 (see Jalal *Sole Spokesman*); and the secession of the provinces of Bengal from Pakistan initiated by the assembly elections in 1970. The dates given in the story, so closely linked to these two prior and deeply traumatic partitions, mark the points at which these historical events were, in a sense, signalled but not yet irrevocable, potential but not yet 'known'. But they also signal an unknown personal history that cannot be measured precisely by national histories: Das rightly warns in trauma studies against sliding too easily from the personal to the collective (Das 102).[4] The expected violence of Partition, the trauma of migration, or indeed the armed ethno-nationalist movements in Pakistan at the time the story was being written (Shaikh 114) – all of these are nowhere mentioned. What Partha Chatterjee has called 'the place of history in the present' has been effaced (Chatterjee and Ghosh 15). Rather, since the story does not endorse a later explanation of the original suicide, we are left with a history of violence that cannot be known or located in a single moment, only by a relation between two juxtaposed 'unknowns'. To that extent, it is a true history of trauma. In contrast to the referential work of historiography, such a history is always 'referential precisely to the extent that it is not fully perceived as it occurs; or to put it somewhat differently, that a history [of trauma] can be grasped only in the very inaccessibility of its occurrence' (Caruth 18).

The most significant parallel between the two given moments in 'The Refugees' is that they are the scenes of the telling, or double-telling, of the same story between different generations. On 20 June 1940, father and son walk out into the countryside together for an afternoon, and the father, now a devout Muslim, tells a story of his youth as an actor in a Bombay film, a story in which he mimes a nineteenth-century British cavalry massacre of Muslims, re-enacting his role as a mounted British soldier in the film. The original event is thus already multiply displaced, only available in the distorted forms of story – and yet its self-violence is implicitly echoed in the incomprehensible suicide that follows later that afternoon. Remembering the day exactly 30 years later, Aftab decides to fulfil a long-held plan to return to the spot and retell the story of that day, this time to his own son, in the process crossing back for the first time from his migrant's destination in Lahore. Inevitably, Aftab discovers the hometown he knew gone 'for good' (68), the countryside obscured by new growth. Only the tree under which his father had told the story remains essentially unchanged. This, he now realizes, is because it had been 'frozen in the moment of its death' (72); its 'mutilated' and 'mangled' aspect (74) precisely mimes the unclaimed experience of trauma.

The narrative is thus poised on a recognizable trope of recovery. A superficial reading might expect that the story he tells to his son will enable Aftab to trace his own 'mind paralyzed for thirty years' (70) back to its 'frozen moment of time' (74), to reawaken his 'numb' heart (75). But Aftab chooses not to tell the story as a family event; he withholds his father's name. The double-telling of the story resides in this omission, a story that intimately concerns his son, which connects and directs the generations, is offered up instead as an absent address, an account that cannot be answered or understood because it is not fully heard. When he asks his son for an explanation of the suicide, the boy replies simply: 'Perhaps he loved horses' (76). The collaborative, hitherto unknown, event that takes place between the two surviving generations is therefore not the fleetingly disclosed epiphany of his father's mounted past, but Aftab's more disturbing new knowledge of what will be 'forever hidden' (77) about its violent aftermath, all that storytelling may not reveal. Laub reminds us that repetition 'bears witness not just to a [traumatic] history that has not ended, but, specifically, to the historical occurrence of an event that, in effect, does not end' (Laub 67). In place of transcendence, the absent history is here filled out by a renewed and unaccountable sense of bodily violence in the present. At the close of the story, just as his own father had sat sweating in his sealed room before he killed himself, Aftab is discovered by his son laid out like a corpse in the hotel room, 'drenched with sweat' (78). No explanation can be offered, because what is taking place for the first time is an essential experience of trauma, the violence of its forgetting (Caruth 17).

Crucially, in Hussein's story, this can no longer be an isolated experience. In the double-telling of its loss, the recovery of this knowledge of displacement implicates the narrator in the changing history of another (Caruth 24). If the trauma of his father's suicide has shaped or deformed Aftab, his telling of the story imbricates his own traumatic history with that of his son. The equivocal ending is thus one of uncomprehending agency, as well as a tentative glimpse of a now contemporary burden. With the anxious offer to 'put on the fan' (78), the boy raises his father from the dead.

Being here: a missing history of the present

Hussein was a young first-generation witness to Partition; his family, resident in West Punjab, had been left relatively unaffected (see Ansari; Saint 136). Perhaps for this reason, this late story is able to locate both of its protagonists as inheritors of an unknown history, one marked by ruptures or gaps that cannot be fully identified. In doing so, Hussein's story signals its own transition point from first- to second-generation testimony. Describing representations of trans-generational trauma, Marianne Hirsch notes in them 'at once incomprehensibility and presence, a past that will neither fade away nor be integrated into the present' (40). Hussein's story is an illustration of one of the moments in which trauma is passed on through the generations, leaving behind the 'incomprehensibility' that Aftab's son must experience, the trauma of his father's death that awaits him when he turns on the light in the hotel room.

The first generation thus opens up its history to the alteration of others. To that extent, we might further specify the contemporary Pakistan which Aftab's son has inherited as the absent address which once again changes the meaning of Partition. Alongside the divided time scheme of the story, the title 'The Refugees' (*Muhajirin*) offers just an imprint, as opposed to a snapshot, of its displaced subject. The story was written at exactly the time the Muhajir Qaumi Movement (MQM), formed in 1984, turned to armed militant acts on behalf of 'Muhajirs' (migrants from India during Partition), claiming for them a distinct ethnicity as a platform from which to counter the longstanding *ressentiments* of indigenous ethnic groups in Sind and Punjab (see also Verkaaik). The title of the story is clearly a reminder of what is at stake and what has been forgotten in the appropriated term, its intense and divisive contemporary connotations whose violent roots in Partition the story probes but cannot name. In this context, the haunting vision given to Aftab beside the dead tree, of a horse and rider soaring 'into space in such unison that it seemed they were a single body which would jump across the length of the earth in one gigantic bound' (77), metaphorically resituates a prior partition in the impossible fissiparous territory of his son's immanent contemporary inheritance.

As Surendra Prakash's repeated crucifixion story indicates, however, for the next generation the traumatic legacy of Partition is more directly intensified by a present violence. In Pakistan, for instance, the writer Ikramullah's story 'Jungle' (1990) presents a similar scene of graphic and mysterious violence as a man wanders blindly through a dense forest at night, literally knocking himself bloody and senseless trying to find a path home that he had once known by heart. The 'great tree' (56) from his childhood by which he attempts to orient himself is more immediately lethal than in Hussein's story, and in the final lines the morning sun comes up on his unrecognizable corpse (63). In the Indian writer Syed Muhammad Ashraf's story 'Man' (*Aadmi* 1994), the protagonist returns to the path he had taken daily home from school in his childhood through a grove, to find that the anonymous ghostly figure of a farmer who had once, he imagined, protected him, stands now with his rifle raised in warning. The importance of missing genealogical connections locates Partition as a common absent signifier between these second-generation stories: the first crucifixion, the lost paths. However, the sources of violence are also closer to home, more recurrent and resistant to articulation.

The reverberation of motifs of self-destruction reflects their conjoint contexts in the communalization of politics across South Asia in the 1980s (see Gould). The masculinist, militant nature of the religious and ethno-nationalist movements of the period mirrored each other across political borders, not only in terms of their common spectacular opposition to increasingly centralized and authoritarian South Asian states, but also in terms of mutual incitement and emulation (see Jaffrelot 369–71; Nandy). Living in Bombay in the 1980s, Prakash would have witnessed first-hand the divisive rise in political power and locally rooted presence of the sectarian Hindu right-wing Shiv Sena (Army of Shiva). At the same time, in Karachi the writer Asif Farrukhi drew directly on the descent into violence that marked the capital of Sind in the 1990s. When he wrote 'The Homebound' (*Ghar Ghusna* 1995), the sensational violence of the MQM and its opponents was generating a weekly mortality rate not seen in the city since Partition. The description of innumerable daily nameless corpses in this story thus carries a more literal referent than Prakash's allegorical tale of crucifixion. Indeed, the Urdu title Farrukhi chose, *Ghar Ghusna*, invokes connotations of violent forced entry in the verb *ghusna*: these are not just 'homebound' protagonists, as the closing lines hint, they are under assault.

While the general context of his contemporary Karachi is clear, from whom, or what, they are under assault in Farrukhi's story is never quite specified. Despite the immediacy of newspaper reports and the importance of Karachi as a city under siege, what is striking about this story is its troubling dislocations, the way in which it cannot hold fast to, cannot even name, its literal object. The causes of the deaths which the narrator's joint family bet on over the breakfast table cannot be defined. Sectarianism, political calculation and gambling debts are proffered, hinting that even the effort to discriminate is implicated, that the breakfast gamblers are not only complicit with the perpetrators but potentially numbered among the dead: 'Well, I have to account for the gambler too,' the narrator admits: 'I know I will have to pay' (124). This insistent, self-conscious interrogation of language as a complicit event foregrounds the issue of narrative and testimony. Simple recitations become impossible: 'What did happen yesterday? I try hard to recall. Despite trying, I cannot. With an apology I hang up the phone' (126). Gradually, the failure to enclose and specify in language encourages the spatial instability, the vulnerability, of the 'home-bound'. Narrating the passing of a day within a single home in the city, the story begins with the ritual unfastening of door and window locks, and ends with uncontainable linguistic thresholds:

> And this ring ... no, it is not the telephone but the doorbell perhaps [...] What kind of sound is this? Someone has jumped into the house. Running off at close distance ...
> And those chasing him ...?
> The knocks on the door are gradually turning into strikes.
> I have not responded to it. (129)

As 'home-bound' and 'home-penetrated' merge, the narrative is rendered immobile, unable in the last lines to judge anything but its own apparent failure: 'I do not even move from my bed. I do nothing and I feel it is the right thing' (129).

That 'nothing' is neither glib nor, in any simple sense, provocative; it contains the full force of the narrative. Nothing concrete has been told, no concrete action, not even a telephone call, has been completed. So what can it mean when 'nothing' becomes 'the right thing' for a witness to traumatic violence? Where is its structural, its collective and 'civilized' response? The problem of interpretation lies partly in whose violence is being addressed here. The references to recent ethnic cleansing would seem to locate the story in the wake of the bitter ethnic conflict that arose in the city in 1989, following the breakdown of an accord between the ruling PPP party and the MQM, a situation which then prompted devastating military operations in 1992 as the city spiralled out of control and the death toll rose (Samad 68–70). The conversations that surround the narrator, however, dislocate these events, parsing them instead as more distant, autobiographical narratives from his parents. 'I can't tell you how I felt that day,' the mother relates about the recent violence, as though of an event that antedates the grown-up narrator's infancy: 'Cruelty would reach its zenith' (127). The father later takes over the story, narrating perhaps another event entirely: 'A silent terror hovered over the city that evening. It seemed the city would drown in a sea of blood' (128). The actual content – a possibly state-sponsored 'clean out' of 'entire localities' (128) – suggests the enthno-nationalist violence in contemporary Karachi, but the cadence of the words seem to, as Hirsch puts it in another context, 'affirm the past's existence and, in their flat two-dimensionality, [...] signal its unbridgeable distance' (23). The parents as survivors already occupy, in this sense, the figural position of a 'speaking corpse' common to survivor testimonies (Schwab 15).

That 'death-in-life' quality (Schwab 19) signals the cryptonomy at work, a past secret encoded in their language. Their voices moreover have been intertwined with the narrator's own thoughts on the current crisis. In the middle of a phone call his 'memory brings strange forgotten things from the past' (126). This is a 'memory' of his father's voice speaking of his own great-uncle mixing industrial quantities of arsenic at some indeterminate point in the late colonial past, then succumbing to the poison himself. 'He had the prescription' (26), the father's voice repeats within this uninterpreted 'memory'. That this oblique reference to another form of mass suicide might invoke Partition is less significant than its arrival in a 'dead' story form now transferred wholesale to the narrative voice itself, now part of its own conscious attempts to make sense of the violent events of the moment. Its own language of interpretation, its psychic space, is thus colonized long before the home is penetrated.

Gabriele Schwab has identified this kind of linguistic cryptonomy – the 'death-in-life' of a trapped and encoded memory of trauma – as central to what she calls 'trans-generational haunting'. Second-generation writers, she argues, can inhabit the position of the 'speaking corpse' not because they imagine the traumatic thing itself, but because 'something of the quality of "death-in-life" has been transmitted to them in a complex transference from those who were actual witnesses and survivors' (19). It is this deadened and deadening language, designed to expunge traumatic loss through narrative fetishism (see Santner), which is experienced as a form of violence by the succeeding generations (Schwab 21). In a study of the children of Holocaust survivors, Nadine Fresco records the reception of their parents' spoken histories as the 'incomprehensible attacks of pain […] concealed behind a screen of words, again, always the same words, an unchanging story, a tale repeated over and over again, made up of selections from the war' (quoted Laub 64). Farrukhi's story speaks to just this kind of received and yet absent violence. The words of the narrator's parents assault him as so much 'chitter-chatter [that] comes cascading down – like the firing in the city' (127). When the mother relates an incident with the observation 'death is far better than such a life', the narrator's reaction is as if to a literal demand she has just made on his life:

> I cannot bear to listen to any more. Why should I pray for this death, and then pray for how many more.
> I turn away from the wall. I am in the house. (129)

Speaking from within the location of trauma – its absent address in the language of his parents – the narrative reveals the event as already within the walls of the home. It is present as the 'nothing' that determines the narrator's response, the absence, gaps and walls in the language of trauma that both colonize and evacuate his articulation of the present context. This is a learnt culture of amnesia, the story suggests, forgetting itself in language – and so repeating its story even as it tells it.

Trans-generational survivor narratives often contain this trope of what Schwab calls linguistic 'spatiotemporal splitting' (23). The violent 'splitting' effect of the language, displacing the immediate context into other absent violent histories (23), is in the end literally instanced by the coming apart of the home in Farrukhi's story, displaced from pressures within as much as answering those from without. As a creative response to the dissociative language of survivor testimony, it is the form of the story that is the civilized 'right thing', speaking to a collective trans-generational context and seeking to break open the repetitive framework of traumatic histories by exposing their lethal, self-protective patterns of articulation.[5] Like the murderous empty jungle in Ikramullah's story, and Prakash's 'speaking corpse', it is a formal and cross-communal response to the absent address of trauma, long evolved and already encoded within the Urdu short story. These stories emerge from an earlier complex literary history of self-consciously concealing and contextualizing storytelling; and as in the Euro-American modernist short story, their disunifying effects of ambiguity and ellipsis work here precisely to reconnect text and context (Head 2). But they are distinct in posing a trans-generational structural critique of absence: '[t]imes are different now', Prakash's bewildered narrator is told by his father: 'and then when you become a father, your sons will tell you stories' (160). Reading forwards from the first towering generation of Urdu short story writers in the 1940s, Aamir Mufti has valorized the modern genre as a whole for its dissent from the teleology of the nation in South Asia. If the 'willed' and structural narrative response to writing violence is to be understood today, we must begin to take account of these more contemporary Urdu evolutions in which the divisive teleologies of Partition are still being transmitted and re-encountered, an 'epic' struggle still being 'unwritten' in a literature of post-national dissent.

Notes

1. See, for example, the interventions in reconstructing lost Partition archives in Bhalla; Butalia; Kamra; Kaul; Talbot; Talbot and Singh; Tan and Kudaisya; and Zaminder.
2. For the further effects of socio-religious movements on the development of Hindi in the twentieth century, see Rai.
3. For the history of the modernist Urdu short story, see Ahmad; Gopal; Kumar *Narrating Partition* and *Conversations on Modernism*; and Mahmud.
4. Conversely, it is remarkable that in one of the few critical interpretations of this important story by a writer best known for his Partition novel *Udas*

Uslein (1963), it is read as a Proustian study of memory that floats free of all context, including the violence it recalls (see Phillips).
5. For the importance of these dissociative tropes in cross-cultural testimonies, see the essays collected in Rhoades Jr. and Sar.

Works cited

Ahmad, Aijaz. *Lineages of the Present: Ideology and Politics in Contemporary South Asia*. London and New York: Verso, 2000.

Ansari, Rehan. 'A Conversation with Abdullah Hussein' *Chowk* (2000). 11 February 2012. http://www.chowk.com/Views/A-Conversation-With-Abdullah-Hussein-Part-One

Ashraf, Syed Muhammad. 'Aadmi.' *Mapping Memories: Urdu Stories from India and Pakistan*. Ed. Sukrita Paul Kumar and Muhammad Ali Siddiqui. New Delhi: Katha, 1998. 193–204.

Ayres, Alyssa. *Speaking Like a State: Language and Nationalism in Pakistan*. Cambridge University Press, 2009.

Bhalla, Alok, ed. *Partition Dialogues: Memories of a Lost Home*. Oxford University Press, 2006.

Butalia, Urvashi. *The Other Side of Silence: Voices from the Partition of India*. New Delhi: Viking, 1998.

Caruth, Cathy. *Unclaimed Experience: Trauma, Narrative, and History*. Baltimore and London: Johns Hopkins University Press, 1996.

Chatterjee, Partha and Anjun Ghosh, eds. *History and the Present*. London: Anthem Press, 2002.

Chughtai, Ismat. 'Communal Violence and Literature.' *Annual of Urdu Studies* 15 (2000): 445–56.

Craps, Stef. 'Wor(l)ds of Grief: Traumatic Memory and Literary Witnessing in Cross-Cultural Perspective.' *Textual Practice* 24.1 (2010): 51–68.

Craps, Stef and Gert Buelens. 'Introduction: Postcolonial Trauma Novels.' *Studies in the Novel* 40.1/2 (2008): 1–11.

Dalmia, Vasudha. *The Nationalization of Hindu Traditions: Bharatendu Harischandra and Nineteenth-Century Banaras*. Oxford University Press, 1997.

Das, Veena. *Life and Words: Violence and the Descent into the Ordinary*. Berkeley: University of California Press, 2007.

Datta, Pradip. 'Historic Trauma and the Politics of the Present in India.' *Interventions* 7.3 (2005): 316–20.

Eaglestone, Robert. *The Holocaust and the Postmodern*. Oxford University Press, 2004.

Farrukhi, Asif. 'The Homebound.' *A Letter from India: Contemporary Short Stories from Pakistan*. Ed. Moazzam Sheikh. New Delhi: Penguin, 2004. 122–9.

Franklin, Ruth. *A Thousand Darknesses: Lies and Truth in Holocaust Fiction*. Oxford University Press, 2011.

Ghosh, Amitav. *The Imam and the Indian*. Delhi: Ravi Dayal, 2006.

Gopal, Priyamvada. *Literary Radicalism in India: Gender, Nation and the Transition to Independence*. London and New York: Routledge, 2005.

Gould, William. *Religion and Conflict in Modern South Asia*. Cambridge University Press, 2012.

Hansen, Kathryn and David Lelyveld, eds. *A Wilderness of Possibilities: Urdu Studies in Transnational Perspective*. Oxford University Press, 2005.

Head, Dominic. *The Modernist Short Story: A Study in Theory and Practice*. Cambridge University Press, 2009.

Herrero, Dolores and Sonia Baelo-Allue, eds. *The Splintered Glass: Facets of Trauma in the Post-Colony and Beyond*. Amsterdam: Rodopi, 2011.

Hirsch, Marianne. *Family Frames: Photography, Narrative and Postmemory*. Cambridge MA: Harvard University Press, 1997.

Husain, Intizar. 'An Unwritten Epic.' *An Epic Unwritten: The Penguin Book of Partitions Stories from Urdu*. Ed. Muhammad Umar Memon. New Delhi: Penguin, 1998. 153–78.

Hussein, Abdullah. 'The Refugees.' *Fear and Desire: An Anthology of Urdu Stories*. Ed. Muhammad Umar Memon. Oxford University Press, 1994. 50–78.

Ikramullah. 'Jungle.' *A Letter from India: Contemporary Short Stories from Pakistan*. Ed. Moazzam Sheikh. New Delhi: Penguin, 2004. 52–63.

Jaffrelot, Christophe. *The Hindu Nationalist Movement and India Politics 1925–1990s*. London: Hurst, 1996.

Jalal, Ayesha. *Democracy and Authoritarianism in South Asia*. New Delhi: Foundation, 1996.

—— *The Sole Spokesman: Jinnah, the Muslim League, and the Demand for Pakistan*. Cambridge University Press, 1985.

Kabir, Ananya Jahanara. 'Subjectivities, Memories, Loss of Pigskin Bags, Silver Spittoons and the Partition of India.' *Interventions* 4.2 (2002): 245–64.

Kamra, Sukeshi. *Bearing Witness: Partition, Independence, End of the Raj*. New Delhi: Roli, 2002.

Kaul, Suvir, ed. *The Partitions of Memory: The Afterlife of the Division of India*. Delhi: Permanent Black, 2001.

King, Christopher. *One Language, Two Scripts: The Hindi Movement in Nineteenth Century North India*. Oxford University Press, 1994.

Kumar, Sukrita Paul. *Narrating Partition: Texts, Interpretations, Ideas*. New Delhi: Indialog Publications, 2004.

——, ed. *Conversations on Modernism*. Shimla: Indian Institute of Advanced Study, 1990.

Laub, Dori. 'Bearing Witness, or the Vicissitudes of Listening.' *Testimony: Crises of Witnessing in Literature*. Shoshana Felman and Dori Laub. New York and London: Routledge, 1992. 57–74.

Mahmud, Shabana. 'Angare and the Founding of the Progressive Writer's Association.' *Modern Asian Studies* 30.2 (1996): 447–67.

Memon, Muhammad Umar. 'Partition Literature: A Study of Intizar Husain.' *Modern Asian Studies* 14.3 (1980): 377–410.

—— 'Urdu Fiction from India.' *Annual of Urdu Studies* 26 (2011): 236–8.

Metcalf, Barbara D. 'Urdu in India in the 21st Century: A Historian's Perspective.' *Social Scientist* 31.5/6 (2003): 29–37.

Mufti, Aamir. 'A Story Greater than God: Genre, Gender and Minortiy in Late Colonial India.' *Subaltern Studies XL: Community, Gender and Violence*. Ed. Partha Chatterjee and Pradap Jeganathan. New Delhi: Permanent Black, 2005. 1–36.

Nandy, Ashis. *Bonfire of Creeds: The Essential Ashis Nandy*. Oxford University Press, 2004.

Oesterheld, Christina. 'Entertainment and Reform: Urdu Narratives in the Nineteenth Century.' *India's Literary History: Essays on the Nineteenth Century*. Ed. Stuart Blackburn and Vasudha Dalmia. Delhi: Permanent Black, 2004. 167–212.

Padamsee, Alex. 'Uncertain Partitions: Undecidability and the Urdu Short Story.' *Wasafiri* 53.1 (2008): 1–5.

Palakeel, Thomas. 'Partition Stories: Epic Fragments and Revenge Tragedies.' *Annual of Urdu Studies* 16 (2001): 329–44.

Pandey, Gyanendra. 'In Defense of the Fragment: Writing about Hindu–Muslim Riots in India Today.' *Representations* 37 (1992): 27–55.

——— *Remembering Partition: Violence, Nationalism and History in India*. Cambridge University Press, 2001.

Phillips, Robert. 'The Spotted Snake of the Past: Time and Memory in "The Refugees" and "The Back Room".' *Annual of Urdu Studies* 11 (1996): 259–65.

Pollock, Sheldon, ed. *Literary Cultures in History: Reconstructions from South Asia*. Berkeley: University of California Press, 2003.

Prakash, Surendra. 'Wood Chopped in the Jungle.' *The Tale of the Old Fisherman: Contemporary Urdu Short Stories*. Ed. Mohammad Umar Memon. Washington: Three Continents Press, 1991. 159–63.

Pritchett, Frances W. *Nets of Awareness: Urdu Poetry and its Critics*. Berkeley: University of California Press, 1994.

Rai, Alok. *Hindi Nationalism*. Hyderabad: Orient Longman, 2007.

Rhoades Jr., George F. and Vedat Sar, eds. *Trauma and Dissociation in a Cross-Cultural Perspective: Not Just a North-American Phenomenon*. Binghamton: Haworth Press, 2006.

Saint, Tarun K. *Witnessing Partition: Memory, History, Fiction*. New Delhi and Abingdon: Routledge, 2010.

Samad, Yunas. 'In and Out of Power But Not Down and Out: Mohajir Identity Politics.' *Pakistan: Nationalism Without a Nation?* Ed. Christophe Jaffrelot. Delhi: Manohar Publishers, 2004. 63–83.

Santner, Eric L. *Stranded Objects: Mourning, Memory, and Film in Postwar Germany*. Ithaca NY: Cornell University Press, 1990.

Schwab, Gabriele. *Haunting Legacies: Violent Histories and Transgenerational Trauma*. New York: Columbia University Press, 2010.

Shaikh, Farzana. *Making Sense of Pakistan*. London: Hurst, 2009.

Talbot, Ian. *Freedom's Cry: The Popular Dimension in the Pakistan Movement and Partition Experience in North-West India*. Oxford University Press, 1996.

Talbot, Ian and Gurhapal Singh, eds. *The Partition of India*. Cambridge University Press, 2009.

Tan, Tai Yong and Gyanesh Kudaisya, eds. *The Aftermath of Partition in South Asia*. London and New York: Routledge, 2000.

Van der Veer, Peter. 'Writing Violence.' *Making India Hindu: Religion, Community, and the Politics of Democracy*. Ed. David Ludden. Oxford University Press, 2005. 250–69.

Verkaaik, Oskar. *Migrants and Militants: Fun and Urban Violence in Pakistan*. Princeton University Press, 2004.

Zaminder, Vazira Fazila-Yacoobali. *The Long Partition and the Making of Modern South Asia: Refugees, Boundaries, Histories*. New York: Columbia University Press, 2007.

2
'Sheddings of light': Patricia Grace and Māori Short Fiction

*Michelle Keown**

This chapter offers an overview of Māori short fiction in English published in Aotearoa/New Zealand from the early 1970s to the present, focusing in particular on the work of Patricia Grace, one of the most prolific and influential Māori short story writers. The chapter contextualizes Grace's work alongside that of other influential 'first-generation' Māori short fiction writers such as Witi Ihimaera (also an editor of multiple volumes of Māori fiction), as well as more recent or 'emerging' writers such as Alice Tawhai.

The Māori short story in English has its origins in the 1950s, emerging at a time when, following the Second World War, large numbers of Māori migrated from rural and coastal settlements to the cities in search of employment and educational opportunities. Previous representations of Māori in short fiction had been produced by Pākehā (ethnically European) New Zealanders, from the late nineteenth-century tales of Alfred A. Grace (who characterized the Māori variously as a doomed race of noble savages, cannibalistic warriors and likeable rogues), to Noel Hilliard's and Roderick Finlayson's more sensitive attempts to explore the effects of rapid social change upon Māori in the decades before and after the Second World War (see Ihimaera *Where's Waari*; Pearson).

The first wave of Māori short fiction in English was galvanized by the founding of *Te Ao Hou*, a magazine for Māori – established in 1952 by the New Zealand Government's Department of Māori Affairs – that began publishing short stories by Māori authors from 1955. Regular short story contributors in the 1950s and 1960s include Arapera Blank, Rowley Habib, Harry Dansey, Riki Erihi, Barry

Mitcalfe and Hirini/Sidney Moko Mead, as well as J.C. Sturm, who became the first Māori writer to have her work anthologized when her *Te Ao Hou* story 'For All the Saints' (1955) was reprinted in C.K. Stead's *New Zealand Short Stories: Second Series* (1966). Patricia Grace and Witi Ihimaera, who began publishing stories in *Te Ao Hou* and other periodicals from the late 1960s and early 1970s respectively, became the first Māori writers to publish single-authored collections of short stories: Ihimaera's *Pounamu, Pounamu* in 1972 and Grace's *Waiariki and Other Stories* in 1975.

As they quickly rose to national literary prominence, Ihimaera and Grace clearly felt the burden of responsibility conferred upon them as 'representative' Māori authors, and early in their careers both identified an explicitly counter-discursive strand in their work, which posed a challenge to Romantic and negative stereotypes of Māori produced in much Pākehā literature (Beavis 53; Grace 'Maori in Literature' 80). Grace's and Ihimaera's first publications emerged during the early years of the 'Māori Renaissance', a politico-cultural movement intended to revive and promote Māori cultural 'traditions' and to improve opportunities for Māori within Pākehā-dominated urban society. The movement was galvanized by a growing awareness of the ways in which urbanization had widened the socio-economic gap between Māori and the colonizing Pākehā culture.[1]

With both cultures living and interacting closely on a larger scale than before, interracial tensions had developed, and there were many instances of overt discrimination against Māori in employment, housing provision and public services (Keown 138; King 474–5). Many of the Māori who migrated to the cities were channelled into manual and unskilled labour, forming what was to become an established urban underclass vulnerable to unemployment in times of economic uncertainty. Post-war urbanization also had a radically destabilizing effect on the structures of 'traditional' Māori society, given that in little more than a generation, Māori became an 'overwhelmingly urban people': whilst only 11.2 per cent of Māori were urban dwellers in 1936, this rose to 25.7 per cent by 1945, and to 81 per cent by 1996 (King 473). It was becoming clear by the 1970s that many urbanized Māori had begun to lose contact with their tribal communities and their 'traditional' ideologies and social practices, and an important language survey undertaken in the early 1970s revealed a drastic reduction in the numbers of speakers of Māori as a first language, not least due to the fact that many urbanized Māori felt pressured to prioritize English as a means of educational and social advancement (Keown 138).

Spurred to action by these sobering statistics, throughout the 1970s urban Māori began to establish supra-tribal organizations in order to replace the traditional infrastructures of the dwindling rural communities, while political activists petitioned Parliament for the establishment of courses in Māori language and culture in schools, and for the government to honour its obligations under the 1840 Treaty of Waitangi (which secured Britain's annexation of New Zealand). The Treaty existed in two versions: the Māori translation promised Māori tino rangatiratanga (full chiefly authority) over their lands, villages and taonga (treasures), while in the English version – which the British Government subsequently took as the sole authoritative document – Māori were promised only 'full exclusive and undisturbed possession' of their lands, forests and fisheries, and ceded sovereignty to the British Queen (whereas the Māori version translated 'sovereignty' as 'kāwanatanga', which meant 'governorship' and therefore appeared to Māori to guarantee custodianship rather than absolute sovereignty). As increasing numbers of British settlers arrived in New Zealand in the 1850s, outnumbering Māori by 1858, settler demand for land far outstripped Māori willingness to sell, and the failure of the colonial government to honour the terms of the treaty led to a devastating series of 'land wars' in the late nineteenth century, after which huge tracts of Māori land not already in Pākehā hands were confiscated. It was not until 1975, following vigorous lobbying by Māori activists, that a Waitangi Tribunal was established to investigate Māori land claims and, eventually, to begin negotiating restitutive settlements with various Māori iwi (tribes) in the 1990s (Keown 56–7, 139). Apart from questions of land ownership, for many Māori the objective of tino rangatiratanga (here best translated as 'self-determination') in other areas of Māori life became, and has remained, a key objective.

Grace and Ihimaera, like many of the other *Te Ao Hou* authors of the 1960s and 1970s, engaged closely with the immense social changes of the post-war and Māori Renaissance period in their early work. A dominant strand in writing of the period is a nostalgic focus on rural Māori life (commonly represented as fast-disappearing), as well as a preoccupation with the social pressures faced by urbanized

Māori. Early stories by Grace and Ihimaera also index the Māori struggle for socio-political equality and self-determination: Ihimaera's story 'Clenched Fist' (1977), for example, focuses on a young Māori man who has adopted the rhetoric of the African-American Black Power movement in his battle against white racism, and stories such as 'A Sense of Belonging' (1977) and 'The Other Side of the Fence' (1972) feature Pākehā characters who discriminate against Māori. Early stories by Grace such as 'A Way of Talking' (1975) and 'Journey' (1980) feature similar themes, and significantly, her 1975 story 'Parade' links the task of Māori literary representation with the politics of self-empowerment. The story is narrated by a young Māori woman participating in a Māori performance event during a community carnival. The costumes and dances are those associated with a pre-colonial warrior culture long-romanticized and fetishized by Pākehā (particularly since the 1890s, when falling Māori population figures fuelled popular social Darwinist theories on imminent Māori 'extinction'), and the narrator fears that Pākehā observers are viewing the Māori performers as they would 'Animals in cages', or museum exhibits (*Collected Stories* 88). However, one of the narrator's elders advises her that 'It is your job, this. To show others who we are' (*Collected Stories* 91), and the statement becomes a manifesto for Grace's own role as a Māori writer, also resonating with assertions made by other postcolonial authors such as Chinua Achebe, who in his 1965 essay 'The Novelist as Teacher' expressed an impulsion to 'help my society regain belief in itself and put away the complexes of the years of denigration and self-abasement' (3). Part of the task of representation for both Grace and Ihimaera has been to engage with some of the major historical injustices against Māori since colonization (such as the alienation of Māori land, and the denigration of Māori language and culture) in order to create Māori-centred alternatives to Pākehā dominant discourse.

These impulses have left a lasting legacy in Māori short fiction: as late as 1999, Grace identified in her work an enduring focus upon 'dislocation, people removed from their groups, the breakdown of communities and the forming of new ones as people find themselves on the fringes' ('Influences' 71), while Ihimaera has repeatedly returned to the scenario described in his 1977 story 'Passing Time', in which urban Māori, bereft of ancestral land and family connections, have become 'after-hour people, fringe-suburb people, bottom drawer people who [live] on the periphery of existence' (*Kingfisher* 213). Such social patterns are redolent of those described in *The Lonely Voice* (1962), Frank O'Connor's landmark study of the short story in which he argues the form is germane to 'submerged population' groups on the 'fringes of society', expressing 'an intense awareness of human loneliness' and putatively endemic within (post) colonized societies such as those in Ireland, the Caribbean and the Americas (18–20). Social marginalization and solitude have long been common themes in New Zealand creative production more generally (from John Mulgan's bush-sojourning hero in the novel *Man Alone* (1939), to the tortured isolates within the novels and short stories of Janet Frame, or the films of Vincent Ward and Jane Campion), and a considerable body of Māori fiction has focused upon some of the more extreme examples of Māori social deprivation. Alan Duff's controversial bestselling novel *Once Were Warriors* (1990), a harrowing account of a working-class Māori family wracked by domestic violence, child abuse and alcoholism, spawned a new generation of short fiction exploring these themes. Since 1995, for example, the Māori publisher Huia has held regular short story competitions and published the most highly rated submissions in anthologies, and a significant proportion of these stories (by authors such as Jacqui Brown, Phil Kawana, Michelle Manning and Maraea Rihari) explore Māori social deprivation and dysfunction.

Yet while applicable to a substantial tranche of Māori short fiction, O'Connor's theories have little relevance to the large body of Māori writing that – in contrast to the Anglo-American modernist tradition against which O'Connor writes – celebrates communal Māori values and social practices. Indeed, Grace, Ihimaera and other prominent Māori writers such as Keri Hulme – in her Booker Prize-winning novel *The Bone People* (1983), as well as in some of her short fiction and poetry – have celebrated Māori spirituality and whanaungatanga (strong family or community ties) in counter-discursive opposition to the putative spiritual poverty and individualism of Pākehā society (Keown 144–5). It is also the case that, while many contemporary Māori writers – such as those publishing with Huia, or in various recent short story anthologies edited by Witi Ihimaera and others – have continued to explore political themes associated with the Māori Renaissance and the continuing drive for Māori self-determination, many others feature Māori in more quotidian or humorous social settings (which, incidentally, have also been explored extensively in Grace and Ihimaera's work).

A major point of continuity between the *Te Ao Hou* generation and contemporary Māori short fiction is the centrality of Māori oral storytelling traditions to many of these narratives. *Te Ao Hou* was described in its inaugural issue as a 'marae on paper' (Anon. n.p.), a metaphor that draws attention to the importance of whaikōrero or speechmaking as a central facet of ritual occasions on marae (the sacred ground in front of the wharenui or meeting house within traditional Māori communities). Whaikōrero customarily involves multiple speakers offering individual perspectives on a topic of discussion, and *Te Ao Hou* similarly invited Māori to submit compositions or commentaries that could form the basis of ongoing debates within the post-war Māori community. This is significant in view of the fact that an engagement with oral traditions is common to a wide variety of postcolonial short fiction, often as a counterpoint to hegemonic Western narratives. A wide array of postcolonial fiction – from the Onitsha market literature of Nigeria to Raja Rao's and Salman Rushdie's experiments with the digressive 'looping' trajectories of South Asian oral narratives – indexes such traditions.

Māori short fiction foregrounds the continuing importance and relevance of Māori oral traditions in various ways. Writers such as Patricia Grace and Ngahuia Te Awekotuku, for example, have produced a variety of narratives that invoke and rework traditional Māori mythological figures and folktales, often in situations involving postmodern play or a reinterpretation of gender roles. Grace's 'Sun's Marbles' (1994), for example, is a playful retelling of a Māori myth in which the demi-god and trickster Māui ensnares the sun and forces it to slow its passage across the sky so that people can enjoy longer daylight hours. The opening of the story gives a sense of its demotic register, as though written to entertain a new generation of worldly wise young Māori:

> When Maui booby-trapped Sun then clobbered him over the head with a hunk of bone shaped like two parts of a bootmaker's last, he won, for all time, high praise as the pioneer of daylight saving. (*Collected Stories* 11)

Grace has explored and recontextualized the Māui myth-cycle elsewhere in her work (most extensively in her 1986 novel *Potiki*), and has also referenced powerful female mythological figures such as Mahuika (goddess of fire) and Hine-nui-te-Pō (the goddess who guards the gateway to the underworld). Her 2006 tale 'Moon Story' retells a folktale in which a woman named Rona is kidnapped by the moon (cast as another powerful female mythological figure) after she trips over at night and curses the moon for going behind a cloud. Again, the opening of Grace's story signals its playful revision of the ancient myth for a contemporary audience: 'On the night that Rona bad-mouthed Moon she did it because she wasn't in her right mind. Even before she tripped and fell she was feeling stressed' (*Small Holes* 111).

Another retelling of the Rona myth appears in Ngahuia Te Awekotuku's short story collection *Ruahine: Mythic Women* (2003). In an italicized section preceding the story, Te Awekotuku draws attention to the story's original significance as a 'lesson' to 'take care in what you say', but indicates that her retelling is 'different', reinterpreting Rona's experience as an enlightening odyssey in which she meets sky-beings who 'still feature' in the genealogies of Te Arawa and Tainui (two tribal confederations of the North Island of New Zealand (*Ruahine* 17)). Like Ihimaera, Te Awekotuku has also explored gay and lesbian Māori relationships extensively in her fiction, and in 'Hinemoa', another story in *Ruahine*, she uses a variation on the commonly heteronormative myth of lovers Hinemoa and Tutanekai as the basis for a retelling in which Hinemoa (a high-born woman from the Te Arawa tribe of Rotorua) masquerades as a man in order to seduce Tutanekai, who favoured a male 'intimate friend' named Tiki ('Kia Mau' 288). Te Awekotuku's retellings of Māori myths, like Grace's, underscore the continuing relevance of pre-colonial oral traditions to contemporary Māori society by reinterpreting familiar myths in contexts attuned to contemporary values and audiences.

Another way in which Māori short fiction writers engage with the legacy of oral traditions is by indexing the practice of whaikōrero. Ihimaera's 1972 story 'Tangi' and Grace's 'Waimarie' (1987), for example, feature characters who speak at tangihanga (funeral) ceremonies on their marae. Grace's novel *Potiki* similarly incorporates fragments of speeches made during a tangihanga, and is also – like her novels *Cousins* (1992) and *Baby No-Eyes* (1998) – structured into discrete chapters narrated by multiple family members who offer differing yet overlapping perspectives on particular events, in a manner comparable to the tradition of whaikōrero.

One of the most palpable formal ways in which writers such as Grace and Ihimaera index Māori oral traditions is through the use of Māori words and phrases in predominantly English-medium narratives. This practice has served an important cultural function during and beyond the Māori Renaissance period, contributing to a wider process of Māori language revival that has included the establishment of kohanga reo and kura kaupapa Māori (Māori-medium preschool, primary and secondary school language programmes) and, more recently, Māori-administered universities (whare wananga) and adult literacy programmes. Although, as has been argued in the introduction to this collection, the oral and communal elements within tale-telling cannot be replicated in a written document, among New Zealand's Māori writers who draw upon oral traditions, Patricia Grace comes closest to bridging the gap between oral and written narratives.

As I have argued elsewhere, Gilles Deleuze and Félix Guattari's model of 'minor literature' offers a useful basis upon which to analyse the politics of language in Grace's work. In particular, it sheds light upon the ways in which her writing foregrounds and employs Māori language in order to advocate Māori cultural revival and self-determination. In *Kafka: Toward a Minor Literature* (1975), Deleuze and Guattari argue that when a 'minor' writer uses a 'major' or dominant language, a process of 'deterritorialization' takes place when grammatical and conceptual categories from the writer's own 'minor' language infiltrate the syntax of the 'major language'. This process, they argue, undermines any sense of univocal authority and shifts the parameters of meaning towards the 'minor' writer's own cultural milieu (Deleuze and Guattari 26). While the terms 'major' and 'minor' are problematic in their association with processes of domination and subjection in colonial discourse, Deleuze and Guattari's arguments are nevertheless useful to a reading of the linguistic strategies used in Grace's fiction.

One of the more obvious ways in which deterritorialization takes place in Grace's writing is in her frequent use of code-switching between English – her main or 'dominant' mode of expression – and the Māori language. Grace was born in 1937 to a Māori father and

a Pākehā mother, and like many of her generation, she recalls her
Māori relatives avoiding using the Māori language in front of her due
to the common belief that it was more advantageous for Māori children to grow up speaking English (Tausky 90). In spite of this, Grace
recalls some degree of exposure to Māori, and reveals that she has
incorporated Māori words and phrases into her 'English sentences'
throughout her life ('Influences' 72). This practice of code-switching
between English and Māori is pervasive in Grace's fiction, used as
a marker of cultural identity among older characters in particular
(in keeping with the mid-twentieth-century decline in the use of
Māori among the young). In her early fiction, Grace accommodates
non-Māori-speaking readers – a substantial number of whom are
potentially Māori – by including glossaries of Māori words, or offering contextual translations of Māori phrases appearing within her
narratives. An example of the latter appears in Grace's 1975 story
'The Dream', in which a Māori man, Raniera, discusses a nocturnal
vision with a friend. In the excerpt below I provide my own translations in square brackets:

'E Hika! He aha te moemoea?' [Hey mate! What's the dream?]
called Ben as Raniera stepped from the taxi and waved to the
driver.
'What's the dream?'
'E tama, he tuna.' [It was about an eel, man.]
'Ei! Kia tika ra!' [Wow, really?]
'Yeh! A big one this eel. Ka nui te kaita!' [It was huge.]
He showed Ben with his hands the size of the eel of his dream.
(*Collected Stories* 29)

In this extract, a number of Māori phrases are used, and although
the translations Grace provides in adjacent sentences are not exact,
a monolingual reader would be able to gain a good sense of the
tenor of the conversation through context. Examples of this type of
translation are widespread in Grace's stories throughout the 1970s
and 1980s, but significantly, from the publication of her novel *Potiki*,
Grace has made far fewer concessions for non-Māori-speaking readers,
and has more recently argued that writers from 'small population cultures' should not have to 'other' their languages and cultures by providing glossaries and other explanatory information ('Influences' 71).

In considering Grace's linguistic strategies at a deeper structural level, a more sophisticated process of deterritorialization takes place in narratives in which Māori grammatical and conceptual codes are transferred into the syntax of English sentences, creating what Deleuze and Guattari describe as 'linguistic Third World zones by which a language can escape, an animal enters into things, an assemblage comes into play' (26–7). For example, Māori is categorized as a 'VSO' language (with sentence constituents ordered as verb, subject, object in contrast to English which is SVO (subject, verb, object)). Using a VSO pattern in her English sentences is one way in which Grace signals that her older Māori characters speak Māori as a first language. An example of this occurs in her 1975 story 'Toki', where the elderly male narrator, in recounting a fishing expedition he took as a young man, states 'But sat quietly, I, to wait for morning' (*Collected Stories* 19). Here, the first verb precedes the subject as it would in Māori. Another form of grammatical transference in this story involves agent deletion, which commonly occurs in Māori narratives in which the identity of the subject has already been established earlier in the text. An awareness of this grammatical process may account for the absence of subject pronouns in the following sentence: 'To the hills next morning, and from there saw the little boat head straight for the deep' (*Collected Stories* 19). (In Standard English this sentence would read '*I* went to the hills ... and from there *I* saw the little boat ...'.) A similar process is at work in Grace's story 'At the River' (1975), in which a similarly elderly narrator tells of a dream in which she has a premonition of her husband's death during an eeling expedition: 'To the tent to rest after they had gone to the river, and while asleep the dream came' (*Collected Stories* 20).

Another example of grammatical 'interference' in Grace's work is the rendering of mass and count nouns, which are not differentiated in Māori. For example, 'a book' and 'some food' would be expressed using the same indefinite article 'he' (as in 'he pukapuka' and 'he kai'), although in English 'book' is a count noun and 'food' is a mass noun. In Grace's 1987 story 'Waimarie', again an elderly Māori speaker carries this rule over into her English, asking her niece to 'get me *a* leaves from my little tree' (*Collected Stories* 193; my italics), while in her 1975 story 'Holiday' a group of adult siblings who code-switch between English and Māori use the same grammatical rule as they joke with their mother:

> 'You made *a* bread, Mum?' they say.
> 'You got any meat? Gee-ee, Macky forgot to get us *a* meat for the weekend.' (*Collected Stories* 37; my italics)

While these examples of grammatical transference imbue Grace's writing with a sense of socio-linguistic realism, and exemplify the 'deterritorializing' strategies Deleuze and Guattari describe, in some cases her language strategies are also put to more explicitly political purposes (Keown 168–9). In her 1980 story 'Letters from Whetu', for example, a disjunction between Māori and English grammatical patterns is explored in order to challenge the adherence to prescriptive grammatical rules within the English-medium education system. The story is epistolary, comprising a series of letters written by a Māori high school student named Whetu-o-te-moana (which translates as 'Star of the Sea') to allay his boredom during class time. Whetu addresses his letters to various Māori and Pacific Island friends who have either failed to get into sixth form (Whetu's current cohort), or have left school altogether. Whetu expresses his bemusement at the fact that his teacher, Ms Fisher, has taken him under her wing as 'her honourable statistic, her minority person MAKING IT' in an education system in which Māori students frequently drop out as soon as they reach legal school-leaving age (*Collected Stories* 122). In order subtly to undermine the well-meaning but patronizing behaviour of his teacher, Whetu sometimes uses putatively 'incorrect' grammar:

> I sometimes do a bit of a stir with Fisher, like I say 'yous' instead of 'you' (pl.). It always sends her PURPLE. The other day I wrote it in my essay and she had a BLUE fit. She scratched it out in RED and wrote me a double underlined note – 'I have told you many times before that there is no such word as "yous" (I wonder if it hurt her to write it). Please do not use (yous heh heh) it again.' So I wrote a triple underlined note underneath – 'How can I yous it if it does not exist?' (*Collected Stories* 122)

Here, Whetu's mischievous sally makes a serious ideological point. The word 'yous' as a second person plural pronoun is often associated with non-standard dialects of English within the United Kingdom, for example, but in New Zealand it is also strongly associated with Māori ethnicity. The usage possibly stems from the fact that unlike modern English, Māori has separate singular, dual and plural second-person pronominal forms, meaning that the modern English pronoun 'you', which is used for all three pronominal forms, has three counterparts in Māori: 'koe' (you, singular); 'kōrua' (you two) and 'koutou' (you plural), and is therefore not only a legitimate plural form in certain non-standard varieties of English, but also arguably indexes an existing (and more complex) number distinction in Māori. Whetu's behaviour therefore foregrounds the way in which non-standard usages in Māori English are proscribed by the Pākehā-dominated education system, exacerbating the sense of exclusion experienced by Māori students (Keown 168–9).

Within this context, it is significant that Whetu also satirizes his teacher's obsession with the stories of Katherine Mansfield:

> She's trying to make us enjoy KM. Kay Em is what she calls Katherine Mansfield, as though she and KM were best mates. Well I suppose Fisher could be just about old enough to have been a mate of KM's.... She's prancing about reading like she's gonna bust.... Sometimes she flaps the book about and makes circles in the air with it ... [and] doesn't stop 'reading', so I suppose that means she knows her KM off by heart, bless her HART (Halt All Racist Tours), punctuation and all. (*Collected Stories* 122)

Here, Whetu ridicules the teacher's elevation of Mansfield to canonical status, and implies that she is attempting to indoctrinate the students with material Whetu clearly considers to be irrelevant to his generation, and arguably associates with a colonial ethnocentrism that Mansfield herself satirizes in her story 'How Pearl Button Was Kidnapped' (1912). The grouping together of Mansfield, Ms Fisher and HART (a New Zealand organization that formed in 1969, in protest against rugby union tours to and from South Africa) makes a light-hearted but potentially subversive association between the teaching of 'English' literature and the processes of racial exclusion that characterized the apartheid era. Significantly, Grace has pointed out that during her own childhood 'teachers had low expectations of my intellectual ability because I was Maori', and she also recalls reading some of Mansfield's short fiction, finding certain images and settings resonant but ultimately feeling that Mansfield's work was 'far removed from me in time and social class as well as culture' and therefore not something she 'identified with' (Kedgley 50–1; Tausky 91). (By contrast, Ihimaera produced a short fiction collection, *Dear Miss Mansfield* (1989), which was inspired by her work.) Grace's work is avowedly inspired more by the working-class characters and demotic register adopted by New Zealand writer Frank Sargeson, in whose stories (written during and beyond the 1930s Depression era) she heard 'the New Zealand voice' in literature for the first time (Tausky 91). Indeed, one of the defining characteristics of Grace's work is her ability to capture the idioms of a wide demographic of Māori and Pākehā speakers, but her work also achieves the kind of painterly luminosity that is often associated with Mansfield's symbolist writing. Take, for example, the ending of 'Waimarie', in which the eponymous elderly woman, wearing a circlet of green leaves customarily used at Māori funerals, performs the karanga (a keening call of welcome) that inaugurates a tangihanga ceremony on her marae:

There was hot sun on her lifted face, sun which swathed light through her hair and sifted the circle of leaves into layers of green. And then she called their kinsman to his home, called him to the warmth, the protection of the place where he would be wept for.

The light showed the lines on her face to be deep and hard, and light spun off the gold clasps which clutched the ornaments at her ears. These ornaments hung quivering in the brightness, curving the way her jaw curved, light sculpting them against the contour of her jaw. She called the spirits of the many dead to gather along with the kinsman, so that the dead could all be wept for together.

Light mixed the muted colours of her shawl and glossed the dark clothing. And her voice lifted out, weaving amongst the sheddings of light, encompassing the kinsman and his family, bearing them forward. (*Collected Stories* 195)

The incandescence of this extract is striking, and in the context of Māori spiritual beliefs, draws attention to the transition the deceased is about to make from Te Ao Mārama (the world of light and the living) to Te Pō (the darkness/the afterlife). The shifting optic of the extract emphasizes the fluidity of the movement of the coffin bearers processing in rhythm with the karanga and the 'sheddings of light'. This attention to visual detail is found throughout Grace's work (one of the most recent examples being her 2006 story 'The Kiss', which – in detailing a screen kiss being filmed in Florence – unfolds as though perceived through the lens of a camera). Further, a variety of Grace's stories hinge on a moment of epiphany that transposes the sudden loss of innocence one finds in Mansfield's stories (such as 'Her First Ball' (1921) and 'Bliss' (1918)) to racially inflected settings. In 'Going for the Bread' (1987), for example, a racially motivated assault on a young girl instils in her mother a new determination to fight the 'war' against prejudice (*Collected Stories* 226), while in 'The Hills' (1987), a schoolboy's innocence is violated when racist police arrest him on a pretext and subject him to a spurious anal search on the grounds that he may be hiding drugs.

Such disturbing epiphanies are also central to the work of Alice Tawhai, one of the current 'new' generation of Māori writers who has published three volumes of short stories: *Festival of Miracles* (2005), *Luminous* (2007) and *Dark Jelly* (2011). Tawhai's writing responds to some of the more recent trends in 'ethnic minority' New Zealand literature, such as the exploration of strengthening social networks between Māori and rapidly expanding Asian and Pacific Island immigrant populations. It is also distinctive in finding beauty within bizarre and disturbing scenarios: 'The Festival of Miracles' (2005), for example, sets a baby's death during a house fire against the backdrop of a breathtakingly stellar night sky, while in 'Imagining Winter' (2005), a Lebanese immigrant who murders his girlfriend places her body in a freezer and marvels at the way in which fish scales trapped in the ice 'surrounded her like sparkling snowflakes in a storm' (*Festival* 51). Other stories, particularly within *Dark Jelly*, push themes of mental illness and sexual violence to new limits.

In addition to making its own innovations to the Māori short story, Tawhai's work also responds to the legacy of earlier generations of Māori writers in various ways: indexing through magical realist strategies what Witi Ihimaera calls 'the holistic frameworks of the unreal as well as the real' that inform Māori attitudes to history and culture ('Maori Perspective' 53–4); exploring death, violence and cruelty with the detached precision and linguistic dexterity of Keri Hulme; probing Māori social dysfunction with the brutal honesty of Bruce Stewart and Alan Duff; and delineating the minutiae of place, colour and texture, and the warmth of interpersonal relationships, in a manner commensurate with the work of Grace and Hone Tuwhare. The Māori drive for self-determination is still present in Tawhai's work, but is carefully situated within the complex social dynamics of contemporary Māori society. 'Pale Flower' (2005), for example, features a man who 'wrap[s] himself up in the flag of tino rangatiratanga and drink[s] from brown bottles', on the one hand committed to revitalizing Māori culture and on the other venting his frustrations by beating his girlfriend (*Festival* 131). Many of Tawhai's characters are variations on the 'bottom-drawer people' who feature in Ihimaera's and Grace's narratives, but stories such as 'Butterflies and Moths' (2007), on the other hand, bespeak the existence of a growing body of professional Māori – children of Renaissance era parents – who are confident and secure in their cultural identity. Such scenarios bespeak the continuities and innovations that make contemporary Māori short fiction so dynamic and vital.

Notes

* The author wishes to thank the Carnegie Trust for the Universities of Scotland for funding that enabled her to undertake research for this chapter in New Zealand.

1. Like other British settler colonies such as Australia and South Africa, New Zealand established some degree of constitutional independence from Britain in the early twentieth century, but indigenous Māori have remained subject to various forms of neo-colonial hegemony.

Works cited

Achebe, Chinua. 'The Novelist as Teacher.' *African Writers on African Writing*. Ed. G.D. Killam. London: Heinemann, 1973. 1–7.
Anon. *Te Ao Hou: The New World* 1 (1952). http://teaohou.natlib.govt.nz/journals/teaohou/issue/Mao01TeA/c1.html
Beavis, Bill. 'Brown is Beautiful: Witi Ihimaera.' *New Zealand Listener* 11 January 1971: 53.
Deleuze, Gilles and Félix Guattari. *Kafka: Toward a Minor Literature*. Trans. Dana Polan. Minneapolis: University of Minnesota Press, 1986.
Duff, Alan. *Once Were Warriors*. Auckland: Tandem, 1990.
Grace, Patricia. *Baby No-Eyes*. Auckland: Penguin, 1998.
—— *Collected Stories*. Auckland: Penguin, 1994.
—— *Cousins*. Auckland: Penguin, 1992.

—— 'Influences on Writing.' *Inside Out: Literature, Cultural Politics, and Identity in the New Pacific.* Ed. Vilsoni Hereniko and Rob Wilson. Lanham and Boulder: Rowman and Littlefield, 1999. 65–73.

—— 'The Maori in Literature.' *Tihe Mauri Ora: Aspects of Maoritanga.* Ed. Michael King. Hong Kong: Methuen, 1978. 80–3.

—— *Potiki.* Auckland: Penguin, 1986.

—— *Small Holes in the Silence.* Auckland: Penguin, 2006.

—— *Waiariki and Other Stories.* Auckland: Longman Paul, 1975.

Hulme, Keri. *The Bone People.* London: Picador, 1986.

Ihimaera, Witi. *Dear Miss Mansfield: A Tribute to Kathleen Mansfield Beauchamp.* Auckland: Viking, 1989.

—— *Kingfisher Come Home: The Complete Māori Stories.* Auckland: Secker & Warburg, 1995.

—— 'A Maori Perspective.' *Journal of New Zealand Literature* 9 (1991): 53–4.

—— *Pounamu, Pounamu.* Auckland: Heinemann, 1972.

——, ed. *Where's Waari: A History of the Maori through the Short Story.* Auckland: Reed, 2000.

Kedgley, Sue. *Our Own Country: Leading New Zealand Women Writers Talk About Their Writing and Their Lives.* Auckland: Penguin, 1989.

Keown, Michelle. *Pacific Islands Writing: The Postcolonial Literatures of Aotearoa/ New Zealand and the Pacific.* Oxford University Press, 2007.

King, Michael. *The Penguin History of New Zealand.* Auckland: Penguin, 2003.

Mulgan, John. *Man Alone.* London: Selwyn and Blount, 1939.

O'Connor, Frank. *The Lonely Voice: A Study of the Short Story.* New York: Harper & Row, 1985.

Pearson, Bill. *Fretful Sleepers and Other Essays.* Auckland: Heinemann, 1974.

Tausky, Thomas E. '"Stories That Show Them Who They Are": An Interview with Patricia Grace.' *Australian & New Zealand Studies in Canada* 6 (1991): 90–102.

Tawhai, Alice. *Dark Jelly.* Wellington: Huia, 2011.

—— *Festival of Miracles.* Wellington: Huia, 2005.

—— *Luminous.* Wellington: Huia, 2007.

Te Awekotuku, Ngahuia. 'Kia Mau, Kia Manawanui – We Will Never Go Away: Experiences of a Māori Lesbian Feminist.' *Feminist Voices: Women's Studies Texts for Aotearoa/New Zealand.* Ed. Rosemary Du Plessis. Oxford University Press, 1992. 278–89.

—— *Ruahine: Mythic Women.* Wellington: Huia, 2003.

3
Unmaking Sense: Short Fiction and Social Space in Singapore

Philip Holden

Any account of the postcolonial short story in Singapore needs to begin with a certain amount of necessary groundwork. Singapore's multi-ethnic and multilingual literary culture calls into question the idea of a single cultural tradition for which reference to 'the short story' in the singular might suggest. And while Singapore as a nation-state did emerge from a history of colonization, its future is not necessarily conditioned by that past. An economically developed city-state strategically located between two rising global powers, India and China, Singapore is in many ways hypermodern, having already long encountered many of the contradictions regarding social inequality, multiculturalism and state surveillance that now trouble the postcolonial cities of former colonial powers. If short stories in Singapore defamiliarize readers from the social space of the city-state they also, perhaps more significantly, suggest the need to interrogate the notion of the postcolonial itself, and in particular the implicit privileging of the West in the context of global history. Singapore has literatures in each of its four official languages, but it may be that English-language writing occupies a particularly important nexus within the literary field that we often designate as postcolonial (see below). With this goal in mind, this chapter will explore the short stories of three contemporary Singapore writers – Suchen Lim, Alfian Sa'at and Wena Poon – and the manner in which each writer responds critically to elements of a contemporary Singaporean social space: such examination, however, needs to be prefaced by a brief account of the place of the English-language short story in Singapore.

Short story writing in English by Singapore residents, as opposed to colonial travellers or visitors, has a history of over a century. It begins with a series of short stories published in the *Straits Chinese Magazine* from 1897 to 1907; written by comprador-class intellectuals of Chinese, Eurasian and European descent, these stories were by no means anti-colonialist, yet they did implicitly point out the contradictions of colonialism in denying full equality to educated Anglophone non-Europeans. From the 1930s onwards, and increasingly after the end of the Japanese occupation in 1945, the short story in English became more concerned with the politics of Malayan nationalism. Such politics are central to the short stories of S. Rajaratnam, written in London during the war, but also later stories published in student journals and anthologies at the University of Malaya from 1950 onwards, including the writings of Lloyd Fernando, Kassim Ahmad and Wang Gungwu. During this period, it was widely anticipated that full decolonization would result in the union of Singapore and Malaya, and Singaporean and Malayan Literature at this point are historically inseparable; the short stories of the most sophisticated of Malayan modernists, for instance Lee Kok Liang, were published in the Singapore-based journal *Tumasek,* during the brief period that Singapore was part of Malaysia from 1963 to 1965.

After Singapore left Malaysia and became an independent nation in 1965, short story production continued. Catherine Lim, who would become central to any popular canon of English-language writing in Singapore, first made her name through two short story collections describing life in a rapidly modernizing society. In the late 1980s and 1990s, more critical voices emerged. The short fiction of Philip Jeyaretnam in *First Loves* (1987), for instance, focuses on youth culture, sexual exploration and the transgression of class and ethnic boundaries through personal relations; Claire Tham's collection, *Fascist Rock* (1990), centres on social rebellion.

Writing in English, initially in a colonial and then in a postcolonial public sphere, however, developed in a distinct manner in Singapore. In contrast to the experiences of Britain and the United States, literacy in English in Singapore remained until the 1960s the province of a small elite, and a mass reading public for the short story took time to develop. Singapore's experience in this regard is different not only from colonial metropolitan centres, but from other South East Asian societies undergoing decolonization. In the Philippines, systematic cultural colonization by the United States led to a golden age of the English-language short story in the 1930s, matched by parallel literary production in Tagalog and in regional languages. In Indonesia, the short story was one of the principal forms through which the nation was imagined as Bahasa Indonesia became a national language. Singaporean short stories in English were published in journals – *The Straits Chinese Magazine*, *The New Cauldron*, *Tumasek* and *Singa*, for instance – with circulations of a few hundred copies, and it was not until the popularization of Catherine Lim's stories, partially as school texts, and the popularity of Jeyaretnam's collection that short stories achieved a larger reading public.

The history of the restricted reading public, however, has another aspect, and one more closely connected with an evolving sense of social space. Under colonialism, Singapore, as a colonial entrepôt, was governed as part of the Crown Colony of the Straits Settlements. Rather than the indirect rule through a reconstituted Malay aristocracy that they used as a mode of governance in what is now peninsular Malaysia, the British governed Singapore as a 'plural society', with ethnic groups having their own cultural enclaves, and meeting only through the marketplace. English-language education, with a few notable exceptions, was conceived of as having largely a pragmatic function, in educating clerks and middlemen whose knowledge of the language might oil the wheels of commerce. Yet the English language exceeded colonial designs for it: it became a space where educated Asians from different ethnic groups in Singapore might meet and discuss issues to do with politics, cultural belonging and identity. Singapore lay at the crossroads of maritime travel in Asia, and Asian intellectuals travelling to other countries and making pan-Asian connections, such as Rabindranath Tagore, would often stop there. The language in which they would communicate would be English.

The function of English as a language for the construction of modern Asian cultural communities continued in a different and yet related manner after independence in 1965. The People's Action Party government chose English as the lingua franca, and as the language of administration. By the end of the 1980s, all education was also English-medium. At the same time, in order to prevent cultural deracination, all Singaporeans were also required to learn a 'mother tongue' that corresponded with their ethnicity: for the vast majority, this was one of the three languages Mandarin Chinese, Malay and Tamil. In the schema of multiracialism and a bilingual citizenry, the mother tongue – often not the language spoken at home – gave cultural ballast and a sense of self, while English, as the language of science, technology and commerce, provided a means of entry into an outer, globalizing world. Cultural and literary production in English was thus out of place, since cultural roots were conceived as lying elsewhere, yet paradoxically, with the decline of Malay as a lingua franca, English became the only language shared by a new generation of Singaporeans, and indeed became localized in a variety of written and spoken registers. English-language cultural production in the 1980s and 1990s gained a wider audience, yet also remained a space where modern Asian identities were forged, often in contrast to the state's vision of cultural affiliation based on ancestry. To use Stuart Hall's terminology, English-language writers stressed a process of 'becoming' as well as of 'being', drawing on the experience of Singapore itself as a cultural marketplace rather than on imagined filiations to ancestral homelands (225).

For all this, it would be a mistake to see English-language writing in Singapore as automatically subversive because of its awkward place within the framework of state-sponsored multiracialism. Changing geopolitics from the 1990s onwards have made Mandarin Chinese, for instance, as much a language of regional business and commerce as it is one of cultural belonging for many Chinese Singaporeans. In a parallel development, the state's promotion of culture industries from the 1990s onwards, marked by the founding of the National Arts Council in 1991 and increased funding for the arts, often within the narrow remit of economic development, has seen encouragement being given to English-language cultural production. Yet it is clear that the English language has a particular relation to the social space in Singapore, a relationship that can perhaps best be thought of through the work of Henri Lefebvre.

In *The Production of Space* (1974), Lefebvre analyses the 'abstract space' of modern society that has replaced previous conceptions of space. Space itself, Lefebvre notes, is a social product, in which the mental and physical merge, and are often perceived by individual subjects as continuous. Under the rationalization promoted by capitalism, social space is saturated with 'the social relations of reproduction and production' (32), reflecting biological reproduction through a sacralized family, divisions of labour, and the management of leisure time and historical memory. Concealed by the 'illusory transparency' of such space, Lefebvre notes, is the 'real "subject", namely state (political) power' (51). This observation seems particularly true of Singapore, in which the built environment has been radically transformed in the years after independence. In keeping with the management of ethnicity discussed above, quotas for different communities in public housing have ensured that ethnic enclaves do not form. At the same time, older ethnic areas such as Chinatown, Little India and Kampong Glam have been refurbished and 'themed' for both internal and external tourism. In a conceptual inversion of physical space, the modernist Housing Development Board estates which ring the older city centre are frequently referred to as Singapore's 'heartland', while the city centre is increasingly a space for tourists and transnational white-collar workers, the old colonial buildings dwarfed by edifices such as the new Marina Bay Sands integrated resort. In the management of space, then, we can see the social and economic developmental projects of the national state writ large: ethnicity, language and housing forming crucial components of what several commentators have characterized as Singapore's 'state capitalism' (see Chua 206–11).

Yet Lefebvre's account also registers the complexity of space in modern societies, and the manner in which it might be contested by various actors. In order to explore this aspect of spatiality, Lefebvre develops a 'conceptual triad' to account for the way in which space is experienced. The first element of the triad is 'spatial practice', involving the manner in which space is embedded in dominant social routines: a pertinent example with reference to Singapore is Lefebvre's account of 'the daily life of a tenant in a government-subsidized high-rise housing project' and the means of transport that connect such residences to workplaces (38). Lefebvre's second element, 'representations of space', refers to larger visions of the urban environment, 'conceptualized space, the space of scientists, planners, urbanists, technocratic subdividers and social engineers' (38), explicitly articulated in government reports and developmental plans. The third, 'representational spaces', is more concerned with the symbolic meaning of space 'which the imagination' of its inhabitant 'seeks to change and appropriate' and which Lefebvre describes as coating physical space, converting physical objects into symbols (39). What is important here is Lefebvre's observation that the three elements embody contradictions, both internally and through a 'dialectical relationship [...] within the triad of the perceived, the conceived, and the lived' (39). It is these series of contradictions that Singaporean writers, making use of the architecture of their short stories, take pains to explore.

The first writer considered here, Suchen Christine Lim, is best known as a historical novelist. Her four novels, *Rice Bowl* (1984), *Gift from the Gods* (1990), *Fistful of Colours* (1992) and *A Bit of Earth* (2000), all retrieve alternative histories of Singapore and Malaysia – of political activism, women's stories or differently con-figured ethnicities – that problematize the historical memory of the nation-state. This is in part informed by Lim's own experience: born in 1948 in Malaysia, she moved to Singapore as a teenager, living through the political and social struggles before and immediately after Singapore's independence in 1965. Yet Lim's work also reveals a commitment to history as a way of rethinking what one scholar has described as the 'unfinished business' of various colonialisms in the present, in order to imagine 'alternative [...] futures' (Poon 27). This project is continued in a collection of short stories which Lim published in 2007 as *The Lies that Build a Marriage*. While many of the stories in the collection are narrated in contemporary Singapore, they frequently make use of the processes of memory to excavate alternative understandings of space. In Lefebvre's terms, we might say that special practices and representational spaces in the present are interrupted by those of the past, enabling the remapping of the symbolic nature of space – new representational spaces, as Lefebvre would put it – in the present.

An illustration of how this happens is shown in the story 'My Two Mothers'. Contemporary state capitalist discourse in Singapore frequently constructs Asians – and thus Singaporean citizens – as naturally conservative and Asian societies as built upon the unit of the family. In discussions in the public sphere in Singapore, it is dif-ficult to escape such framing. Debate regarding the repeal of section 337A of the Criminal Code in Singapore in 2007, which essentially criminalizes male homosexuality, for example, largely focused on whether homosexuality was opposed to traditional and putatively Asian social values, despite the fact that the code itself is a relic of British colonialism, and that the most vocal opposition to repeal came from evangelical Christian groups. Lim's short story intervenes in this particular debate in a skilful way. The story is set in the past, within a family. Its narrator's life, as in many Singapore narratives of the past half-century, mirrors that of the nation. Kwai Chee enters school in 1958, the year before Singapore achieved self-rule and elected its first People's Action Party government. The next date mentioned is 1965, the year of independence, when a scene takes place between the protagonist and two school friends; further scenes occur in 1975 and 2000, by which time the narrator has graduated from university in Singapore and has become a successful writer, now writer-in-residence at the University of Iowa.

The story's architecture mirrors a national narrative with its scenes taken as representative of a larger narrative of upward social mobility. The series of concentric circles Kwai Chee moves through – family, friends, nation and then a global community – mirrors the manner in which the Singapore state constructs identity, with the family 'as the basic unit of society',[1] and then an outward movement to community and nation. Furthermore, the protagonist comes from a family of black and white *amahs*, domestic servants who are often celebrated as actors in state capitalist narratives of immigration, devotion to work and eventual success. The spatial practices of the story fill in the framework of the narrative: they are largely domestic, but are linked to a larger world of progress outside. The protagonist eats at home or with friends, but she discusses school work or a politician's comments, or gets ready for her graduation ceremony. We might also note that the spatial design of the story itself reiterates the narrative of state capitalism. The story's scenes are markers in a life of meritocratic success, and move towards a denouement in which the protagonist makes an epiphanic connection with a previous past that she has wished to escape in pursuit of a deracinated modernity. In this she follows the pedagogy of the postcolonial state: having found her place in the modern world, she reaffirms her roots within Asian traditional society.

The nature of the reaffirmed traditions, however, results in a symbolic reconfiguration of social space. As the story's title implies, its narrator is brought up not within a heterosexual nuclear family, but by two mothers, whom she refers to as her aunts. When she grows older, Kwai Chee gets to know two adopted daughters of two women who live together, and notes that 'they were a family. They lived in the same house, drove to school in one car and went home together after school' (22). Not only are the women lesbian, but their relationship is also interracial, cutting across the bounds of community that mark multiracialism. Yet the spatial practices, to use Lefebvre's term, that they and their daughters carry out are those of everyday aspirant middle-class life. Kwai Chee's epiphany comes in the United States, when she reflects on a lesbian couple she knows who have two daughters, and sees herself for the first time as a 'daughter of two mothers' (28).

Yet the story goes beyond a simple accession to a contemporary North American sex-gender system, a homonormativity in which a homosexual relationship is simply imagined as a mirror image of a normative heterosexual one. Kwai Chee's realization reconfigures spatial representations; the sisterhood of black and white *amahs*, with their pledge never to marry, is not retrospectively presented as simply lesbian, but rather disruptively queer. The past is reconfigured: traditions become unmoored from the representional spaces to which they have been assigned, and the past's relationship to the present is reconfigured. Singapore's history of indentured migration and the influence of many different family structures, indeed, has meant that the normative monogamous heterosexual family that is foundational to state capitalist imagination of social space is exceptional: most families have histories of fracture, polygamy or adoption.

Lim's story, and the collection it is part of, represent a conscious effort to intervene in public debate in Singapore concerning the nature of the family; as Lim explains in her postscript, she has been invited to read the stories at church services, to mixed reactions from congregations. Indeed, the stories might be critiqued for being too consciously didactic, and thus not allowing for a prolonged and complex meditation on social space. In this they contrast with the short stories of Alfian Sa'at in the 1999 collection *Corridor*. Alfian, born in 1977, is from a younger generation who grew up well after Singapore's independence, coming to adulthood in a city-state that had already achieved developed-nation status. Much of Alfian's recent work has been in the theatre, but his short story collection was one of two works – the other being the poetry collection *One Fierce Hour* (1998) – that announced his arrival on the Singapore literary scene. While Alfian's work has been centrally concerned with the politics of sexuality and race, his writing is also less overtly didactic than Lim's. There is also a further difference. While Lim critiques the present through a rediscovery of the past, Alfian occupies the spatial practices of the present. His stories are set in Housing Development Board estates, shopping malls, public transport such as buses or MRT (mass rapid transit) trains, spaces that might seem to mirror the 'representations of space' of the developmental state, and yet can be reconfigured symbolically. Toilet cubicles and cars become sites of queer sexuality; characters' dreams reconfigure the symbolic freight of the flotsam and jetsam of consumer culture: computer games, BMW and Mercedes cars, a sandwich-maker or a video camera.

As the title of the collection implies, the centre of this spatial reconfiguration is the Housing Development Board estate. Most of the older HDB blocks, especially those containing smaller flats for lower-income residents, feature a common corridor on each floor, which links the individual flats. In older developments in which the interior spaces of the flats are small, the corridor becomes an extension of the flat's living space, much like the 'five-foot ways' or covered walkways that front traditional shop-houses in South East Asia. On newer estates, however, the common corridor is often in the interior of the building, rather than on its exterior: doors are shut, and living space more fully interiorized. Much of Alfian's early fiction and poetry explores the landscapes of HDB estates as a site of alienation in which efforts to create community are either artificial, or fleeting.

Alfian's short story 'Video' features a recently widowed mother, Maimon, and her daughter, Jamilah, now married and childless. Both act out spatial practices that seem to fit almost seamlessly within planned representations of space. Jamilah participates in Community Centre aerobics classes, watches game shows on television and visits her mother regularly. Most of the story's action takes place in her mother's flat, which is saturated with objects which are symbolically representative of domesticity and scarcely realized social aspirations: a sofa set with 'wooden armrests and brown velvety cushion covers', a television with a 'crocheted white cover' underneath a 'cuckoo clock [...] with two pendulous handles' (15). Religiosity as a marker of state-sanctioned ethnic identity also saturates the flat: on the walls are 'two white plates [...] from a bazaar in Malacca; one reading "Allah", and the other "Muhammad" in Arabic'

(15). Jamilah and Maimon also seem imprisoned by gender roles that fix them within a social order, and in particular their attempts to live up to their expected roles of wives and mothers.

The spatial ordering of the estate and the interiors of the flat are, however, disrupted by the discovery of an item that at first appears to be another symbol of consumption: a video camera. The camera has been bought by Maimon's husband, Abu Bakar, before his sudden death, in anticipation of a planned trip on the haj to Mecca, a fact which Maimon and Jamilah discover when inspecting the suitcase he has packed in anticipation of his journey. Initially, it seems as though the video camera will simply be a tool through which existing social practices will be reinforced, catching the first time a 'baby learns to speak or walk' or making a home video to send to a television show (14). Yet when Jamilah returns to her mother's flat for a subsequent visit the video camera becomes an entry-point into a different way of perceiving space. Jamilah practises filming with the camera, and then plays back the results on the television. Maimon watches, at first recognizing herself, her face 'a drought-stricken landscape tormented by the blinding memory of her husband' (16), and then watching the camera pan away to other parts of the flat: the kitchen with 'Milo tins, ketchup bottles, and even the woks and aluminium pots on the cooker' (16). Space is reconfigured: the consumer goods which previously cohered symbolically now appear as nothing more than litter. Maimon sees a figure wander back into the frame and commence cooking, sobbing all the while, but she no longer recognizes herself.

Such spatial dislocation intensifies as the story progresses. Jamilah teaches her mother how to use the video camera, and Maimon makes a series of recordings of areas of the flat associated with memories of Jamilah's childhood, but which are now empty, stripped of meaning. She plays these back to Jamilah who, overcome by emotion, cannot watch the video tape through to its conclusion:

> As she was watching the screen, she sensed how there were actually four people in the living room. Both mother and daughter felt it and felt themselves shudder with the knowledge. They were watching, and at the same time being watched, by a child who was not yet born and a husband not yet gone. They were in the company of ghosts. (21)

Such affective dislocation of habitual spatial practices, however, is not the last word in the story. In a final scene, Maimon presses the camera on Jamilah, who reluctantly takes it, but then leaves it on a park bench in the HDB estate. She returns again to switch it on, and is then framed in its viewfinder, becoming smaller and smaller as she heads towards a nearby MRT station.

If Lim's story ends in epiphany, Alfian's ends in a paradox. The story up to this point has been focalized entirely through Jamilah and Maimon, and yet in the conclusion of the story, the focalizer can only be a spectre staring through the viewfinder of the abandoned camera. Jamilah's diminution in size is a common rhetorical device with which movies end: Alfian's use of the trope gives us a sense of how individual lives, despite their seeming autonomy, are often conditioned by social scripts. Thus the spatial structure of the story itself intersects with the spatiality of the world it depicts: the story itself is a representational space that offers the possibility of reconfiguration or re-symbolization of meanings. What Alfian's story suggests – and in this it is more subtle than Lim's – is that such a process is not simple: using Lefebvre's metaphor, a fictional text cannot simply repaint a previously existing space, coating it with new symbolic meaning. Rather, the attachment of spatial practices to spaces of representation occurs through affective ties – those between parent and children, or between lovers: disturbance of these connections is painful, and re-symbolization not an easy or straightforward process. The most a story can do, perhaps, is to defamiliarize, to create a disruption in narratives that would see the postcolonial city as undifferentiated representational space mirroring the project of state capitalism.

As Lim's and Alfian's stories show, history and the built environment are vital elements in the conceptualization of postcolonial space in Singapore. Wena Poon's short story 'Justin & the Cenotaph' (in the collection *The Proper Care of Foxes*) introduces a third element: the manner in which Singapore's cityscape is marked by a conflux of flows often described as globalization, and which exist in uneasy tension with postcolonial elements (see also Krishnaswamy). Poon's two collections of short stories, *Lions in Winter* (2007) and *The Proper Care of Foxes* (2009), are both relentlessly transnational in location, moving between the United States, Canada, Singapore, Hong Kong and a host of other locations, with many stories revolving around a visit to another country, or a situation of exile or migrancy. In the latter collection, in particular, space comes to play a central role. The story 'Reuse, Recycle', for instance, dramatizes tensions within a family through its setting: a home that unites a family whose unity has only ever been imaginary, and which is in the process of being sold off for demolition, its contents commodified for sale on eBay.

'Justin & the Cenotaph' approaches such questions from another angle, in its appropriation of the spaces of representation of the colonial and developmental states. The plot of Poon's story has three distinct time periods yoked together by processes of memory. In the present, Justin, the story's central consciousness and a successful architect in modern Singapore, is commissioned to build a new cenotaph for the city-state, since the old one is to be removed to build a new highway. He goes to London to look at Lutyens' original memorial, and is hosted there by his niece, Rebecca, who is studying in the English capital. Justin's encounter with Rebecca triggers memories of his own sojourn in London in the 1980s as a government scholar, at a time when the built environment of Singapore was being transformed. As Justin recognizes the sites of London that he inhabited some two decades before, he telephones his mother. This introduces a further mapping of space and historical memory, through her memories of watching, as an eight-year-old girl in Singapore, the Coronation of Elizabeth II on television. At the end of the story, Justin returns to Singapore and replays a recording of the Coronation Rebecca has found on YouTube to his mother.

If in both Alfian's and Lim's stories the spatial practices and associated representational spaces of state capitalism are defamiliarized, Poon's suggests a different possibility: the separation of spaces of capital from those of the nation. Justin does not initially realize that there is a cenotaph in Singapore – it is small, neglected, tucked away on the Esplanade, which formerly looked out onto the harbour but is now hemmed in by bridges, tall buildings and reclaimed land:

> He tried to remember what Singapore's Cenotaph looked like, and couldn't. He looked at a photo on the Web, then got up from his seat and looked out of the window.
>
> There it was, right in the middle of his view. He had worked in this office for five years and never once saw it. (176)

The Cenotaph itself is clearly an example of the representations of space that undergirded both colonialism and nationalism. Justin speaks of its symmetry reverentially, how its horizontal lines follow the curvature of the earth, and how its verticals 'slope up to meet at a point a thousand feet in the air' (183). The Cenotaph is clearly evocative of the project of nationalism, and gains emotional power through its spatial condensation of affect: 'You cannot trust your own eyes,' Justin tells Rebecca. 'You must trust the architect to build the grander design around you' (183). Indeed, when Benedict Anderson comes to talk of nationalism's appeal to the transcendental in 'a strong affinity with religious imaginings', he chooses a closely associated memorial, the Tomb of the Unknown Soldier (51).

Yet the paradox implied by the concept of the cenotaph is that it is easy to render invisible: it is an empty tomb, a strange inversion of space that haunts a polity that has left many of the ideals of nationalism behind. Poon does not seem here to be concerned with a specifically Singaporean postcolonial nationalism: unlike other writers, she does not make use of the early ideals of nationalism as a standard against which to critique the inequalities of the present-day nation-state. The Singapore Cenotaph was built by the British after the First World War, and has not been centrally incorporated into the memory of the nation-state, and its neglect stands in contrast to the visibility of Leong Swee Lim's more starkly modernist Civilian War Memorial, which commemorates victims of the violence during the Japanese occupation of 1942 to 1945. However, like the memory and video of the Queen's coronation, it haunts the present. What both the Coronation and the Cenotaph signify, perhaps, is the ability for remembered collective affect to re-symbolize space, to remake representational spaces, or to coat them with different meanings from the commoditization of the present. New technologies, such as the mobile phone and video file sharing, have the capacity to shrink space and time, to make one aware of how present space is saturated by the symbols of the past. In the sense that this re-symbolization makes use of elements from a colonial period but is no longer concerned with their coloniality, it might be felt to be truly postcolonial. In this reading, then, the colonial past is made to serve the needs of the present: its coloniality is acknowledged, but it is fundamentally irrelevant to its present symbolic function.

The conclusion to Poon's story, however, undercuts such optimism regarding postcolonial reconfigurations of space. Justin manages to negotiate a larger budget from the government to build his new Singapore Cenotaph: he puts away earlier blueprints and decides to opt for a 'new design' (192). Yet the story ends here, and readers are given no clue as to what such a design might be. After its various historical analepses, the story returns to the present, and to an architectural project which is, despite Justin's own personal recollections and investments, initiated by the state. There remains the possibility that the representations of space of state capitalism will effortlessly incorporate the representational spaces that Justin and his mother have briefly inhabited: the past, too, is susceptible to commoditization.

Lim's, Alfian's and Poon's stories, in their connection to Singapore, emerge from a unique historical experience, yet it is an experience that is likely to become more representative in time. The economic rise of China and India in the past two decades within a neoliberal global system has undermined an association between modernity and the West that undergirded much earlier postcolonial writing and criticism. Postcolonial writers, under the circumstances of new urban modernities, are often less concerned with 'writing back' to a perceived centre, or with the revival of national traditions. In the urban spaces they inhabit, the moral authority of nationalism has been eroded, along with its appeal to an imagined community of the people. If the hope for transcendence provided by nationalism may always be revived through affective appeal, such appeals are submerged by everyday governmental spatial practice. In this context, it may be helpful to see the short story as an urban, rather than a national, form, often culturally out of place, dwarfed by the monuments of a national culture, but preserving and indeed reinscribing many of the constituent tensions of postcolonial urbanism on a global scale. In the colony, writers often migrated from the countryside to the city, seeing the city as not only a place of decadence and colonial subjection but also a place generative of national autonomy. The short story, in this context, often became a way of fixing and reframing the past within the context of the modern. In the postcolony, the modern developed city is an equally contradictory space, marked by the spatial practices of a state capitalism that attempts to appropriate all affective life, and yet still haunted by the possibilities of transcendence. The short story's own features – longer than a poem, but shorter than a novel – offer the reader a temporary immersion in another life-world that is concluded soon after it is begun, throwing the reader back into the spatial practices of the everyday. And yet, as we have seen, the architecture of the short story itself, with its re-symbolization of the everyday, offers at least the possibility of reimagining spatial practices that constitute the self. To Lefebvre's triad of perceived, conceived and lived, we might add a fourth element that tugs on the sleeve of the reader as s/he puts down the book and heads for work: the remembered.

Note

1. The quotation is drawn from the five national Shared Values that were adopted by Parliament in Singapore on 15 August 1991, as the result of the report of a parliamentary committee on national ideology and shared values set up in 1989.

Works cited

Alfian Sa'at. *Corridor: 12 Short Stories*. Singapore: SNP, 1999.
Anderson, Benedict R. *Imagined Communities: Reflections on the Origin and Spread of Nationalism*. 1983. London: Verso, 1991.
Chua Beng Huat. 'Disrupting Hegemonic Liberalism in East Asia.' *boundary 2* 37.2 (2010): 199–216.
Hall, Stuart. 'Cultural Identity and Diaspora.' *Identity: Community, Culture, Difference*. Ed. J. Rutherford. London: Lawrence and Wishart, 1990. 222–37.
Krishnaswamy, Revathi. 'Postcolonial and Globalization Studies: Connections, Conflicts, Complicities.' *The Postcolonial and the Global*. Ed. Revathi Krishnaswamy and John C. Hawley. Minneapolis: University of Minnesota Press, 2007. 2–21.
Lefebvre, Henri. *The Production of Space*. 1974. Trans. Donald Nicholson-Smith. Oxford: Blackwell, 1991.
Lim, Suchen Christine. *The Lies that Build a Marriage: Stories of the Unsung, Unsaid and Uncelebrated in Singapore*. Singapore: Monsoon, 2007.
Poon, Angelia. 'Mining the Archive: Historical Fiction, Counter-modernities, and Suchen Christine Lim's *A Bit of Earth*.' *The Journal of Commonwealth Literature* 43.3 (2008): 25–42.
Poon, Wena. *The Proper Care of Foxes*. Singapore: Ethos Books, 2009.

4
Vancouver Stories: Nancy Lee and Alice Munro

Ailsa Cox

Alice Munro: scenery, suburbs and basements

The British Columbian city of Vancouver, on Canada's Pacific coast, is regarded by some as an archetypal postmodern metropolis. In his introduction to *Vancouver: Representing the Postmodern City* (1994), Paul Delany interrogates what is already a presumption of its place as a 'vanguard city of postmodernism' (23). *City of Glass* (2000), Douglas Coupland's quixotic travel guide/memoir, characterizes his home town as a vibrant, idiosyncratic young city, where East and West meet: 'in a poetic way, it feels as if human history, which began in Asia and moved ever westward across the centuries, is now making the final connection by hooking up western North America with Asia' (26). Although the cyberpunk author William Gibson has situated very little of his fiction in an explicitly Vancouver setting, his hi-tech cityscapes, with their networks of disparate communities, may also be read in the context of fusion culture in the place where he has lived for 40 years. This chapter examines female encounters with postcolonial Vancouver which subvert or problematize that version of the ultra-modern global city, seen in Coupland, Gibson and other male writers such as Timothy L. Taylor.

Alice Munro needs no introduction as Canada's most influential short story writer, and a figure whose worldwide canonical status has become incontestable. Her work is most frequently associated with her home territory, in small-town, semi-rural Ontario, but she has also set a number of her stories in Vancouver, where she lived at the start of her first marriage, later moving to the city of Victoria, on Vancouver Island, before returning to South West Ontario in 1973.

In the linked story sequence, *The Beggar Maid* (published in Canada as *Who Do You Think You Are?* (1978)), Munro's protagonist Rose follows a similar trajectory, transplanted to this same alien territory when she marries Patrick. Her first adulterous kiss takes place at a West Vancouver party, her face wet from one of the city's notorious rainstorms. In this story, 'Mischief', British Columbia is divided between the suburban conformity Rose encounters in Vancouver and the symbolic wilderness beyond the city. Rose flies to a secret assignation with her lover on Vancouver Island, a journey which is fraught with false assumptions, guilt and failed connections. The complications of the journey stand for the moral and emotional complexities that she must negotiate on unfamiliar ground. In 'Material' (1974), the narrator reads the biography of her ex-husband Hugo, a macho Vancouver-based writer:

> He lives on the side of a mountain above Vancouver. It sounds as if he lives in a wilderness cabin, and all it means, I'm willing to bet, is that he lives in an ordinary comfortable house in North or West Vancouver, which now stretch far up the mountain. (*Something* 29)

In 'Mischief', Rose and Patrick's house – a house in which he takes a special pride – is 'a stone and cedar house in a suburb called Capilano Heights, on the side of Grouse Mountain' (*Beggar Maid* 115). 'Memorial' matches the Native American and Inuit artefacts inside a house with its much-lauded view, suggesting that both are consumed as simulacra. Munro's comments in a recent interview, 'I love the landscape, not as "scenery" but as something intimately known' (Munro 'Conversation'), implies a distinction between 'scenery' which is devoid of memory and external to the subject and an experience of landscape which itself contributes to subjective identity.

Munro divides her fictional Vancouver according to a widely acknowledged demographic. North and West Vancouver linked to downtown Vancouver by the Lion's Gate Bridge, which crosses Burrard Inlet, represents the smug and prosperous suburbs. Early in her marriage to Hugo, the narrator of 'Material' lives at a less socially desirable address, in a shabby house on Argyle Street, well to the other side of the inlet. Their landlady's daughter, Dotty, has a flat in the basement. A figure of fun to the young marrieds, she becomes the model for a character in a story Hugo publishes several years later, and the class divide between Argyle Street and North Vancouver is one of the unstated reasons for the narrator's unease concerning her transformation by Hugo.

Munro has returned to Vancouver in more recent collections, drawing on both earlier impressions and more current observations; since the late 1980s she has spent a good part of the year on Vancouver Island. The later stories revisit some of those earlier themes, portraying Vancouver and its surrounding territory as an alien environment, negotiated by protagonists who have often migrated from small-town Ontario. For these women, the city externalizes her protagonists' self-doubt and tests a cultural identity grounded in the pioneer values they were brought up with. The inauthenticity of suburban life, signalled through landscape and architecture, is reiterated. For many of her protagonists the city represents a transitional space rather than a place where they can assimilate.

In 'Cortes Island' (1998), it is the 'little bride' herself who lives underground in a basement, emerging onto the streets like a revenant:

> Winter in Vancouver was not like any other winter I had ever known. No snow, not even anything much in the way of a cold wind [...] I walked along Hastings Street where there wouldn't be another woman walking – just drunks, tramps, poor old shuffling Chinese. Nobody spoke an ill word to me. I walked past warehouses, weedy lots where there wouldn't even be a man in sight. Or through Kitsilano, with its high wooden houses crammed with people living tight, as we were, to the tidy Dunbar district, with its stucco bungalows and pollarded trees. And through Kerrisdale, where the classier trees appeared, birches on the lawns. Tudor beams, Georgian symmetry, Snow White fantasies with imitation thatched roofs. Or maybe real thatched roofs, how could I tell? (*Love* 127)

This haunting, rhythmic passage evokes a trance-like state, as Munro's young *flâneuse* passes through these sparsely populated streets, in a timeless zone, beyond the sharp seasonal contrasts of home. The city starts to come to life as the day wears on:

> In all these places where people lived, the lights came on around four in the afternoon, and then the streetlights came on, the lights in the trolley buses came on, and often, too, the clouds broke apart in the west over the sea to show the red streaks of the sun's setting – and in the park, through which I circled home, the leaves of the winter shrubs glistened in the damp air of a faintly rosy twilight. (*Love* 127)

In a travel piece for the *New York Times*, David Laskin contrasts the neighbourhoods Munro inhabited from the 1950s to the early 1960s with the territory now populated by sushi bars, joggers and coffee machines: 'Young but hopelessly uncool, lustful without being sexy, dowdy, white, blind to its own staggering beauty, Ms. Munro's Vancouver is an outpost where new wives blink through the rain and wonder when their real lives are going to begin' (Laskin n.p.). As Laskin points out, Munro tends to disregard or resist the visual splendours of the city's location, looking westwards over the Pacific, and set against the dramatic backcloth of the snow-topped mountains. The 'little bride' lifts her gaze to the sunset very briefly, before lowering her horizons to circumscribed, domestic pathways. The imagined landscape of Cortes Island, some hundred miles north which becomes associated in the narrator's mind with the tale of a violent and unsettling incident, is more vivid than her actual memories of Kitsilano. The Tudor beams and 'imitation [...] or maybe real thatched roofs' (*Love* 127) indicate her abiding distaste for architecture which either replicates traditional English style or reduces the colonial experience to mere affectation.

In 'Post and Beam' (2001), Lorna's cousin Polly from Ontario mocks her house, built somewhere off Capilano Road in North Vancouver, and specially designed in 'contemporary' style:

> 'So I really started out on the wrong foot, Brendan, wait till you hear what I said. Lorna and I are walking down the street from the bus stop and I'm saying, Oh shoot, this is a pretty classy neighborhood you live in, Lorna – and then I say, But look at that place, what's it doing here? I said, It looks like a barn.' (*Hateship* 197)

Like Munro's other young brides, Lorna has found the move westwards traumatic, and remains acutely aware of the social divide between the middle-class world she has married into and the folks back home. While Lorna is able to assimilate – superficially, at least – Polly is a misfit, and at one point during her extended visit Lorna even imagines that she might hang herself. Figuratively speaking, Lorna is haunted by the ghost of her pioneering forebears, voicing the commonsense values she was brought up with. Timber-frame 'post and beam' houses are modern reinventions of a colonial style which was, indeed, used for building barns; Polly misreads – or pretends to misread – its significance as a self-conscious cultural marker.

While Munro tends to present the Vancouver landscape as simulacrum without depth, she does sometimes invest the 'scenery' of British Columbia with more ambiguous qualities. Passing over the Lion's Gate Bridge, on her way home from a family trip, Lorna catches a glimpse of Vancouver Island. The image of 'those blue, progressively dimmer, finally dissolving mounds that seem to float upon the sea' (*Hateship* 212) is typical of Munro's use of liminal space to evoke a diffuse and mobile reality, something seen more often in her Ontario stories. The hazy landscape of the Georgia Strait heralds a small epiphany, as Lorna reaches home to find that Polly has not hanged herself after all, but that she herself must face up to the fact that her marriage and her migration westwards have brought her to a dead end. As Coral Ann Howells puts it, '[Munro's] stories make readers see that there is always something else which is out there unmapped, still "floating around loose"' (5).

Nancy Lee and contemporary Vancouver

Nancy Lee is a young, Vancouver-based writer, born in the UK, with Chinese and Indian ancestry. The stories in her first collection, *Dead Girls* (2002), are loosely connected by the presence in the city of a serial killer, prefiguring the capture of Robert Pickton shortly after its Canadian publication in 2002. Speaking about the setting of *Dead Girls*, Lee has described a geographical and social divide in the city, and the invisibility of those on the wrong side of the line:

> In my previous life, when I worked as a publicist, my office was right on the border between the downtown and the East Side,

where all these Skid Row girls were stumbling down the street, hovering in doorways, shooting up. I would often pass Main and Hastings, or Pigeon Park, and see these girls, so thin, so young, and imagine what they would look like if they were in regular shape, sitting at the mall, doing whatever, and I thought what a shame that this is going on, that really no one outside this area cares. It made me very sad. I would walk around Vancouver, such a beautiful city, and I'd see the water and the mountains, and think, at the same time, there are these horrible things going on. (Wigston n.p.)

Hastings is, of course, the street walked by the 'little bride' in Munro's 'Cortes Island', 'where there wouldn't be another woman walking' (*Love* 127). Lee seems to share some of Munro's ambivalence towards the allure of the natural landscape – 'such a beautiful city' – which she contrasts with the experience of the city streets as a gendered space. A sharp distinction between the bourgeois western suburbs and the less affluent east side is mapped out in the story 'East':

Then she said, Everything bad is east [...] As you move east the population gets poorer, there's religious fanaticism, racial intolerance. What else did she say? Oh, yeah, book bannings, drive-by shootings, murder suicides. That's why they put the prison out there. (149)

However, Lee challenges the east/west dichotomy along with other simple dualities in the moral mapping of Vancouver. While several stories deal directly with lives of the girls on Skid Row, others ('Associated Press', 'Young Love') use the figure of the killer, Thomas Coombs, to explore ways in which a range of female characters have internalized the pervasive threat of sexual violence. The centre of gravity for this violence lies not in the socially stigmatized parts of town but in its respectable outskirts, where Coombs' victims are buried in a suburban backyard.

In 'East', two friends out on a spree swap jokes about the killer's photo in the paper: 'Am I totally sick, or is there something kind of attractive about that man?' (135). Here the figure of Coombs is just one of the male antagonists who crop up in conversation or in person as they cruise the city in a minivan, grazing on junk food, cigarettes and candy. The spur-of-the-moment decision to throw rocks at the jail where he is being held seems motivated by anger, not just at Combes but at unreliable boyfriends, irresponsible ex-husbands, boors, predators, men in general; and at the 'puppy-killing bitch' (155) who ran over a dog belonging to one of the women. Ultimately, it is directed towards the designation of 'East' itself, as a receptacle for the 'other' Vancouver, the site of abjection and of their own impotence. Even the women's anger rebounds on themselves, as they lash out against two policemen, and are handcuffed and assaulted. The story's final sentence describes the inmates looking on, 'crowded into their tiny windows, scratching at the glass, hungry for the taste of angry girl' (158). The positions of viewer and spectacle, subject and object, have been reversed, the women's status changed from avenger to perpetrator, their faces pushed in the ground, and their transgressive behaviour fetishized.

In his article, 'Remapping Vancouver: Composing Urban Spaces in Contemporary Asian Canadian Writing' (2008), Glenn Deer aligns Lee with a new generation of Asian Canadian writers, including Madeleine Thien, Kevin Chong and Larissa Lai, who 'speak from greater socially mobile positions than their predecessors' (119), and thus are able to map out a more diverse and fluid urban space, informed by a globalized culture. This is not to claim that race and ethnicity are irrelevant in Lee's fiction. The two young women in 'Sisters', only one of whom survives sexual exploitation, are Native Americans, brought up in poverty. Coombs himself, 'a balding, dough-faced man with small eyes that receded like pressed raisins' (9), is middle-aged, middle-class and evidently white, cruising the streets in a spotless white car. However, the ethnic background of most of her characters remains undetermined. In an interview with her Canadian publisher, Lee draws attention to the fact that most of the teenage prostitutes working in Vancouver have migrated from elsewhere in Canada (Anon. n.p.), positioning them in terms of the opposition between small town and big city rather than global diaspora.

Interviews with Lee stress her research into the circumstances surrounding the murder of sex workers, and her political aims for the collection: 'if instead of dismissing those involved as "them," we examine the very things that scare, disgust and horrify us, we can come to a more honest understanding of who we are and what we consider important' (Anon. n.p.). This drive towards realism is accompanied by the evocation of heightened interior states, shaped by fantasy, sexual arousal and mood-altering substances. In this Lee is aided by the elliptical nature of the short story form, which lends itself to the fragmentary and inexplicable.

'Young Love' describes the misadventures of a volunteer first-aider at a school dance-a-thon. Her consciousness skewed by the pills she keeps popping, she tries to seduce first Janet's husband and then a teenage patient, only to be caught *in flagrante* by the husband, Paul. But these events take place in a seemingly arbitrary fashion without any pattern of cause and effect. Why does the narrator deliberately damage her hand? What has made her self-destruct? Explanations are withheld, and the story closes cryptically with the image of the killer in captivity:

> I fell asleep, eventually, sometime between four-thirty and five a.m. The last thing I remember thinking about was the dentist, Coombs, imagining him, cold and uncomfortable in a jail full of strangers, wishing for his white lab coat, anxious over who would play him in the movie of his life and whether or not they would get it right. (188)

Coombs' appearance at this point follows a kind of dream logic, recapitulating casual conversations from earlier parts of the story; there are rumours of a film, starring Martin Sheen or maybe Gene Hackman. This final passage includes thematic echoes from elsewhere in the story – the nurse's uniform worn by the narrator, the suggestion of childish play-acting. But these symbolic echoes are diffuse and attenuated. As Clare Hanson has said, 'Within the novel [...] each image as it appears resumes something of what has preceded it in the text. In the short story foregrounded details or "images" tend to resist such interpenetration and integration' (23).

The heterogeneity celebrated in Coupland's homage to the 'fractal' city (151) is incorporated into the formal characteristics of this loosely linked sequence. The drive through Vancouver in 'East', with its seemingly random detours and abrupt shifts in conversation, is representative of Lee's approach to structure within individual stories and across the collection as a whole. However, in Lee's representation of the city as a gendered space, with the choices available constricted by power relationships, this heterogeneity and fragmentation also generates social isolation, alienation and the destruction of traditional communities. In the next section, I shall go on to discuss images of severance and fragmentation in Lee's 'Dead Girls', going on to compare her treatment of estrangement between mother and daughter with Munro's handling of a similar theme in 'Silence' (2004).

The broken and the missing: 'Dead Girls' and 'Silence'

Images of the dismembered or decomposed female body recur in *Dead Girls*. 'Sally, In Parts' is an anatomical reassembly of its protagonist, each constituent part ('Sally's Ears', 'Sally's Feet', etc.) yielding further revelations about the protagonist. Sally is alive; but this forensic reconstruction mirrors the work of identifying the individual victims, buried in Coombs' backyard; and when Jemma's and Annie's faces are pushed into the mud at the end of 'East', readers may also be reminded of 'those girls [...] stuffed into the ground, clawed and eaten by the dead' (81). The closing image of 'East', 'hungry for the taste of angry girl' (158), echoes the description of police mug shots in 'Dead Girls', portraying 'thin, angry girls' (104). All the women in the collection are potentially 'disposable girls' (99).

Images of dismemberment and severance in *Dead Girls* may be linked to the fracturing of connections between self and other, including family structures and local communities. In the title story, the TV news follows the attempts to identify each of Coombs' 23 victims. The coverage is watched by the unnamed protagonist, whose drug-addicted daughter, Clare, is also missing. Lee uses second-person, present-tense narration to universalize the mother's story through indeterminacy; the technique also suggests urgency, repetition and compulsion, as in the opening line: 'You are addicted to television news' (99).

Much of the story is seen through the camera's eye:

A live camera pans through a backyard with cedar fencing, past a white plastic patio set and a painted picnic table to a huge rectangular dirt pit, its muddy sides reinforced with wood planks; small orange flags dot its surface. To you it looks like the beginnings of an in-ground swimming pool. The camera moves in closer.

Protruding here and there beside the orange flags, pale slivers and rounds, the bones of the unexhumed. Drowning hands. (104)

Still photos are also used extensively. Mug shots, taken from police records, are contrasted with high-school photographs. The mother tries to read Clare's identity through contradictory images – one of them a snapshot taken outside a police station:

> On the sidewalk, you showed the Polaroid to your daughter, asked her, 'Is this really you?' Clare held the photo in her dirty hands, squinted through cigarette smoke, shrugged and handed it back to you. The white bottom of the Polaroid was smudged with her thumbprint, a dark trail of swirls and circles that seemed to lead nowhere. (112)

Clare is absent even when physically present, the thumbprint standing for the futility of the mother's search not just for her missing daughter, but for the reasons behind her behaviour. She shows the polaroid to the other girls; she scrutinizes Clare's expression in earlier photographs for clues to her addiction, and retrieves images from her childhood and adolescence that are stored in her memory. The scopic element introduced by the use of cameras and photographs is sustained through frequent references to the eye and the gaze, for instance when the mother watches the streetwalkers opening their coats to advertise their bodies to the cars cruising past.

The externalized, partial eye of the camera is implicit in the narrative viewpoint:

> It is the shuffle and clink against the car that startles you. Some one squeezing by. You look up and catch the backs of a man and girl walking. The girl, in a white leather coat that almost covers her short white skirt, takes long strides on high chunky heels; the man, thin and older, in a tight-fitting suit, follows quickly behind, looking around himself as he goes. (117)

Despite the man's precautions, she is unobserved when she gets out of the car and follows them into an alley. It is as if the mother herself is transformed into a hidden camera, recording the transaction in minute detail. Towards the end of the story, having suddenly initiated rough sex with her husband, she replays the scene for his benefit:

> You tell him about the alley, the smell, the needles. The girl, her arms, her knees, the man, her hair in his hands, her buried face. The wet sounds, the jingle of her bracelets. You tell him that she looked thin, but not too thin, not sick, not hurt. (120)

The figure of the girl – her face concealed, glimpsed only in fragments – appears to be Clare herself. However, this sighting may be no more than provisional, in a narrative marked by misrecognition, for instance the misreading of grandchildren as children on a waitress' novelty button (114).

This difficulty in reading visual signs may be linked with a failure or refusal to hear. The aural is also strongly invoked in this story – the TV turned up loud, the whispering of the real-estate agent as she shows potential buyers round the family home. Because the silence in Clare's old room is unendurable, her mother installs a CD player, set to continuous play: 'you try to select five CDs that Clare would like, but you don't know what Clare likes, so you buy numbers one to five from the Weekly Top Ten rack' (108–9).

The sale of the house, necessitated by the expense of Clare's failed treatment at a recovery programme, intensifies the crisis between the protagonist and her husband, as their daughter's room is emptied, obliterating the last remaining traces of her presence. This character is always referred to as 'your husband', never as a father, although Clare calls him 'Daddy' (103). The protagonist is especially annoyed by the 'whisper' of his pencil as he does the household accounts (101), an action which prefigures Coombs' keeping of an inventory of his victims. Silence and averted eyes signal the couple's estrangement: 'each regards the other's suffering as something foreign and solitary' (105). The silence is broken after their brutal resumption of sex by her speech and his sobs. The rough sex uses physical pain to break through senses muted and repressed by emotional suffering, but the cathartic effect for the mother may also entail a substitution for her missing daughter in the re-enactment of rape and sexual assault. The closing paragraph again uses sound – 'traffic and sirens, rain on the pavement, some one's radio' (121) – and the image of the city washing over the mother, as if reclaiming and absorbing her, detaching her from a potential reconnection with the husband.

Munro's 'Silence' also centres on the figure of an absent daughter, who has severed connections with her mother. 'Silence' is the third and last of the 'Juliet' stories in *Runaway* (2004). The earlier stories, 'Chance' and 'Soon', describe how Juliet first met her daughter's father and, in a tangential way, Penelope's babyhood, but the abrupt temporal shifts between stories disrupts continuity and the sequence of cause and effect.

In 'Chance', Juliet travels by train from Ontario to take up a teaching position at a private school in Vancouver. The journey is rather similar to Rose's journey from South West Ontario to Toronto in *The Beggar Maid* ('Wild Swans'), in that the shy, inexperienced girl is accosted by an over-friendly male passenger, her embarrassment compounded by an anxiety that she may be overreacting or behaving inappropriately. Juliet's self-lacerating sense of shame is redoubled when the stranger commits suicide, and this leads to a second, more fateful encounter when she confides in another passenger. This is her future partner, Eric Porteous, a fisherman who lives on the coast north of Vancouver. In this bucolic setting, Eric represents a rugged masculine type, who would not be out of place in a romantic novel (he even has an invalid wife). However, Juliet's reactions to the British Columbia landscape and domestic architecture reiterate the responses of previous migrants from Munro's Ontario:

> Nothing is much to her liking on this coast. The trees are too large and crowded together and do not have any personality of their own – they simply make a forest. The mountains are too grand and implausible and the islands that float upon the waters of the Strait of Georgia are too persistently picturesque. This house, with its big spaces and slanted ceilings and unfinished wood, is too stark and self-conscious. (83)

'Silence' marks a rapid temporal shift to Juliet in middle age. The classics teacher in 'Chance' is now a presenter on local TV. She is on a ferry to Denman Island, one of the smaller islands in the Georgia Strait, where her daughter has been on a six-month retreat. When she arrives at the Spiritual Balance Centre, she is informed that Penelope has left without giving a forwarding address. The Centre is based at an old church, divested of its pews and other ecclesiastical furnishings. Both the building and the cult members seem disarmingly mundane and characterless. With its empty stage and darkened windows, it resembles a lonely theatre.

Juliet's fruitless voyage to Denman Island may be contrasted with her first visit to Eric at Whale Bay, a journey almost as fraught as Rose's adulterous peregrinations in 'Mischief'. Although the logistics of the bus ride to Whale Bay, and the taxi-ride to Eric's may seem daunting, Juliet does find help on the road, and the story ends with a lovers' meeting. The name 'Penelope' reflects Juliet's classical interests, and the Homeric references in 'Chance', but there is no metaphoric homecoming on Denman Island.

Through a series of overlapping analeptic passages, we discover that Eric drowned in a storm about eight years previously, when Penelope was 13. It is widowhood that has prompted Juliet's move back to Vancouver and her TV career. Despite her grief, the move is liberating, and seems to draw her closer to Penelope, who becomes her confidante, taking on a nurturing role in their shared apartment. This makes the rupture all the more inexplicable to Juliet. Following the trip Juliet receives no further word from Penelope except for an unsigned greetings card sent annually, on her own birthday, until this communication also comes to an end.

Like the protagonist of 'Dead Girls', Juliet is baffled by the irreversible change in her daughter, but Juliet does not preserve the empty bedroom as a shrine. She seals it away, banishing all reminders of her daughter's existence – including photographs – to the periphery. Although she is not able to bring herself to throw away the memorabilia when she moves to a high-rise apartment, she is able to cast off the role of Penelope's mother, at least superficially. The transience of life in Vancouver, 'the cleanness, tidiness, and manageability of city life' (*Runaway* 146), agrees with Juliet. Friendships, even sexual liaisons, are fleeting and essentially pragmatic.

Juliet's high rise is no doubt rather similar to those glass towers described in *Dead Girls* ('Associated Press', 'Sisters'), offering their inhabitants a vantage point over the city. Juliet stays there until she gives up her job in television, retreating to a basement flat – a basement more salubrious in the new Vancouver than the old Vancouver of the 'little bride', but which symbolically conceals her underground. Juliet is divesting herself of personal ties and returning to her previous studies in classical literature. The anonymity of the city helps her to achieve this. In fact the representation of Vancouver in 'Silence' is short on sensual and topographic detail. The narrative structure, based on interlocking elliptical passages, focalized through Juliet, lends itself to a temporal and spatial indeterminacy, matching the rootlessness of the main character.

Yet even at the beginning of the story, when mother and daughter have been apart for no more than six months, Juliet has an elemental need for her daughter, expressed by an intense internal monologue: '– all this time I've been in a sort of desert, and when her message came I was like an old patch cracked of earth getting a full drink of rain' (*Runaway* 128). At the Spiritual Balance Centre, Juliet's attempts to track down Penelope are blocked by a psychopomp she nicknames 'Mother Shipton'. In a phrase that haunts Juliet, this character claims that 'she [Penelope] has come to us here in great hunger' (*Runaway* 132), a hunger Juliet interprets as a spiritual need, but which the reader may connect to Juliet's own self-absorption and the reversal of the mother/daughter roles after Eric's death; the metaphorical 'hunger' mirrors Juliet's metaphorical thirst for her daughter.

Finally, when years have gone by, Juliet bumps into Heather, one of Penelope's old school friends, who mentions meeting Penelope in Edmonton. She has five children now, and has flown down 'from that place way up north' (*Runaway* 154). Juliet is left speculating about these few details and what kind of lifestyle they might indicate. She tries to convince herself that whatever kind of person she has become, 'who had changed in face and body so that Heather did not recognize her, was nobody Juliet knew' (*Runaway* 157). But, like the mother in 'Dead Girls', she finds the irrecoverable breach with her daughter intolerable, and the inability to express that loss makes any other intimacy impossible.

Juliet disappears into the city – once a highly visible TV personality she relishes the anonymity of working in a coffee bar. She has reverted to the figure of the lone *flâneuse*, portrayed in 'Cortes Island'; and is also incorporating some aspects of her missing daughter's life in order to feel closer to her; the story's final sentence echoes the spiritual discourse she ascribes to Penelope in the lingering hope that she might hear from her, 'as people who know better hope for undeserved blessings, spontaneous remissions, things of that sort' (*Runaway* 158). In the globalized city, it is possible to lose yourself in the crowd; and that is both the cause of these mothers' sufferings and a consolation.

Works cited

Anon. 'Author Interview.' 2003. http://www.mcclelland.com/catalog/display. pperl?isbn=9780771052514&view=auqa

Coupland, Douglas. *City of Glass*. Vancouver: Douglas & McIntyre, 2000.

Deer, Glenn. 'Remapping Vancouver: Composing Urban Spaces in Contemporary Asian Canadian Writing.' *Canadian Literature* 199 (2008): 118–44.

Delany, Paul. 'Introduction: Vancouver as a Postmodern City.' *Vancouver: Representing the Postmodern City*. Ed. Paul Delany. Vancouver: Arsenal Pulp Press, 1994. 1–24.

Hanson, Clare. '"Things out of Words": Towards a Poetics of Short Fiction.' *Re-Reading the Short Story*. Ed. Clare Hanson. London: Macmillan, 1989. 22–33.

Howells, Coral Ann. *Alice Munro*. Manchester University Press, 1998.

Laskin, David. 'Alice Munro's Vancouver.' *The New York Times*, 2006. 27 July 2011. http://travel.nytimes.com/2006/06/11/travel/11footsteps.html

Lee, Nancy. *Dead Girls*. London: Faber & Faber, 2003.

Munro, Alice. *The Beggar Maid*. London: Allen Lane, 1980.

—— 'A Conversation with Alice Munro.' 2008. 27 July 2011. http://reading-group-center.knopfdoubleday.com/2010/01/08/alice-munro-interview/

—— *Hateship, Friendship, Courtship, Loveship, Marriage*. London: Chatto & Windus, 2001.

—— *The Love of a Good Woman*. London: Chatto & Windus, 1998.

—— *Runaway*. London: Chatto & Windus, 2005.

—— *Something I've Been Meaning to Tell You*. London: Penguin, 2006.

Wigston, Nancy. 'Dead Girls: Lament for those Lost and Forgotten – Interview with Nancy Lee.' http://www.booksincanada.com/article_view. asp?id=1973. 2002.

5
'And did those feet'? Mapmaking London and the Postcolonial Limits of Psychogeography

Paul March-Russell

In his *Independent* review of Iain Sinclair's anthology *London: City of Disappearances* (2006), Ian Thomson criticizes its colour blindness: 'of 59 authors, only the Trinidad-born Vahni Capildeo writes of West Indian London. Commonwealth immigrants [...] are conspicuous by their absence.' He associates this myopia with a depoliticized view of history: 'an overwhelmingly white man's metropolis, filtered through a rose-tinted nostalgia' (Thomson paras 1 and 2). In two respects, Thomson's criticisms are misguided. Firstly, he devalues Sinclair's anthology on the grounds of positive discrimination, despite this being potentially condescending to Afro-Caribbean settlers and their offspring. Secondly, Thomson glosses the political content of Sinclair's work. As Sinclair describes in a discussion with Kevin Jackson and Will Self:

> It was in the Thatcherite era when there was [...] a kind of occulted state in politics, demonic energies, and things so impacted and grim. And everything was being wiped out, old values, so it became necessary to provoke the human imagination. There were ways of resurrecting tools of resistance and one of them [...] was the notion of psychogeography. (Jackson para. 88)

Nevertheless, despite the attempts of critics such as Robert Bond and Alex Murray to reclaim Sinclair as a politically engaged writer, problems of race – and class and gender – recur: 'We do not think of Sinclair's London as associated with the proletariat, women, ethnic or other oppressed and oppositional social groups' (Brooker 227).

Sinclair has responded by arguing that 'I can only speak for myself. I have no obligation to speak on behalf of other people. That idea is too compulsory, extremely patronising and politically correct' (quoted in Groes 96). This chapter will argue that, on the contrary, 'other(ed) people' are nevertheless integral to Sinclair's work. It will attempt to get beyond the polarized positions of Sinclair and his critics, first, by indicating the limitations of psychogeography in the context of postcolonialism, and second, by advocating a more nuanced understanding of the concept through a discussion of Syed Manzurul (Manzu) Islam's collection *The Mapmakers of Spitalfields* (1997).

Broadly speaking, the work of writers such as Self and Sinclair can be described as examples of contemporary *flânerie*. In his inaugural lecture as Professor of Contemporary Thought at Brunel University, Self is explicit on what he sees as the politics of *flânerie*: 'The contemporary flâneur is by nature and inclination a democratising force who seeks equality of access, freedom of movement and the dissolution of corporate and state control' (Self para. 15). This re-politicized description of *flânerie* has its immediate root in Michel de Certeau's essay 'Walking in the City' (1984). De Certeau distinguishes between 'the urban *fact*' and 'the *concept* of a city' (*Practice* 94). The Concept-city is rationally organized, transparent and integrated from a central administration. In practice, however, tensions emerge between an idealized urban control and the capacity of individuals to either negotiate or resist those ruling structures. Likening the behaviour of pedestrians to that of the speech act, de Certeau argues that the various modalities associated with walking amount to 'a process of *appropriation*', 'a spatial acting-out' and the implication of '*relations* among differentiated positions' (97–8). Taken together, they form a 'chorus, changing from step to step, stepping in through proportions, sequences, and intensities which vary according to the time, the path taken and the walker' (99); 'a way of being in the world' that is 'forgotten' within the panoptical gaze of the Concept-city: the inscription of 'a totalizing and reversible line on a map' that 'has the effect of making invisible the operation that made it possible' (97). De Certeau's critique of orchestrated forgetting can be compared to similar laments in the work of his contemporaries such as Jean-François Lyotard and Paul Virilio, but also to the employment of reification by Frankfurt School thinkers such as Theodor Adorno and Walter Benjamin. As with Benjamin, de Certeau's retrieval of everyday practices can be read as an exercise in brushing 'history against the grain' (Benjamin 248). Likewise, Sinclair's weaving of forgotten histories into the textuality of his *oeuvre* is hardly 'nostalgia' but an attempt to dispel politically managed amnesia (see also Mengham).

In *Lights Out for the Territory* (1997), Sinclair states that 'time on these excursions should be allowed to unravel at its own speed [...] To shift away from the culture of consumption into a meandering stream' (7). Sinclair's invocation of drift distinguishes his project from that of the idle stroller and instead associates it with the calculated, if also in effect haphazard, migrations of psychogeography. Sinclair replaces the figure of the *flâneur* with that of the stalker 'walking with a thesis. With a prey' (75). This redefinition had already been aired in the graphic short story 'The Griffin's Egg' (1996), in which the writer, Norton, is pursued through the London streets by the photographer, Turner, whom Norton has employed to enter and photograph the penthouse apartment of the novelist and political operator Lord Kawn (a thinly disguised Jeffrey Archer). Although the stalker carries with it sexual overtones, like Vaughan, the anti-hero of J.G. Ballard's *Crash* (1973), inhabiting the media-saturated environment of the city, it is more profitable to compare the figure with that of Wyndham Lewis' alter ego of 'the Enemy' (Lewis being an important early influence on Sinclair), a persona that David Ayers has described as 'a sniper at the outskirts of Western civilisation' (196). More recently in Sinclair's work, the modernist/postmodern sniper-stalker has given way to the Romantic figure of the crazed, spontaneous walker: '*Fugueur* was the right job description for our walk, our once-a-month episodes of transient mental illness' (*London Orbital* 147).

Despite the Romantic origins to what Self and Sinclair describe as their particular brand of psychogeography, the term was popularized by Guy Debord in his 'Introduction to a Critique of Urban Geography' (1955): 'Psychogeography could set for itself the study of the precise laws and specific effects of the geographical environment, consciously organized or not, on the emotions and behaviour of individuals' ('Introduction' 5). Following Ivan Chtcheglov's 'Formulary for a New Urbanism' (1953), Debord's aim was to encourage an urban space that did not delineate between formal architectural design and the imaginative play of its consumers. As Chtcheglov declared:

> The principal activity of the inhabitants will be the CONTINUOUS DÉRIVE. The changing of landscapes from one hour to the next will result in complete disorientation. (4)

Debord subsequently glossed the *dérive* as 'a technique of transient passage through varied ambiences' ('Theory' 50); in effect, the exploration of an urban district by drifting through its environment and observing what had previously passed unnoticed. Unlike Chtcheglov, Debord sought to disorientate the individual only to recapture a new sense of the urban milieu and of its possibilities. There is a resonance here between Debord's project and the psychogeographical wanderings of Self and Sinclair in that the aim is ultimately one of reorientation.

It is significant that, despite Self's emphasis upon the solitary walker, Sinclair usually walks with others. To some extent, this collaborative ethos echoes the group nature of the *dérive*, but whereas, for Debord, collective action was constituent of political activism, for Sinclair the emphasis is upon the forging of interpersonal relationships and group identities in reaction to the abstracted forces of centralized economic and political control. In other words, whereas Debord imagines political change in the period before 1968, in the wake of post-Thatcherite economics Sinclair writes of recuperation, of drawing attention to those historical, cultural and communal ties that have not been broken. Although Peter Brooker argues that this tendency identifies Sinclair with a modernist desire 'to order, map and *re-align* what is perceived as chaos' (232), within his cartography Sinclair associates fugitive poets such as Brian Catling and Aaron Williamson 'with other avatars of unwisdom: scavengers, dole-queue antiquarians, bagpeople, out-patients, muggers, victims, millennial babblers' (*Lights Out* 247). They become the contemporary equivalents to the mad, dispossessed and forsaken figures valorized by Romantic poets such as Charlotte Smith and William Wordsworth, and embodied by the Romantics William Blake and John Clare, key players in texts by Sinclair such as *Lud Heat* (1975) and *Edge of the Orison* (2005). Even if Sinclair begins his project of remapping London with modernist intentions – a call to order more apparent in Peter Ackroyd's magisterial studies such as *London: The Biography*

(2000) – what he produces are characteristically Romantic accounts in which the 'Other' is reproduced as the visionary, or shamanic, outcast. In some cases, these shamans are also ethnic minorities, in particular Jewish figures such as the mysterious David Rodinsky, subject of Sinclair's collaboration with Rachel Lichtenstein, *Rodinsky's Room* (1999), or the poet Grace Lake/Anna Mendelssohn, collected alongside the likes of Catling and Williamson in Sinclair's anthology *Conductors of Chaos* (1996). For Brian Baker, Sinclair's valorization of the outsider is marked by the influence of the anti-psychiatry movement led by R.D. Laing (Baker 3–10) and, as Sinclair recalls, the Dialectics of Liberation Conference, the subject of his first publication *The Kodak Mantra Diaries* (1971):

> A big term was 'psychopolitics', which was a way of heating up politics, and taking it away from corporate entities, and I think the same sort of thing happened with geography. (Jackson para. 15)

As Baker argues, Sinclair's growing interest in the spirit of urban space, although inspired by such occult practices as ley lines, complements the work of postmodern geographers such as Mike Davis and Edward Soja writing against the socio-economic policies of Ronald Reagan and Margaret Thatcher (10–15). Yet, as Kristin Ross suggests, a precedent can be found during the Paris Commune of 1871: Arthur Rimbaud's valorization of the vagabond and his personal resistance to rectilineal unities of time and space (52–5). As Simon Sadler suggests, the disorientation induced by the *dérive* can be likened to Rimbaud's derangement of the senses (94).

Sinclair's disorientation of what passes for home occurs in the context of what Patrick Wright has termed 'Deep England': an inchoate series of myths that reify English history and re-present it as timeless (*On Living* 81–7). Sinclair's use of ley lines and treatment of texts as if they were divinatory tools may suggest complicity in this ideology but, as Simon Perril argues, mysticism 'is inverted into a study of power and oppression' (313). Nevertheless, the agents of shamanism through whom Sinclair operates in order to re-vision his readers' understanding of historical London locates his work within the nexus of a conceptual centre (the centralized administration outlined by de Certeau) and a hypothetical periphery (the *fugueurs* with whom Sinclair is a fellow – and often – a literal traveller). Sinclair's own ambiguous role as the mass media's psychogeographer of choice (see also Brooker 235) emphasizes that this is less an opposition of forces than a dialectic. The title, for example, of Sinclair's 2009 account of his stamping-ground of Hackney performs a Situationist-styled *détournement* by rebilling the London outpost – which, in the 1960s, acted as an escape for Cambridge academic poets and an intersection with London's fugitive poetry scene – as 'that rose-red empire'.

In his composite novel, *Downriver* (1991), Sinclair dramatizes the elision between the centre and the periphery through the use of Joseph Conrad's *Heart of Darkness* (1899) as a recurrent paratext. A copy of Conrad's novella is first spied by the narrator amongst 'the beached detritus of the Imperial Dream' (*Downriver* 15), the remaining stock of the Nigerian book-dealer, Iddo Okoli. Okoli's initial appearance, 'savage in Middle Temple mufti' (14), recalls Marlow's description of the African fireman as 'a dog in a parody of breeches' (Conrad 70). Okoli is lured into a scam that sells 'all the tribes of brutalized' white goods to developing nations, amongst them Nigeria (*Downriver* 15). The money is 'laundered through a government-funded education programme: heavyweight Industrial Training Films', staffed by Dutch instructors who 'have to deal in black-market primitive art to survive' (16). Sinclair's narrator describes a nexus of neo-colonial exploitation, in which the postcolonial subject (Okoli) plays the willing dupe, and which acts as an analogue to Conrad's own theme of ruthless imperialism. The narrator concludes this section by asking the reader 'to imagine, as you go under, Claudius bringing his legions over from the Kent shore', words that echo Marlow's account of the Roman commander with 'nothing but Thames water to drink' (Conrad 30). Later, the narrator's companion, Joblard, composes an imaginary rewrite of both Conrad and Sinclair, '*Joblard's HEART OF DARKNESS. A Narrative in Twelve Postcards*' (*Downriver* 25): rewriting being their only escape from 'the sullen gravity of Tilbury Riverside' and 'the World's End [...] once the baggage store where troops crossing the river left their equipment' (17). Sinclair's fractured and compulsive retelling of stories involving the Australian Aboriginal cricket team of 1868, Pocahontas and Rodinsky works against the neutrality of a hypothetical 'Museum of Immigration':

As if immigration could be anything other than an active response to untenable circumstances – a brave, mad, greedy charge at some vision of the future; a thrusting forward of the unborn into a region they could neither claim nor desire. (136)

As Robert Sheppard suggests, 'only the immigrant [...] may speak authentically with a subaltern voice' (67).

This silence is embedded in what might be called the cosmopolitanism of Sinclair's neo-modernist style: 'the limits of perception and the waning of a confident epistemology, the conflict between the exhaustive and the ineffable, the appeal of the trivial, the political consequences of uniformity and variousness in meaning, the fragmentation of perspectives, and the disruption of social categories' (Walkowitz 20). For Robert Spencer, the self-consciousness, irony and scepticism of modernist discourse, allied to its receptivity to 'numerous clashing perspectives and voices' (10), renders it a viable form through which to begin considering 'trans-national relationships embodied in structures and institutions' (6). Yet, Sinclair's cosmopolitanism has its roots in what he regards as the Ur-source for psychogeography – Thomas De Quincey's description of the 'northwest passage':

And sometimes in my attempts to steer homewards, upon nautical principles, by fixing my eye on the pole-star, and seeking ambitiously for a north-west passage [...] I came suddenly upon such knotty problems of alleys, such enigmatical entries, and such sphynx's riddles of secrets without thoroughfares [...] I could almost have believed [...] that I must be the first discoverer of some of these *terrae incognitae*, and doubted, whether they had yet been laid down in the modern charts of London. (53)

Until its successful navigation in the 1900s, the north-west passage had represented the illusory dream of European colonial nations to find a commercial sea route past North America and into Asia. De Quincey's deployment of the metaphor is consequently bound up with imperial and economic desires, and although his intended destination goes astray, he finds new territories that he describes in orientalist terms ('sphynx's riddles'). As has been much discussed, De Quincey's text is filled with orientalist imagery – the Malaysian drug-pedlar, the hallucinations of jewelled crocodiles, Eastern gods and sacrificial rites – but more profitably, De Quincey's addiction situates him, however marginally, within a nexus of economic and imperial relations that underlie the opium trade.

In other words, although Sinclair's cosmopolitan writing does open itself out to other, ex-centric voices that he (perhaps respectfully) does not try to mimic, it has also evolved from discourses that were situated metaphorically in the history and desires of colonialism. Sinclair's replacement of the *flâneur* with the image of the *fugueur* has made this connection to Romantic exoticism all the more apparent. And although, following Perril's distinction, the shamanic means are never an end in themselves, they still reveal that Sinclair's writing is dialectically engaged with the legacy of colonialism to varying degrees of self-awareness. Furthermore, despite Sinclair's critique of memorialization, in Geoff Nicholson's novel *Bleeding London* (1997) Nicholson satirizes the ways in which an occult version of London's history can be inducted into national heritage. In his interview though, for Nicholson's *The Lost Art of Walking* (2008), Sinclair is aware of 'psychogeography as a franchise' (94), one that Nicholson later critiques during his visit to the Conflux festival in New York. Rebecca Solnit too criticizes the 'abstraction of contemporary theory': 'Much of the terminology of location and mobility [...] are not attached to specific places and people; they represent instead ideas of rootlessness and flux that seem as much the result of the ungrounded theory as its putative subject' (28). As Solnit remarks of her own experiences of walking late at night in San Francisco: 'the world was full of strangers who seemed to hate me and wish to harm me for no reason other than my gender, that sex so readily became violence, and that hardly anyone else considered it a public issue rather than a private problem' (241). Threats of sexual violence pierce the veil of abstract theory and remind Solnit of her own corporeality – of being a physical body moving through a demarcated city space. Although Benjamin is justly remembered for his theorization of the *flâneur*, he also offers an image of walking that runs counter to de Certeau:

> Moving through this traffic involves the individual in a series of shocks and collisions. At dangerous intersections, nervous impulses flow through him in rapid succession, like the energy from a battery [...] Whereas Poe's passers-by cast glances in all directions which still appeared to be aimless, today's pedestrians are obliged to do so in order to keep abreast of traffic signals. (171)

Despite Benjamin's use of electrical metaphors, his aim is to reveal the extent to which the individual has been compelled by the built environment into 'a complex kind of training'. There is an emphasis upon 'the tiny, fragile human body' (84) as also expressed towards the start of his essay 'The Storyteller' (1936).

Both Benjamin and Solnit, despite their contrasting approaches, experience the city as a physical entity, an embodiment that – for all his talk of ley lines – is also apparent in Sinclair: 'all lines of energy and intelligence move out from that particular cluster' (the memorials to William Blake, John Bunyan and Daniel Defoe at Bunhill Fields) (Nicholson 95). As John McLeod has argued, it is 'the inseparable relations between the material and the invented' (8), which is to say, between the life-world and its shifting portrayal, which constitutes postcolonial London. 'Postcolonial', in this sense, exists as a site of contest between the actuality of lived experience and its discursive representation: as also in Sinclair's readings of the city, it is not exclusively semiological play. Instead, as in Spencer's usage of cosmopolitanism, the material basis of the postcolonial grounds discourse analysis in an historical process of social and political change. The very facts of racism and Islamophobia, in the wake of 9/11 and the 7/7 bombings in London, are an anxious reminder for a would-be psychogeographer such as Self:

> But then again, if I was walking to the airport in Delhi I think I would probably attract more attention for being white-skinned [...] Actually anybody walking out of J.F.K. is in some serious shit, I can tell you that (laughs), it doesn't matter what [your] gender or ethnicity is (laughs). (Jackson para. 103)

A similar unease is to be found in *Downriver* written in the wake of the *fatwa* imposed upon Salman Rushdie. In an instance of Sinclair's Rabelaisian humour, the narrator dwells upon 'the mysterious attraction of the west window' of the Monster Doss House (Tower House): a 'grimy porthole' at which 'the incarcerated onanist' could pleasure himself (*Downriver* 123). Now, though, his view would be obstructed by 'the ochre-brick "Espresso Mosque" [...] grafted on to Whitechapel Road' whose *muezzin*'s 'exotic arias [...] had captured the townscape': 'to curse, to anathematize, to hurl fire and brimstone on to the sublimely indifferent heads of sinners'. Sinclair courts the charge of racism only for his narrator to reveal that the mosque is, in fact, a simulacrum: 'a Disneyland mosque', 'the summons [...] pre-recorded' (124). Similarly, when 'the perished dream of Spitalfields' is said to have been replaced by 'Banglatown' – 'vulture priests, percolating hatred beneath their turbans', 'fundamentalist guards' patrolling 'the border tracks' – Sinclair locates this balkanization of London within 'the occult logic of "market forces"' that have 'dictated a new geography' (265). In what might be another example of *détournement*, Sinclair appropriates the crassness and nightmare scenarios of tabloid journalism to satirize the very loss of multicultural ideals at the expense of market economics. Nevertheless, an anxiety persists that the 'Imperial fantasy' (121) represents one of the 'old values' that Sinclair laments in the apparent victory of Thatcherism – Tower House having since been converted into a block of luxury flats.

For a more effective critique readers could turn to the debut collection from Syed Manzurul (now Manzu) Islam, *The Mapmakers of Spitalfields* (1997). Unlike the form of the composite novel in *Downriver*, which allows Sinclair to trace and retrace overlapping story arcs that cross between the 12 narratives that produce the text, Islam's stories focus upon individual characters and situations. The sense of atomization is also reflected in the structure of the collection which is divided between four stories set in England and three in Bangladesh, a separation that reflects on the fractures within the postcolonial experience – embodied in the title of Rushdie's collection *East, West* (1994) – and the restrictions imposed upon compartmentalized lives as, for example, in Samuel Selvon's pioneering collection, *Ways of Sunlight* (1957). In the London stories, the flawed attempts of the immigrants to make lives of their own echo the fault-lines to be found in the protagonists of other postcolonial texts, such as Hanif Kureishi's *The Buddha of Suburbia* (1990), a novel that evolved initially from a short story. Indeed, Islam's own collection prefigured the themes of his first novel, *Burrow* (2004), as well as Monica Ali's celebrated *Brick Lane* (2003). The blind spot of critics towards the short story, such as McLeod whose otherwise admirable study of postcolonial London includes novels, poems and screenplays, means that a crucial treatment of the postcolonial condition has been omitted. Other notable collections of the 1990s include Doris Lessing's *London Observed* (1992), Pauline Melville's *The Migration of Ghosts* (1998) and Courttia Newland's *Society Within* (1999).

Three other important factors underwrite Islam's collection. Firstly, he is the son of Syed Nazrul Islam, Acting President of Bangladesh during the 1971 war of independence and later assassinated in 1975, the year that his son migrated to England. Secondly, following Islam's graduation from the University of Essex, he worked in the East End as a racial harassment officer at the height of the National Front's campaign against the Asian communities in the early 1980s. Thirdly, he went on to an academic career at the University of Gloucestershire and so, unlike Sinclair who is cognizant but sceptical of critical theory, Islam's fiction is actively informed by postcolonial thought. Rather than producing a mannered product, the engagement with theory provides a creative dynamic with Islam's literary practice.

In his critical text, *The Ethics of Travel* (1996), Islam draws upon a range of thinkers to explore the notions of cross-cultural encounter and Otherness. He dwells at one point on Michel Foucault's figure of the *Stultifera Navis*, the ship of madmen imprisoned on 'the inside (both driven out of the city and confined within the boat)' and on 'the outside (of the passage and sea)' (*Ethics* 29). Islam explains this paradox in terms of Gilles Deleuze's concept of the fold: what is outside is folded so as to be on the inside. Madness is outside the norms of regulated, transparent society – de Certeau's 'Concept-city' – but it is reincorporated by the very act of being expelled. Yet, upon the inmates' arrival, the lines of control emanating from the colonial centre are stretched thin: however precarious, the inmates could create a new identity for themselves elsewhere (as in the apt case study of enforced migration to Australia offered by Robert Hughes in *The Fatal Shore* (1987)). Foucault's historical instance effectively dramatizes the process of de- and reterritorialization described by Deleuze and Félix Guattari. Yet, it also has clear affinities with the Situationist technique of *détournement* while Foucault's example echoes André Breton's claim that 'Columbus should have set out to discover America with a boatload of madmen' (5–6), a statement consistent with Sinclair's use of the Romantic *fugueur*. In other words, the immediate reference-points for the theorists that Islam calls upon are from the European avant-garde rather than the postcolonial experience. Islam has to perform his own *détournement* to make use of these ideas within his fiction.

As Islam has commented in an online interview, the stories recount 'the symbolic mapping process' through which a 'hostile

[...] colonial metropolis' was turned 'into a home' (Kabir para. 2). This hostility is conveyed in 'The Tower of the Orient' where a young immigrant couple experience the transient joy of moving into their first home – on the seventeenth floor of a tower block. Islam frames this tale with allusions to T.S. Eliot's *The Waste Land* (1922) and William Wordsworth's 'Daffodils' (1804–7):

> How can you say that April is the cruellest of months and the land is the land of the dead? There were lines of daffodils contemplating in yellow from thin, green stalks [...] Mixing memory and desire – she had discovered that this strange land had flowers too – made her dreamy-eyed again. (*Mapmakers* 89)

Soraya's husband, Munir, sniffs them and comments: 'All pretty pretty without sweet smell. I call them heartless flowers' (90). With the smash of a falling bottle, possibly an allusion to a similar incident in J.G. Ballard's *High-Rise* (1975), they wake to their surroundings and to the undead imagery of Eliot's modernist text: the lift is likened to 'a metallic grave, ready to devour her in its airless, timeless trap' (90). Unlike Sinclair's use of modernist techniques to reassemble the city, Islam draws upon modernist examples of entrapment and claustrophobia.

For instance, the opening story 'Going Home' begins with a chance encounter amidst 'a cloud of jostling city-gents' (9), not unlike the 'crowd' that flows 'over London Bridge' (Eliot 65) in Eliot's poem, and continues: 'we had carefully avoided each other's shadows and haunts, used different survival-kits to get by, put on different illusions', a process of deception that echoes Prufrock's injunction 'to prepare a face to meet the faces that you meet' (Eliot 14). Whereas Sinclair uses the spectral in order to reveal an unofficial version of London, Islam's use of the ghostly acts as a commentary upon the postcolonial condition of migration, 'this ghost dance' (*Mapmakers* 25) as the narrator calls it. Central to this experience is the narrator's dream, in which he and three companions slip 'into a subterranean darkness', labyrinthine sewers 'full of shit gushing towards us' (22). Turning into 'a single tunnel', they hear the amplified voice of a tour-guide: 'you've hit upon the ancient one-way street, leading to our magnificent heritage, the famous/infamous towers of the black ravens [...] intrepid travellers, or shall I say archaeologists' (22–3). Although a literal submerged London has been a popular trope with fantasy writers such as Neil Gaiman and China Miéville, it is possible to read this sequence as a satire on psychogeography: the metaphorical 'north-west passage' that guides the excavators to the doubled Tower of London. Instead of stumbling upon the occult truth, however, they are swept away by further 'waves of shit' (23). But, for the narrator, the dream acts as an analogy for the 'same old routine' of urban living: 'clock-time, black-time, brown-time – licking a living from this shit-hole', 'swept along by the rushing crowd' at Kings Cross, with only a tenuous network of friends preventing him from 'being swamped on the margins' (26).

The title story begins within such a supportive environment, 'the Sonar Bangla cafe', and its intrusion by 'two blond men in white overalls' (61), who might be medical orderlies or, equally, doc-marten-wearing Aryans. They are in pursuit of Brothero-Man whose origins are mysterious but who, possibly, was 'one of the pioneer jumping-ship men, who landed in the East End and lived by bending the English tongue to the umpteenth degree' (69). Brothero-Man resembles one of Foucault's mad seafarers who, in the terminology of Deleuze and Guattari, deterritorializes the master language. At one point, asked 'why he never went inside the mosque' (possibly the same mosque in Brick Lane that Sinclair dismisses as a simulacrum), Brothero-Man replies:

Inside/Outside what a fussing-wussing talk. Have you any idea, you shit head, where that mosque be? Right in me inside. Well, well, now tell me, you mother-fucking donkey, how can I go inside of the inside? (73)

In other words, Brothero-Man embodies the fold of which Deleuze writes. He is less of a *fugueur*, though, and more another key figure in the thinking of Deleuze and Guattari: the nomad, the sedentary traveller 'who moves without moving', who effectively takes his/her home with them, and who dwells 'by learning how to live a life without rigid boundary, by leaving the door open onto the outside, and by erasing the savage polarities of the *same* and the other' (*Ethics* 10). Brothero-Man seems to have no other possessions than the clothes he wears:

Look at the funny way he dresses. My God – the colours! Tell me something, how can a sane person walk about all day so aimlessly? And where does he go? Absolutely nowhere. (*Mapmakers* 66)

His clothing associates Brothero-Man with another literary nomad – the Russian who, in *Heart of Darkness*, wanders the river 'for nearly two years alone, cut off from everybody and everything' (Conrad 91):

> He looked like a harlequin. His clothes had been made of some stuff that was brown holland probably, but it was covered with patches all over, with bright patches, blue, red, and yellow, – patches on the back, patches on the front, patches on elbows, on knees. (90)

Contrary to Islam's passing comments on Marlow in *The Ethics of Travel*, Marlow's reaction to the Russian is nomadic in its affinity: he appreciates the beauty of the other's patchwork appearance.

Brothero-Man resembles the nomad in another respect: by distributing 'himself in a smooth space', 'he occupies, inhabits, holds that space' in contrast to the urban environment 'striated, by walls, enclosures, and roads between enclosures' (Deleuze and Guattari 420). In placing 'one foot in front of the other with the utmost precision [...] sketching delicately, with the skill of a miniaturist, a map at the very heart of this foreign city' (*Mapmakers* 63), Brothero-Man smoothes striated space into what Foucault describes as a heterotopia: 'a strange new city, always at the crossroads, and between the cities of lost times and cities of times yet to come' (69). In this respect, *Downriver*'s rhizomatic structure of continual tracing and retracing would seem to perform this ambition more effectively than Islam's text. Yet, in keeping with the figure of the nomad, Islam too transgresses his collection's striated structure. For example, the title story features the names of characters from other stories: Shafique from 'Going Home', and Munir and Soraya from 'The Tower of the Orient'. Are these the same characters and, if so, does the title story occur before or after? Details do not correspond: Munir and Soraya now have a son, Tariq, and are living on the seventh, not the seventeenth, floor. As Brothero-Man remarks, 'it's an either-neither place' (80), which is also applicable to Islam's text.

Yet, Brothero-Man is also more than the nomad. He is compared to a trickster entertaining the local children, whose Bengali 'hums and lullabies' mix 'with the *hickory dickory dock* of those English ones' (65); a cartographer noting 'topographical details' (70); 'a holy man' (72) whose divine vision contrasts with the celebrity madness of 'the wacko guy Jacko' (67); 'a white horse with a long flowing mane / galloping through the veins of your city' (75) in the words of 'my friend the poet' (73); a poltergeist who, 'as if from thin air' (79), forcibly silences the fundamentalist preacher Mulana Abdul Hakim; 'a commandante' (81) fighting the fascist skinheads; and a murderer with allusions to both Jack the Ripper and Spring-Heeled Jack. His excessive identity is further complicated by the narrator mistaking him for Jamir Ali, who 'one day, possessed by the evil bobby-spirit [...] stopped speaking and [...] made himself a police uniform' (77), when the latter is caught by the mad-catchers. Then in a *coup de grâce*, although one clearly signposted earlier in the text, the ending suggests that the narrator is after all Brothero-Man himself. This conclusion, which echoes one possible reading of Edgar Allan Poe's seminal text, 'The Man of the Crowd' (1840), also undercuts everything that has gone before. Just as Poe's titular character is not truly a *flâneur*, in that he pursues his own isolation from, rather than within, the crowd, so to theorize Islam's mapmaker as a nomad, let alone Sinclair's preferred terms of the stalker or *fugueur*, is to rationalize his singularity. As Islam argues, 'the discourse of othering masks the virtual encounter with the other' (*Ethics* 115) such that the process of becoming-other entails the recognition of what Deleuze and Guattari refer to as 'the intermezzo' (419), the liminal or in-between for which the short story is such an effective form of representation.

Works cited

Ayers, David. *Wyndham Lewis and Western Man*. Basingstoke: Macmillan, 1992.
Baker, Brian. *Iain Sinclair*. Manchester University Press, 2007.
Benjamin, Walter. *Illuminations*. Trans. Harry Zohn, ed. Hannah Arendt. London: Fontana, 1992.
Bond, Robert. *Iain Sinclair*. Cambridge: Salt Publishing, 2005.
Breton, André. *Manifestos of Surrealism*. Trans. Richard Seaver and Helen R. Lane. Ann Arbor Paperbacks/University of Michigan Press, 1972.
Brooker, Peter. 'Iain Sinclair: The Psychotic Geographer Treads the Border-lines.' *British Fiction of the 1990s*. Ed. Nick Bentley. Abingdon: Routledge, 2005. 226–37.
Certeau, Michel de. *The Practice of Everyday Life*. Trans. Steven Rendall. Berkeley: University of California Press, 1984.
Chtcheglov, Ivan. 'Formulary for a New Urbanism.' *Situationist International Anthology*. Ed. and trans. Ken Knabb. Berkeley: Bureau of Public Secrets, 1981. 1–4.

Conrad, Joseph. *Heart of Darkness*. London: Penguin, 1983.
De Quincey, Thomas. *Confessions of an English Opium-Eater and Other Writings*. Ed. Barry Milligan. London: Penguin, 2003.
Debord, Guy. 'Introduction to a Critique of Urban Geography.' *Situationist International Anthology*. Ed. and trans. Ken Knabb. Berkeley: Bureau of Public Secrets, 1981. 5–8.
—— 'Theory of the *Dérive*.' *Situationist International Anthology*. Ed. and trans. Ken Knabb. Berkeley: Bureau of Public Secrets, 1981. 50–6.
Deleuze, Gilles and Félix Guattari. *A Thousand Plateaus*. Trans. Brian Massumi. London: Continuum, 2004.
Eliot, T.S. *Collected Poems 1909–62*. London: Faber, 1974.
Groes, Sebastian. *The Making of London: London in Contemporary Literature*. Basingstoke: Palgrave Macmillan, 2011.
Hughes, Robert. *The Fatal Shore: A History of the Transportation of Convicts to Australia, 1787–1868*. London: Collins Harvill, 1987.
Islam, Syed Manzurul. *The Ethics of Travel: From Marco Polo to Kafka*. Manchester University Press, 1996.
—— *The Mapmakers of Spitalfields*. Leeds: Peepal Tree Press, 1997.
Jackson, Kevin. 'Psychogeography: Will Self and Iain Sinclair in Conversation.' Transcribed Karian Schuitema, ed. Steven Barfield. *Literary London* 6.1 (2008). http://www.literarylondon.org/london-journal/march2008/sinclair-self.html
Kabir, Ekram. 'Manzu Islam: Creator of the First Literary Map for Brick Lane.' (2008). http://www.scribd.com/ekram.kabir/d/3503550-Manzu-Islam-Creator-of-the-first-literary-map-for-Brick-Lane
McLeod, John. *Postcolonial London: Rewriting the Metropolis*. Abingdon: Routledge, 2004.
Mengham, Rod. 'The Writing of Iain Sinclair.' *Contemporary British Fiction*. Ed. Richard J. Lane et al. Cambridge: Polity Press, 2003. 56–67.
Murray, Alex. *Recalling London: Literature and History in the Work of Peter Ackroyd and Iain Sinclair*. London: Continuum, 2007.
Nicholson, Geoff. *The Lost Art of Walking: The History, Science, Philosophy and Literature of Pedestrianism*. New York: Riverhead, 2008.
Perril, Simon. 'A Cartography of Absence: The Work of Iain Sinclair.' *Comparative Criticism* 19 (1997): 309–39.
Ross, Kristin. *The Emergence of Social Space: Rimbaud and the Paris Commune*. Basingstoke: Macmillan, 1988.
Sadler, Simon. *The Situationist City*. Cambridge MA: MIT Press, 1999.
Self, Will. 'Walking is Political.' *The Guardian* (30 March 2012). http://www.guardian.co.uk/books/2012/mar/30/will-self-walking-cities-foot
Sheppard, Robert. *Iain Sinclair*. Tavistock: Northcote House, 2007.
Sinclair, Iain. *Downriver*. London: Vintage, 1995.
—— 'The Griffin's Egg.' *It's Dark in London*. Ed. Oscar Zarate. London: Serpent's Tail, 1996. 43–52.
—— *Hackney, That Rose-Red Empire*. London: Penguin, 2009.
—— *Lights Out for the Territory*. London: Granta, 1997.

—— *London Orbital*. London: Penguin, 2003.

Solnit, Rebecca. *Wanderlust: A History of Walking*. London: Verso, 2001.

Spencer, Robert. *Cosmopolitan Criticism and Postcolonial Literature*. Basingstoke: Palgrave Macmillan, 2011.

Thomson, Ian. '*London: City of Disappearances*, edited by Iain Sinclair.' *The Independent* (7 December 2006). http://www.independent.co.uk/arts-entertainment/books/reviews/london-city-of-disappearances-edited-by-iain-sinclair-427442.html

Walkowitz, Rebecca L. *Cosmopolitan Style: Modernism beyond the Nation*. New York: Columbia University Press, 2006.

Wright, Patrick. *On Living in an Old Country: The National Past in Contemporary Britain*. London: Verso, 1985.

6
The Short Story in Articulating Diasporic Subjectivities in Jhumpa Lahiri

*Antara Chatterjee**

This chapter will examine the use of the short story by the Indian-American writer Jhumpa Lahiri, two of whose three works, *Interpreter of Maladies* (1999) and *Unaccustomed Earth* (2008), are short story collections. *Interpreter of Maladies* won critical acclaim and was awarded the Pulitzer Prize and she followed up the superb act with *Unaccustomed Earth*. Though writing from a vantage point distinctly embedded in an American cultural space, Lahiri can definitely be called a key practitioner of the contemporary postcolonial short story. She can be seen as perpetuating a literary tradition of short fiction in Indian-American women's writing, specifically among Bengali-American women authors in the works of her predecessors like Bharati Mukherjee and Chitra Divakaruni, who also write from a similar position and often about similar experiences. She thus not only affirms the centrality of the short story in American literature, but reveals how this form is being adapted by contemporary diasporic authors to write 'America'. Lahiri is distinguished from writers like Mukherjee or Divakaruni by virtue of being a second-generation immigrant in the US, which makes her work different despite their similarities. This chapter attempts to unpack some significant questions in this literary tradition, such as whether the short story becomes an enabling genre for diasporic authors like Lahiri, by investigating what motivates this formal choice and what this medium offers which distinguishes it from the novel. I aim to analyse if Lahiri's choice is to be viewed in the context of a North American tradition of short fiction or if her work can be considered within a broader South Asian or even postcolonial ambit.

96

Lahiri had once, in an interview, expressed her incomprehension of what she had described as 'a terrible hierarchy [...] between stories and novels'. She said:

> There is a sense that bigger is better and smaller is a diminutive, lesser thing [...] I don't understand it [...] Some of the most remarkable works of fiction are short. (Wagner, para. 3)

Lahiri's bafflement at this hierarchy in fiction is understandable since some of her own most striking writing has arguably been in her short stories. Her fiction is predominantly about the Bengali diaspora in the US, ranging from the experiences of new immigrants to the complexities of growing up as a second-generation Bengali-American like herself. Her diasporic articulation of Bengal and Bengaliness concentrates mainly on the private space of the Bengali home and how that is reconfigured in the US, a process which symbolizes the broader reformulation of Bengali cultural identity in the American cultural space. Her fiction recreates a microcosmic Bengali world transplanted to the diasporic space of North America and voices typical diasporic concerns like identity and displacement, the physical and psychological dislocation of immigration, the conflicts of cultural assimilation and the tangled ties between generations. Exploring issues such as the complicated connotations of 'home' and the complexity of national and cultural affiliations in the present world of global migrations and dis/replaced homes, Lahiri not only examines the Bengali diasporic predicament in contemporary America, but also comments on a wider human condition in this day of global capital and mass migrations, where displacement, both physical and emotional, is a much more widespread human phenomenon than it was ever before. Arguably, in voicing these diasporic preoccupations of dislocation and the pressures of cultural negotiation, it is the medium of the short story which helps her.

Paul March-Russell says about the contemporary short story: 'Increasingly, it seems that dislocation rather than locality, has become the dominant trait of the short story' (148). This statement is apt for Lahiri's short stories as they try to capture this dislocation inherent within the human condition. Thus her fiction, though almost invariably against the backdrop of Bengali immigrant life in the United States, ultimately explores universal complexities of human relationships. And the short story collection, which appears to be more fragmentary and disjointed than a novel, by virtue of its being a group of disparate narratives about a range of different characters though each short story might have its own internal unity and be a complete artistic piece in its own right, becomes an appropriate medium for expressing the fragmented and transient identities of these diasporic characters. We can thus see a powerful intersection of form and content in Lahiri's short fiction. The novel, at least the kind of fairly traditional, realist novel that Lahiri herself wrote with *The Namesake* (2003), gives a greater impression of wholeness, being an elaborate exploration of her protagonist Gogol's journey from childhood to adulthood. It offers her the space for a more detailed and sustained examination of her protagonist's life, through the form of a *Bildungsroman*, whereas her short story collections, being a series of fragmentary images of different characters, drive home more powerfully the feelings of fragmentation and dislocation experienced by those characters. Her collections are thus like a mosaic of portraits or photographs, offering fleeting yet sensitive glimpses into immigrant lives, ultimately having the effect of a photomontage. The form of the short story plays an important part in Lahiri's craft and her commentary on diasporic experiences becomes more vivid through her use of this genre, since she offers a cross-section of immigrant life – frozen moments delving into the complexities of identities and relationships in her diasporic characters. The formal qualities of the short story like compression and concentration heighten this intensity of effect, in which respect the novel, though longer, could be an inadequate medium. As Valerie Shaw has observed, the structural features of the short story enable a convergence of brevity and intensity, richness and concision, suggestiveness and hard outline (11).

Physical and emotional dislocation sets the predominant mood in Lahiri's *Interpreter of Maladies*. Three of the stories are set in India, the rest in the United States, mostly in the Boston area. All of them, except two, are about Bengali-Americans and their cultural and emotional negotiations. March-Russell observes that, 'Jhumpa Lahiri's *Interpreter of Maladies* (1999) emphasises the theme of self-division by dividing the content between different regions while, at the same time, reflecting upon the displacement of their characters' (148). Displacement is indeed one of the key preoccupations which set the emotional register for the collection. Many of the stories like

'Mrs Sen's', 'When Mr Pirzada Came to Dine' and 'The Third and Final Continent', which are about the experiences of new immigrants to America, reveal the dislocation which comes with immigration. Some of them explore the additional pressure of the Indian institution of the 'arranged marriage' by focusing on the predicament of the wives who have followed their husbands to America, for whom the disorientating experience of immigrating to a new culture only doubles the apprehension and uncertainty of an 'arranged' marriage to a stranger, women Lahiri had herself described in an interview as 'women [...] who were basically living in the United States because of their husbands and didn't have an identity or a purpose of their own here' (Ciuraru and Frankfort 132). And though some of the other stories in the collection like 'A Temporary Matter', 'This Blessed House' and the title story 'Interpreter of Maladies' are about second-generation Bengali-Americans and their lives and relationships and not overtly about the experience of immigration, dislocation is nonetheless a preoccupation which comes out in most of them. 'A Temporary Matter' and 'Interpreter of Maladies' are about dysfunctional marriages, for instance, and 'This Blessed House' reveals the demands of adjustment and accommodation required of a newly married couple very different in their personalities. The collection thus, because of the wide range of predicaments that it reveals, is a nuanced exploration of the different connotations of the immigrant experience. And this vividness of effect in examining the various cultural and emotional implications of immigration in different characters is precisely because of its form of a short story collection whereby it offers the reader a series of poignant glimpses into the lives of these characters, while at the same time revealing the fragmentation of their emotional lives through its own fragmentary nature.

Perhaps the most representative of Lahiri's typical preoccupations about the space of the Bengali home and how that is problematized by being transposed into American culture in *Interpreter of Maladies* is the story 'Mrs Sen's', which offers an excellent glimpse into her work. The story revolves around Mrs Sen, the wife of a university professor who has come to the United States with her husband as a recent immigrant. Suddenly transported to a new and unfamiliar place, she finds herself bewildered, intimidated by the American way of life. Feeling pangs of loneliness and desperately missing her life and family back in Calcutta, Mrs Sen is a classic prototype of the recent immigrant. The story describes the bond developed between Mrs Sen and an 11-year-old American boy, Eliot, whom she looks after in her house.

In the figure of Mrs Sen, Lahiri projects the emotional dislocation caused by physical displacement, and the confusing and painful process of acculturation. For Mrs Sen, 'home' is still in Calcutta, the place she has left behind, the image of which she tries to retain through her memories. When she comes to America, this space of the home is problematized since it has to be refashioned in a new location. This implies, in effect, that her Bengali cultural identity is destabilized or threatened. To Mrs Sen, her identity is still about being Bengali and somehow retaining that in a new atmosphere. This 'adherence to an insistently Bengali identity' (Mitra 193) is important to her as it becomes almost an act of self-preservation which validates her individual identity, and her sense of self. She feels lost without the familiar cultural norms and gendered social roles that she has been conditioned to mould herself in. When called upon to fashion a new 'home' in a different location, she tries to recapture that distant home, that domestic space of secure identity and emotional refuge. Her attempts to recreate a Bengali home in America through re-enactments of Bengali customs and traditions are, therefore, acts of nostalgia for her lost 'home'. They embody her attempted imaginative recuperation of that remembered space, which she tries to transpose to her new setting. Everything about Mrs Sen, from her appearance to her home and kitchen, is evidently 'Bengali'. Perhaps one of the most enduring images of the entire collection is of Eliot watching Mrs Sen chopping vegetables 'seated on newspapers on the living room floor', with a typical Bengali blade known as a 'bonti':

> Instead of a knife she used a blade that curved like the prow of a Viking ship, sailing to battle in distant seas. The blade was hinged at one end to a narrow wooden base. The steel, more black than silver, lacked a uniform polish, and had a serrated crest, she told Eliot, for grating [...] Facing the sharp edge without ever touching it, she took whole vegetables between her hands and hacked them apart: cauliflower, cabbage, butternut squash. She split things in half, then quarters, speedily producing florets, cubes, slices and shreds. She could peel a potato in seconds. At times she sat

cross-legged, at times with legs splayed, surrounded by an array of colanders and shallow bowls of water in which she immersed her chopped ingredients. (114)

This sight of women chopping vegetables on the floor is a typical one in most Bengali households and, in using that Bengali household article in her new life as an American, Mrs Sen is trying to maintain some contact with her Bengaliness. The blade thus becomes a nostalgic trace, a signifier of her life back in Calcutta.

Madhuparna Mitra notes how Mrs Sen tries to recuperate her Bengaliness through culinary practices, how she attempts to transpose 'Bengali culinary tools and traditions across the oceans' (194). Mrs Sen tries to preserve her Bengali identity through food, the 'bonti' becoming a symbol of that identity. Food, especially fish, the quintessential element in the Bengali diet, is a recurrent motif in the story. Laura Anh Williams comments about these elaborate descriptions of food preparation in the story: 'food preparation becomes a way Mrs Sen can construct her own identity and assert her subjectivity', noting how the stories in *Interpreter of Maladies* 'invest food practices – the things characters eat and the way they eat them, as well as how characters relate to the preparation of food – with significance that speaks to conditions of migration and diaspora' (70). But the agency that Mrs Sen's culinary practices invests her with is finally destroyed because it is ultimately her quest for that 'Bengali' item of fish that leads to the minor tragedy at the end of the story when she has a car accident, bringing to an end her job of looking after Eliot. Rather, it is her connection (though abortive) with Eliot, who becomes her only point of contact with America, though bringing out her sense of cultural alienation, that also enables her to establish a connection with America; and the possibility of transcending the dislocation of immigration lies in such human connections.

Gayatri Gopinath has noted the centrality of the male–male (usually envisaged in the father–son relationship) trope as the primary trope in imagining diaspora. She describes the 'patriarchal and heteronormative underpinnings of the term di-aspora' evident in its etymological roots and its metaphoric link to the scattered seeds of males, observing that this predominant way of envisioning diaspora 'invariably displaces and elides female diasporic subjects' (5). Lahiri's stories, such as 'Mrs Sen's', displace what Gopinath terms such a 'patriarchal' conceptualizing of diaspora by foregrounding the experiences of the elided female diasporic subject, and by positing human connections forged within the diasporic space, which go beyond predominant imaginings of diasporas in terms of connections (economic and communal) between men. In 'Mrs Sen's', such a connection is envisaged in the bond between Mrs Sen and the child Eliot.

It is probably this connection between the Bengali woman and the American child that somehow achieves the productive cultural multiplicity which has the potential to make the diasporic position an empowered one, despite the pain of acculturation. Avtar Brah has said of the diasporic experience:

> The word diaspora often invokes the imagery of traumas of separation and dislocation, and this is certainly a very important aspect of the migratory experience. But diasporas are also potentially the sites of hope and new beginnings. They are contested cultural and political terrains where individual and collective memories collide, reassemble and reconfigure. (193)

Homi Bhabha too suggests that the 'interstitial' 'third space' which diasporic communities occupy enables negotiation and reconfiguration of different cultures through hybrid interactions (207–21). Lahiri's stories certainly express the trauma of dislocation in characters like Mrs Sen. Yet they also reveal the diasporic space as 'sites of hope and new beginnings'. And it is in such cross-cultural, cross-national connections that the diasporic location can become invested with possibility.

Therefore, in 'The Third and Final Continent', the narrator's heart-warming connection with his eccentric 103-year-old landlady Mrs Croft is his first step towards emotionally connecting with a new culture and of feeling at home in that space. In 'When Mr Pirzada Came to Dine', the Indian family's bond with an East Pakistani and subsequently Bangladeshi man, Mr Pirzada, during the Bangladesh War of 1971, is a cultural tie that helps overcome the longing for the homeland at a crucial political and historical moment in that nation, a human connection forged despite nationalistic differences and even hostility. Some of the other most touching images of the collection, like the one of Eliot watching Mrs Sen chopping vegetables, are of such moments of communion, like Lilia's description of her parents and Mr Pirzada during the days of the war, 'the three of them operating during that time as if they were a single person, sharing a single meal, a single body, a single silence and a single fear' (41) or of the narrator of 'The Third and Final Continent' taking his new wife Mala to meet Mrs Croft and her declaring, 'She is a perfect lady!' and of his admitting later, 'I like to think of that moment in Mrs Croft's parlor as the moment when the distance between Mala and me began to lessen' (195–6). These moments of human connection offer the possibility of overcoming the dislocation of migration. The idea that short stories represent fleeting moments of change, insight or revelation or an experience of transition or realization, in short, epiphanic moments, rather than the unfolding process of change, which belongs more to the domain of the novel, is common in short fiction criticism (see May; Shaw). Anthony Burgess, for example, suggests that the difference between story and novel is not one of length, but of structure: revelation is characteristic of the story whereas resolution is characteristic of the novel (31–47). Lahiri's short stories reveal impressionistic images of such defining moments, moments of connection or realization as much as they express the pain of immigration.

After trying her hand at writing a novel with *The Namesake*, Lahiri returned to the short story with *Unaccustomed Earth* (2008), a masterfully crafted collection of stories, quite noticeably more complex, subtle and nuanced than some of her earlier ones. Whether this could be seen as a conscious authorial choice that indicates her preference for one medium over another is debatable. In fact, Lahiri has refrained from talking about her preferred form, saying that she would probably know that only after 30 or 40 years (Battersby n.p.). Arguably, however, she returns to the short story to further explore the space that it offers in voicing her predominant concerns. Once again, all the stories are about urban, highly educated Bengalis in the US, this time all second-generation Bengalis. The centre of her focus is again the changing Bengali family and the complexities of family life and relationships in this new milieu. Yet, though her characters are all Bengali-Americans and her subject matter is still the life of Bengalis in America, she is charting new territory here, by offering us a different trajectory of the Bengali diasporic experience. These characters are all second-generation Bengalis, sometimes new fathers or mothers, often in inter-cultural marriages or relationships, like herself. Their concerns now go beyond the struggles of growing up with conflicting cultural affiliations, and encompass wider emotional struggles in their adult lives as Americans. She explores the subtle intricacies of a whole gamut of relationships ranging from familial ties like the developing bonds of new parents with their children or the relationship between adult children and their ageing parents to ties between siblings and relationships between husbands and wives or lovers. The examination of parenthood, the relationship between immigrant parents and their children, in particular, seems to be a key concern in the collection.

Thus, in *Unaccustomed Earth*, Lahiri's focus widens from exploring the reconstruction of Bengali cultural identity in North America to a broader examination of the intricacies of different relationships in the lives of her Bengali-American characters. In fact, at times, these characters do not have anything distinctly Bengali in their lifestyles or cultural practices, apart from their Bengali names. The names mark them immediately to familiar readers as Bengalis, yet at times this Bengaliness seems so incidental in their lives that readers foreign to Bengali names could very well take them for people of any other ethnicity or culture. They are all cosmopolitan Bengalis who grew up in the United States, geographically and culturally mobile, true twenty-first-century 'global citizens' whose 'Bengaliness' seems to have receded so much into the background as to be almost incidental in their busy and demanding 'American' lives. Yet though Lahiri apparently does not seem to be interested, in the same way as before, in exploring her characters' 'Bengaliness', curiously these characters are still all Bengali. And on a careful reading, we find that in them the implicit traces of their Bengali cultural identities, their legacies of growing up in a culture in which they themselves felt at home but their parents often felt 'foreign', the remnants of a childhood of emotional struggles straddling two different cultural affiliations, are often visible beneath the surface.

Similarly the 'home' which is so often the focus of Lahiri's exploration is now no longer the site of nostalgia for a distant homeland or a recuperative space for recapturing Bengali cultural practices; it is now a sign of their American lives, a space which they often share with American spouses. These 'homes', like Ruma's home in 'Unaccustomed Earth' or Amit and Megan's home in 'A Choice of

Accommodations', though always modern, fashionable and comfortable, somehow appear to be more *impersonal* spaces and are no longer distinctly 'Bengali' like Mrs Sen's home was. Just as Mrs Sen, the new immigrant, clinging to her Bengali way of life, replicating a Bengali home in the US, is perhaps the most enduring figure of *Interpreter of Maladies*, one of the most representative characters of *Unaccustomed Earth* is the rootless and itinerant photographer Kaushik of 'Hema and Kaushik' who, Lahiri tells us, maintained a small abode in Rome which consisted of 'an enclosed staircase leading directly into his small world. The apartment was a room and a bathroom and a two-burner stove' (312) where, 'between assignments, he recovered' (306). The experience of displacement for these characters is not associated with immigration as it was for their parents but is rather a reality of their mobile, globalized existences, which instead of being traumatic, could also be liberating for them. We thus see how the space of the home and the space of diaspora can inscribe different connotations in different generations of diasporic subjects. For first-generation immigrants like Mrs Sen, the home was a recuperative, nostalgic 'Bengali' space, which was nevertheless reconstituted, inscribing new possibilities and reconfigurations, thus embodying both the trauma of dislocation as well as the liberating possibilities of Bhabha's diasporic 'third-space'. For these second-generation Bengali-Americans, however, the space of the home assumes different implications. It is no longer a distinctly Bengali space, yet it is also the space associated with the complexities of their conflicting affiliations, their lineage of growing up 'in-between', negotiating two cultures.

Unaccustomed Earth also explores displacement and dislocation but the contexts seem to be different from *Interpreter of Maladies*. Lahiri's characters here do not speak or dress like Bengalis. We learn that Ruma has given away the 200-odd saris of her mother after her death:

> She kept only three [...] telling her mother's friends to divide up the rest. And she had remembered the many times her mother predicted this very moment, lamenting the fact that her daughter preferred pants and skirts to the clothing she wore, that there would be no one to whom to pass on her things. (17)

In appearance these second-generation Bengalis are therefore distinct from the new immigrants of their parents' generation, like Ruma's

own mother 'who would have stuck out in this wet Northern landscape, in her brightly colored saris, her dime-sized maroon bindi, her
jewels' (11). Usha, another child of North America in 'Hell-Heaven',
describes her mother in these terms: 'my mother was wearing the red
and white bangles unique to Bengali married women and a common
Tangail sari, and had a thick stem of vermilion powder in the center
parting of her hair' (61). Pranab Chakraborty, a young man recently
arrived from Calcutta, recognizes her because of her quintessentially
'Bengali' appearance. Usha tells us he 'noticed the two or three safety
pins she wore fastened to the thin gold bangles that were behind
the red and white ones, which she would use to replace a missing
hook on a blouse or to draw a string through a petticoat [...] a practice he associated strictly with his mother and sisters and aunts in
Calcutta' (61). Hema tells us of her mother: 'She herself never wore a
skirt – she considered it indecent' (231). We also remember the very
'Bengali' appearance of Mrs Sen: 'She wore a shimmering white sari
patterned with orange paisleys' (*Interpreter of Maladies* 112). Eliot had
observed 'the perfectly centered part in her braided hair, which was
shaded with crushed vermilion and [...] appeared to be blushing'
(117). In contrast to the appearance of these recent immigrants, we
have Ruma's father reminiscing in 'Unaccustomed Earth' about the
growing-up years of his American-born children: 'The more the children grew, the less they had seemed to resemble either parent – they
spoke differently, dressed differently, seemed foreign in every way'
(*Unaccustomed Earth* 54).

These Bengali-Americans do not speak the Bengali language either.
Lahiri tells us about Ruma:

> Bengali had never been a language in which she felt like an adult.
> Her [...] Bengali was slipping from her [...] On the rare occasions
> Ruma used Bengali anymore [...] she tripped over words, mangled
> tenses. (12)

They also have ethnically indistinguishable, 'international' food
habits, very different from the typically 'Bengali' food which their
parents ate and cooked. In 'Going Ashore', Hema buys 'lettuce, a
box of spaghetti, and mushrooms and cream to turn into a sauce'
(303); 'carbonara and deep-fried artichokes', 'pumpkin tortelli' and
'bollito misto with mostarda' (312) are some of the other items that

they eat. In 'A Choice of Accommodations', Amit is at home eating 'salmon terrine' and 'plates of prime rib with asparagus and potatoes' (111–13). This is very different from the 'khichuri' which Hema's mother made, 'deep-frying pieces of potato and cauliflower, melting sticks of butter in a saucepan for ghee' (247) or the 'curried mackerel and rice' (61) and 'luchis' (63) which Usha's mother made in 'Hell-Heaven'. In 'Unaccustomed Earth', Ruma does 'away with making dal or served salad instead of a chorchori' (22). Lahiri also tells us that when Ruma's son Akash was smaller, 'she had followed her mother's advice to get him used to the taste of Indian food and made the effort to poach chicken and vegetables with cinnamon and cardamom and clove' but that now, and a bit bigger, 'he ate from boxes' (23).

Williams has observed that 'In Asian American literature, food as metaphor frequently constructs and reflects relationships to racial-ized subjectivity and also addresses issues of authenticity, assimila-tion and desire', noting that in the stories in *Interpreter of Maladies*, 'food is the means for characters to assert agency and subjectivity' (70). Williams' comment about how culinary practices in Lahiri's sto-ries are invested with special meaning, addressing issues like cultural recuperation and nostalgia, is significant. We see how in many of her stories, in both collections, food becomes a powerful and multi-directional symbol to express realities of migration and identity; it becomes a way of constructing identity and subjectivity. In *Interpreter of Maladies*, the kitchen seems to be the most distinctly 'Bengali' space within the immigrant home, since it is associated with one of the most enduring cultural traditions, that of cuisine. Food is thus also necessarily one of the significant cultural aspects in which second-generation Bengalis assert their choices as distinctly different from their parents'. Their food choices symbolize the larger choices in their lives. The different food practices of the two generations of diasporic characters reveal the distinct ways in which they construct their subjectivity and how they relate to both Bengali cultural prac-tices and to American or other more international, global food prac-tices. Charting a kind of gastronomy of desire starting from Mrs Sen to *The Namesake*'s Ashima and Gogol, to the culinary practices of the second-generation Bengalis in *Unaccustomed Earth*, Lahiri's fiction reveals how narratives of food and culinarity can become sites on which issues of nostalgia, adaptation, assimilation, intergenerational conflicts and so on are played out.

Therefore, in *Unaccustomed Earth*, Lahiri still explores Bengali cultural identity in diaspora, but it is dealt with in a different manner. Her characters are now different, though still all Bengali, and her concerns also seem to be shifting. Another noticeable characteristic distinguishing *Unaccustomed Earth* from *Interpreter of Maladies* is the fact that the stories in the former collection are all considerably longer, and the last section, 'Hema and Kaushik', shows an innovative experiment, namely the three interrelated stories about the same characters at different stages of their lives, told from different perspectives. Lahiri here seems to be experimenting formally with the short story and testing and pushing the boundaries of the genre. Her very engagement with Bengali culture appears to be different in this collection because the Bengaliness that she is examining here is itself an evolving and changing one. It is often subdued, imperceptible. Yet this Bengaliness and its associated history of cultural accommodation and negotiation are like an emotional subtext which bestows its own peculiar complexities in the larger lives of her characters. This collection offers a vivid glimpse into the second-generation immigrant predicament, by revealing a mosaic of experiences. Like her first collection, its impressionistic form enables the expression of dislocation and fragmentation in the characters' emotional lives.

This also brings us to an interesting progression in Lahiri's *oeuvre* – a movement from examining the predicaments of new immigrants to the experiences of their children growing up in a cross-cultural milieu, to the adult lives of those children. Though she also describes second-generation Bengali-Americans in *Interpreter of Maladies*, the collection, as a whole, seems more attuned to expressing the experiences of new immigrants. *The Namesake*, on the other hand, is about the growing-up years of her protagonist Gogol/Nikhil, as he works out his complex relationship to his Bengali past. Only in *Unaccustomed Earth* does Lahiri focus almost entirely on the adult lives of her second-generation Bengali characters. When examined in entirety, her *oeuvre* thus reveals a kind of linearity, as if a separate narrative strand can be identified within her fiction, like a meta-narrative (see also Bal; Genette). Being an author who has often publicly talked about the relationship of her work with her own life and experiences, we could perhaps decipher a connection between this narrative linearity and her personal subjectivity as a Bengali-American capturing the

Bengali diasporic experience in the American cultural space in her fiction (see, for instance, Wagner paras 12–13).

To conclude, the form of the short story becomes, for Lahiri, an enabling strategy to articulate the fragmentation and dislocation of diasporic subjectivities. The genre helps her to capture the physical, cultural and psychological displacement of immigration and of growing up in a cross-cultural environment. It also expresses the moments of human communion which can ease the pain of such displacement. Lahiri's short stories are thus fleeting glimpses capturing moments in the lives of her characters, moments which help to shape or define them. She offers a series of snapshots, as it were, of immigrant life and shows very powerfully both the painful and productive possibilities of immigration in the twenty-first century.

Note

* An earlier version of this chapter was presented at the South Asian short story conference held at the University of Kent in September 2010.

Works cited

Bal, Mieke. *Narratology: Introduction to the Theory of Narrative*. Trans. Christine Van Boheemen. University of Toronto Press, 2009.

Battersby, Eileen. 'A Serious Voice in a Brash World.' *The Irish Times*. 27 September 2008. http://www.irishtimes.com/newspaper/weekend/2008/0927/1222419961783.html

Bhabha, Homi K. 'The Third Space.' *Identity: Community, Culture, and Difference*. Ed. Jonathan Rutherford. London: Lawrence and Wishart, 1990. 207–21.

Brah, Avtar. *Cartographies of Diaspora: Contesting Identities*. London: Routledge, 1996.

Burgess, Anthony. 'On the Short Story.' *Journal of the Short Story in English* 2 (1984): 31–47.

Ciuraru, Carmela and Tamara Frankfort. 'A Personal Matter: An Interview with Jhumpa Lahiri.' *Real Simple* (June 2001): 130–3.

Genette, Gérard. *Narrative Discourse: An Essay in Method*. Trans. Jane E. Lewin. Ithaca NY: Cornell University Press, 1980.

Gopinath, Gayatri. *Impossible Desires: Queer Diasporas and South Asian Public Cultures*. Durham NC: Duke University Press, 2005.

Lahiri, Jhumpa. *Interpreter of Maladies*. London: Flamingo, 2000.

—— *Unaccustomed Earth*. London: Bloomsbury, 2008.

March-Russell, Paul. *The Short Story: An Introduction*. Edinburgh University Press, 2009.

May, Charles E., ed. *The New Short Story Theories*. Athens OH: Ohio University Press, 1994.

Mitra, Madhuparna. 'Lahiri's "Mrs Sen's".' *The Explicator* 64.3 (2006): 193–6.

Shaw, Valerie. *The Short Story: A Critical Introduction*. London: Longman, 1983.

Wagner, Vit. 'Why Size Doesn't Matter in Fiction.' *Toronto Star.* 14 April 2008. http://www.thestar.com/entertainment/article/414199

Williams, Laura Anh. 'Foodways and Subjectivity in Jhumpa Lahiri's *Interpreter of Maladies*.' *MELUS* 32.4 (2007): 69–78.

7
The Contemporary Egyptian *Maqāma* or Short Story Novel as a Form of Democracy

Caroline Rooney

This chapter aims to explore the relationship between what might be termed the *maqāma* or short story novel, a genre that defies genre which has come to the fore in contemporary Egyptian literary culture, and the aesthetics of democracy. The two works to receive detailed attention in this chapter are Khaled Al Khamissi's *Taxi* (2008) and Ahmed Alaidy's *Being Abbas El Abd* (2003), texts that I will be reading in translation with some reflection on this circumstance. It is the contention of this reading that it is no accident that these two works, among others that may be related to them, appeared shortly before the Egyptian uprising.[1] However, it is not merely in retrospect that these texts emerge as particular yet contingent precursors of the ensuing democratic movement on the streets. It is rather the case that they constitute self-aware strands of the democratic movement in its barely perceived initial stages, serving to reflect and create the kind of popular consciousness necessary for the Egyptian revolution. What this chapter will go on to explore is the quite different ways in which *Taxi* and *Being Abbas El Abd* contribute to the democratic movement in Egypt, while attempting to explain the formal significance of the *maqāma* novel for its social and political potential.

Simply speaking, *Taxi* consists of 58 accounts of conversations with Cairo taxi drivers conducted by the same lead narrator. In encountering this collection of stories, what is indeterminate is whether it should be read as a work of literary fiction or as a textual form of documentary, one that might be further termed a sociological improvisation or a contemporary folkloric archive. Accordingly, when I interviewed Khaled Al Khamissi in March 2010, I was not prepared for his conversational designation of *Taxi* as a novel. The slight surprise, on my part, over the choice of term reflected both a certain cultural difference over assumptions regarding literary form and the difficulty of assigning a genre to a work such as *Taxi*.

Is *Taxi* a novel? It is clearly a highly creative work and, in certain ways, a literary work (as will be further debated in due course), but is it a novel? In the introduction to *Taxi*, Al Khamissi states the following: 'My role here is certainly not to check the accuracy of the information I collected and wrote down. What matters here is what a particular individual says in society at a particular moment of history on a certain subject because sociology transcends the factual in the scale of the priorities of this book' (12). Thus, the work is designated as a sociological enterprise but one which does not purport to offer a study of Cairo taxi drivers as objects of investigation so much as subjects of a discourse. What here renders the sociological enterprise a literary endeavour is, it may be argued, not a matter of 'fictionality' as opposed to 'factuality', but rather a matter of the dynamics of composition. After all, Al Khamissi stresses the importance of what the individual actually says: what is of less importance in 'the scale of priorities' is whether what is *in fact stated* by the individual and *recorded* by the scribe of the work, allowing for creative licence in the process of transcription, is factually verifiable in a scientific sense.

The compositional dynamic referred to above is one of aurality and orality. *Taxi* is therefore a work that arises from the listening to and transmission of viewpoints and stories. With respect to this, the writer is not an *author* who makes up stories through, as Sigmund Freud proposes, 'day-dreaming' or through fantasy formations (141–53). Nor does the writer appropriate the stories of others to present them as his or her own ideas or concoctions. Instead, what really matters is the reproduced recording of a living collective consciousness, an amalgam of voiced subjectivities. As Al Khamissi states: 'those popular stories and jokes will be lost unless recorded' (11). What further matters as regards this recording of popular lore are an ethics and politics of listening.

This is, of course, a democratic question, even a radically democratic question. The former may be said to pertain especially to freedoms of speech and debate, while the latter goes beyond the consideration of the freedom of the individual in entailing a sense of freedom as a collective or holistic phenomenon. This serves to indicate the necessity for something that could be called a short story novel. The term 'novel' might here be understood in generic terms as the anthology, or the *diwan*. However, what is at stake is more than just a collection of stories. It concerns how the stories are inter-implicated in a unity that exceeds them, which pertains to their novelistic dimension. Regarding this, the writer may be said to function as a conductor, in both the musical and electrical senses of the term. That is, the writer orchestrates and arranges the performance of the stories, while enabling the flow of a current. Here the current is not literally an electric one, although it may be considered electric in metaphorical ways, for instance in terms of that which is inspiring, energizing, enlightening, and so sparks further currents.

As briefly touched on above, there are cultural dimensions implicit in the question of the generic classification of a work such as *Taxi*. Two Arabic cultural forms that are particularly relevant to the text may be put forward. The more obvious of these is that of the *maqāma*, while the more unusual one I wish to propose is that of the cassette sermon. I will now go on to consider *Taxi* according to these genres.

In the same interview in which Al Khamissi described *Taxi* as a novel to me, he also stated: 'I wanted to write in a literary form [that was] not a European literary form [...] I did not want to take the novel or short stories. I wanted to take an Arab form [...] I took the form of a *maqāma*,' adding that such a form allowed for a 'theatre of the streets with taxi drivers constituting a broad cross-section of Egyptian society'.[2] *Maqāma* refers to a serial form of picaresque or loosely related stories, as if the story form itself were a travelling phenomenon of adventures and encounters. This indicates why it constitutes an inspired form for taxi narratives, narratives improvised on the move and about daily movement, stories constituted by and full of chance encounters both serendipitous and unsettling. Western criticism has devised terms such as the short story cycle, short story sequence or composite novel to describe such effects (see March-Russell 104–6), but the *maqāma* or short story novel has particular cultural resonances. The term *maqāma* (from the verb 'to stand') means 'assembly', referring to how the narratives are typically addressed to assemblies (*maqāmat*) of the powerful to impress upon them virtuoso displays of wit and wisdom, with possibly satirical effect. In *Taxi*, the notion of assembly is multifaceted. There is first of all a virtual assembly of the taxi drivers and their stories. This further constitutes a public assembly or civic forum as a means by which the concerns of the day may be aired towards the dialogical establishment of a common sense of a shared history and a common purpose. While this is pervasive in *Taxi*, a few examples may be offered:

> In the old days we used to go out on the streets with 50,000 people, with 100,000. But now there's nothing that matters. How many people are going to step out of their front door for something no one understands? And the government's terrified, its knees are shaking. I mean, one puff and the government will fall, a government without knees. (24)

> 'Didn't you see what happened with the ferry that sank in the Red Sea? People died in droves and the government stood there cheering. Much ado about nothing, pardon the expression. Do you know what people are like in the eyes of the government?'
> 'No,' I said.
> 'Human beings in Egypt are like dust in a cracked cup.' (170)

In terms of address, the addressees of the taxi driver's story are the narrator, and through him, the implied reader. That said, there is an implicit address in the form of complaint or warning to the powerful elite in Egypt, and in spirit this is similar to the provocative rap of El Général, one of the sparks of the Tunisian revolution, spoken directly and electrifyingly to the Tunisian President, for example: 'Mr President, you told me to speak without fear.' This may be placed alongside the following from *Taxi*:

> I'd really like to tell the Minister of Information that we're a thousand times cleverer than him and that we understand the world a hundred times better than him. But where would I see the Minister of Information for me to tell him? (136)

In *Taxi*, the emphasis is less on a direct leadership challenge and more on how people are able to represent, analyse and edify themselves, where this entails a certain DIY spirit. Here, it needs to be explained that the failures of Hosni Mubarak's government had not only to do with authoritarianism but also with a leadership that, in fact, provided no leadership. The apparent paradox is not really one in that, as Frantz Fanon explains in *The Wretched of the Earth* (1961), it is precisely elites that lack the skill and the will to govern effectively that resort to authoritarianism as a default position. In such a situation of what may be termed political negligence, people are left to fend for themselves, and the effects of this are both destructive and constructive. The destructive effects concern the corruption, the loss of dignity, the erosion of civic sociality as individuals try to survive in chaotic conditions. *Taxi* puts forward ample evidence of this, for example:

> It's impossible for anyone in Egypt to make do with his salary. Because how much are salaries? [...] So what's the answer? Either we steal or take bribes or work all day. (99)

> There've been customers taking taxis and asking to go to the Sixth of October and in some remote spot they take out flick knives and take all the driver's money and leave him on the side of the road and steal the car. (104)

However, in spite of these criminal forms of making do, equally there is an individualistic spirit that has the potential to allow for a way out from political dependency on the powerful and the setting up of reasserted collective priorities. Related to this, Maggie Awadalla traces how a preoccupation amongst Egyptian women writers from Latifa Zayyat to Rehab Bassam has been to create meeting points and a common ground 'where the self successfully unites with the whole, in a common public space that is both democratic and collective' (451). In an interview from 2010, Bassam asserts that this is a matter of people waking up to the need to do things for themselves, rather than waiting for 'one person' to come along 'and set everyone free' (475).

The lack of leadership may be said to have promoted anarchy in both negative and positive senses: negatively, as chaos, and positively, in terms of anti-authoritarian, even leaderless, ways of establishing non-hierarchical free associations: as entailed in the random yet meaningful encounter. If *Taxi* serves as a literary equivalent of this, it is therefore a collection where it is more than that in as much as it is a matter of the enfolding of stories into a mutual consciousness. It may be said that the stories have to be told together because each retunes the others. It is as if the narrative were a relay, a form of transmission serving to join up the tellers and receivers of tales, where while the narrator relays the drivers' stories, they themselves are often relaying stories heard elsewhere. Moreover, the sense of this relay is not just diachronic but synchronic, where *Taxi* has a musical sense of composition conveying a position of 'we are all in this together; everyone counts'. While the Western novel typically relies on a progressively unfolding narrative, there isn't this successive temporality within *Taxi*: you could reshuffle all the stories and tell them in a different order where the importance of this is that the stories are contemporary with each other, none having any necessary priority. The role of the author is not simply abolished, as in Roland Barthes' famous claim, but reconfigured as collector and listener. Al Khamissi's approach may be said to effect a collective reflexivity through listening to the tales of everyday life: working to affirm the inspiring ones, to weep with the sad ones, to question the dubious ones. It is narrating as an ethics of listening. Here, the term 'author' could more effectively be replaced by the term 'scribe', the role of the scribe having both a humble and a distinguished pedigree within Egyptian literary culture, and where the term for writer in Arabic, *khitab*, may best be translated as 'scribe' (Jacquemond 4).

Of relevance to an aesthetics of listening is the role played by the cassette sermon in modern Egyptian culture, as addressed by Charles Hirschkind. He begins in literary mode:

> I climb into a taxi cab just outside of the Ramses Mosque in the city center. The driver steers onto the busy thoroughfare of Ramses Street, and listens. A sermon struggles out through the frayed speakers and dust-encrusted electronics of a tape player bolted under the taxi's dashboard, just beneath a velvet-covered box holding a small Quran. The voice careens and crescendos along its rhetorical pathways, accompanied by the accumulated vibration, static, hiss, and squeak inherited from the multiple copies that have preceded the one now in the machine. (1)

Hirschkind goes on to explain:

> As a key element in the technological scaffolding of what is called the Islamic Revival (al-Sahwa al-Islamiyya), the cassette sermon has become an omnipresent background of daily urban life in

most Middle Eastern cities [...] As I will argue, the contribution of this aural media to shaping the contemporary moral and political landscape of the Middle East lies not simply in its capacity to disseminate or instill religious ideologies but in its effect on the human sensorium, on the affects, sensibilities, and perceptual habits of its vast audience [...] For those who participate in the movement, the moral and political direction of contemporary Muslim societies cannot be left to politicians, religious scholars, or militant activists but must be decided upon and acted collectively by ordinary Muslims in the course of their daily activity. (2)

Hirschkind proceeds to explore the spiritual fine tunings effected by the soundscapes of aural media, an *environment* also termed 'an acoustic unconscious' (124), thus not a private, inner unconscious, and he writes: 'Animated or "played" by the rhythms, lyrical intensities, sound figures, echoes, and resonances of the recorded performances, the sensorium acquires a moral orientation' (125).

As set out above, in Cairo, it is not unusual on catching a taxi to find a cassette sermon being played and, accordingly, episodes in *Taxi* represent this everyday occurrence. In one such episode, the narrator, having a headache, asks the driver to turn down the volume level of the cassette player but the driver, misunderstanding the nature of the request, assumes that it has been made because the sermon in question is a Christian rather than a Quranic one. Therefore, he refuses to comply, prompting the narrator to reflect on his own request:

> I held my tongue and he drove on. I thought of talking to him about the principle of moderation in the exercise of one's rights and that his right must end where the rights of others start. But then I remembered that what I was thinking was meaningless nonsense in the streets of Egypt, which ring with shouts of every kind, where loudspeakers surround us and no one can open his mouth.
>
> One side of the tape had ended and the driver quickly put the other side on. Silence reigned for some minutes as we waited at the traffic lights near the High Court building. I noticed that the tensed muscles of his neck began to relax a little. (203)

It could be said that the cassette sermon competes with the cacophony from the Cairo streets less as yet more noise and more as if it were a form of silencing. At least what the above excerpt serves to suggest is that what is desired from the sermon is actually the effects of silence, if not silence itself, as the means to relaxation. This accords with the arguments put forward by Hirschkind, regarding the cassette sermon as a kind of popular acoustic therapy, where furthermore what is particularly aimed for is a 'state of calm and relaxation', termed *inshirah* (literally, 'opening of the chest', although more accurately rendered as *inshirah sadhuru*), through which resentments and frustrations may be dispelled (76).

What transpires in this particular cassette sermon episode from *Taxi* is that the young man is indeed listening to the tape to calm his anger, which turns out to be over repeated discrimination, serving to deny the university advancement of his brother simply on the grounds of his brother being a Copt (a Native Egyptian Christian). The point is that the sermon is not merely being played as an aggressive form of identity assertion, but, as with the Quranic sermon, it is being played to defuse emotional tensions and restore spiritual peace. Another episode in the book supports this understanding: 'By this stage in the conversation the driver was in a highly emotional state. He put on a cassette tape and we started listening to a recitation of Koranic verses' (147).

The very last episode of *Taxi* serves to provide a significant perspective on the above. The anecdote begins with a deliberate use of religious imagery:

> Ramadan, just before the cannon was fired to mark the end of the fast, and I was carrying a big picture, waiting for a taxi to appear, if necessary from the sky. It was about ten minutes before the cannon and it's hard to find a taxi at that time. But divine intervention sent one to me like an angel on the night of Revelation. He was truly a black angel with black wings coming from the black south, the most beautiful part of Egypt, Aswan, with a heart that was black, the colour of purity and beauty. (213)

As it turns out, this black angel is a cosmopolitan lover of art, confessing: 'I've been around, travelled far and wide, been to Spain, Italy and France. I stayed in France [...] There on a Sunday I used to go to the Louvre, because on Sundays it's free. Culture for everyone' (214). When the narrator encourages the driver, as an art lover, to express himself as a painter, we discover that what matters for this taxi driver is the art of everyday living in harmony with your surroundings. For instance, he comments: 'I like very many things. I waste all my money on my hobbies [...] I've planted honeysuckle, hyacinth beans, dieffenbachia and bougainvillea. I've also planted hibiscus with red flowers [...] And I've made an Arabian-style sitting area on the ground, surrounded by the fish tanks and the birds, and in front of me through the window, there's the garden. I feel like I'm in Paradise far from the hell of Cairo' (215).

It is notable that the effect of such words on the narrator is implied to be spiritual, not in a lofty way but precisely in a down-to-earth worldly way. The narrator muses: 'In the end that black angel left the taste of sugar in my mouth and the scent of honeysuckle in my soul. He made me, for the first time in ages, have my breakfast slowly, without haste, contemplating everything around me' (215). With this, the realization may reach the reader that the anecdotes we have been listening to in *Taxi* may function somewhat as mini-cassette sermons, that is, quasi-aural experiences (given much of the text is spoken), serving to readjust the soul through the effects of our words on each other, further serving to retune us to our surroundings. What this conveys is that the sacred, here, is not a question of the beyond but a question of how we live the everyday where slowing down to be present is a matter of attentiveness, of being there, a form of receptivity.

The encounter with the art-loving driver may be counter-pointed with an encounter with another man from Upper Egypt who, sitting next to a taxi driver, weeps as he recounts his woes concerning his inability to pay for some surgery he had to have. This man and the driver are oblivious to the narrator who eavesdrops from the back seat:

Throughout the conversation, they were not aware of my presence, as though I did not exist or perhaps was wearing a cloak that made me invisible. Even when I got out and paid the fare, neither of them paid me any attention or addressed a word to me.

The two were praying, each whispering to each other, turning their faces to the heavens on a chance that a portal would open there and their prayers would reach the One who Listens and Answers. (179)

Two invisible presences are thus counterposed, that of the narrator and that of a God on high. What *Taxi* implies as a whole is that Listening and Answering have to take place amongst the people, as opposed to transcendentally, not as a matter of atheism so much as a matter of what may be described as a re-worlding of the sacred. There is a particular episode in *Taxi* that dramatizes this question. It begins: 'It is very rare that one meets a driver like this one. A man in his 50s, elegantly dressed, close-shaven, smelling of after-shave, with a deep calm voice like a Buddhist priest or an ascetic in the desert or maybe a saint in a remote monastery' (95). As a conversation unfolds, we learn from this saintly presence that: 'You only have to open your heart [*inshirah*] to see the beauty around you. But if you're like most people and you've closed your heart, how can you see the light shining around you? We in Egypt are truly blessed, one of the most beautiful and greatest countries in the world and you live here. And when you open your heart, you'll see unbelievable things in Egypt' (95). When the narrator leaves the taxi, he asks for the driver's name, which arrives as a punchline: 'Before I got out I asked him his name, and that too I will remember: Sharif Shenouda' (96). The punchline is not explained; it is there to be registered as a silent understanding, a moment of telepathy or shared consciousness. However, here, it may be necessary to explain that the name Shenouda would bring to mind Pope Shenouda III of Alexandria, the head of the Holy Synod of the Coptic Orthodox Patriarchate until his death in 2012. It could be further pointed out that Pope Shenouda came out in favour of the succession of Gamal Mubarak, and thus the turning of Egypt's leadership into a dynasty (Al Aswany 95). Shenouda, though, is also a dynastic name, not the Coptic Pope's real name, but one he assumed on his appointment to the leadership of the Coptic Church: Shenouda originally being the name of a Coptic saint. In *Taxi*, sainthood could be said to be returned to the ordinary man in the street. It is further worth pointing out that the original Shenouda, while living a monastic life, was a populist. He is spoken of as a creator of Egyptian nationalism through Coptism, and in regard to his compassionate act of taking besieged refugees into his monastery: 'This event illustrated Saint Shenouda's belief that practical love is above all other monastic virtues' (Saint Shenouda Monastery n.p.).

In *Taxi*, democratic values emerge not only through the exercise of free speech and the frequent criticisms of corrupt authorities.

While Western democracies are non-spiritual in their secularism, what manifests itself in *Taxi* is a kind of spiritual reattunement that has a social dynamic, as indicated, a kind of grounding of the sacred, something that was testified to in the collective spirit of Tahrir Square. In terms of the aesthetics of *Taxi*, one way of accounting for this is in terms of its creation of a form that combines the *maqāma* with 'the opening of the heart', aimed for by the cassette sermon as acoustic therapy. In addition, *Taxi* could also be seen to participate in the popular cultural forms of social networking and blogging, as if it were a taxi blog or a taxi Facebook, although the only explicit reference to the digital media in the book is to the cellphone explosion (see also El Hamamsy 453–66).

When I interviewed Al Khamissi in 2010, having read *Taxi* in the wake of British and American accounts of the dominance of Islamic fundamentalism in Egypt, I remarked to him: 'When I read *Taxi*, I thought this book is democracy [...] I don't think people in England realise that there is this spirit of democracy on the streets in Cairo.' Al Khamissi explained that the writing of *Taxi* had constituted a turning point for him in that it only became possible for him to write the book when he felt the pessimism of the mood on the streets beginning to shift towards a spirit of resistance that occasioned optimism. That is, the act of writing had reacquired an urgency and sense of purpose. Interestingly, Ahmed Alaidy's *Being Abbas El Abd* pertains to a moment just before this shift in mood that blogger Rehab Bassam, in keeping with Al Khamissi, identifies as starting to occur in 2006 (475).

Being Abbas El Abd is starkly different to *Taxi* in two respects. Firstly, it is a much bleaker work, thoroughly permeated with a sense of meaningless and pointlessness. Secondly, the kind of popular culture it is immersed in is that of postmodernist youth culture. That said, the picaresque form of the novel reflects aspects of the *maqāma* form. Instead of following a linear, progressively unfolding plot, the narrative is highly episodic, based on the riffs of its rascally narrator in relation to his alter ego Abbas and their escapades. In order to explain the narrative form the work takes, it will first be necessary to undertake an analysis of it where the term 'novel' will be used as a designation of convenience rather than as a decisive definition.

As acknowledged by Alaidy, the work is indebted to Chuck Palahniuk, including his novel *Fight Club* (1996) and its 1999 film version. At one point the film states: 'We're the middle-class children of history, man. No purpose, no place. We have no great war, no great depression. Our great war is a spiritual war. Our great depression is our lives.' In *Being Abbas El Abd*, Alaidy writes: 'Egypt had its Generation of the Defeat. We're the generation that came after it. The "I've got nothing left to lose generation". We're the autistic generation, living under the same roof with strangers who have names similar to ours' (36). While the sense of alienated malaise on the part of both male youth cultures may be similar, the causes are radically different. In *Fight Club*, the problem is one of being reduced to automaton-like banality in a society of passive consumerism with the attendant feeling of not being properly alive. In *Being Abbas El Abd*, while the novel deals with middle-class youth, the sense of being outside of history concerns the frustrations of lack of access to a forward-moving modernity. The adoption of a postmodernist style could even be seen as symptomatic of a desire for a certain trendiness against a frequent alternative response to economic stagnation in Egypt, namely the appeal to its glorious past. This retro-patriotism is rejected in the following outburst by the character Abbas:

You want us to progress?
So burn the history books and forget your precious dead civilization.
Stop trying to squeeze the juice from the past.
Destroy your pharonic history. (34)

What Palahniuk's and Alaidy's works may be considered to have in common is a sense of failure on the part of the previous generation of fathers to provide adequate role models for their sons. It is arguably for this reason that, in both texts, the protagonists develop doppelganger alter egos through, it could be claimed, a need to fashion ideal egos for themselves, given the lack of such on a social level, except that these ideal egos are, in fact, based on the repressed forces of the id. Put another way, the collapse of male heroism in the paternal generation leads to the creation of private fantasy selves that are characterized by a charismatic rebelliousness that is otherwise repressed.

In *Fight Club*, the captivating alter ego Tyler Durden sets up a fight club as a means of restoring macho-ness to young men but where this thug culture more problematically implies that, in soporific late capitalist America, the only way that people are able to access the real and feel alive is through sadism and violence. For this reason, the implications of the novel, and the film based on it, are considered by some commentators to be fascist, perhaps in ways that recall Theodor Adorno's analysis of fascism as an irrational attempt to restore authenticity to capitalism. It could be further pointed out that Slavoj Žižek, in *Welcome to the Desert of the Real* (2002), appears to uphold the position that access to the real is through violence as if there were no alternative to this dark side of capitalist modernity where Žižek deploys a true (and not necessarily inappropriate) doppelganger logic in identifying Islamic extremism as the violent double, say the Mr Hyde, to the liberal or neoliberal American self, the Dr Jekyll.[3]

In *Being Abbas El Abd*, the narrator first encounters Abbas in a fight where Abbas rescues him from his assailants. However, it is clear that Alaidy's work has a very different relation to violence than that of Palahniuk. In fact, in his anecdotal novel, incidents of violence are presented as symptomatic of the breakdown of civility in Egyptian society, a question of a shameful loss of dignity. At the outset of the novel an incident is recounted that has intertextual resonances with an incident in Robert Louis Stevenson's *The Strange Case of Dr Jekyll and Mr Hyde* (1886). In Stevenson's text the id-driven Hyde mows down a young girl without remorse, indeed with demonic coldness, as narrated in the story: 'the man trampled calmly over the child's body and left her screaming on the ground' (31). In *Being Abbas El Abd*, the following is recounted:

> The minibus stops at a traffic signal and a small barefoot girl goes by [...] She goes up to a red car with a well-off looking guy at the wheel and tries to interest him in buying a packet of paper hankies [...] He pushes her, this well-off looking guy [...] He pushes her so roughly that the little fragile girl can't stand up and falls to the ground, and packets of hankies propagate about her on the grungy pavement. (12)

Alaidy's anecdote serves to identify the obscenity of violence with the dehumanization that accompanies the self-insulation of elitism, a matter of the very loss of sociability. In this novel, the Cairo streets are presented as a stream of everyday aggression: insults flying, bodies pushing and shoving each other out of the way, with Abbas providing the aphorisms for such a world to live by, for example: 'If someone gives you a dirty look, pluck out his eyebrows' (52). As this example indicates, there is a cartoonish humour in the airing of aggressive attitudes, which is partly parodic and partly a matter of the novel's wider sense of enjoyment in flouting taboos. That is to say, the novel partakes of an energetic pleasure, precisely a liberation or cathexis of damned-up emotions, in exposing what a contemporary Egypt has come to. It refuses an escape into nostalgia and, similarly, it refuses to uphold a piously patriotic image of Egypt, as promoted by official discourse, and it implicitly refuses a piously conservative Islam as the solution too. As its translator, Humphrey Davies, comments, the novel features the 'generation of a relaxed religiosity whose presence [...] provides a counterbalance to the discredited pieties of Egypt's establishment and the aggressive rhetoric of fundamentalists' (128). The insistence is that the corruption, cruelty, sexism, hypocrisy and malaise of a dysfunctional society must be faced up to without face-saving cover-ups or makeovers. Interestingly, the character of Abbas is almost composed of a string of preacherly sayings, as he has soundbites for everything, but they are scabrous ones, a mockery of pieties.

While *Being Abbas El Abd* does not engage with religion as such, it may be said to offer a substitute focus in the attention it gives to psychotherapy. What is surprising about this area of the novel is that psychoanalysis and psychotherapy are very marginally practised in Egypt where, as already explored through Hirschkind's study, the role of therapeutic communities is much more of a popular religious domain, extending from local mosques to agony-uncle media *shayks*. However, *Fight Club* constitutes an inspiration for Alaidy's swerve towards alternative therapies in that it depicts desperate Americans trying out the therapy business of gurus, support groups and dubious cures. In *Being Abbas El Abd*, the narrator's uncle, Uncle Awni, is a psychiatrist and psychotherapist who may be read as both an inner projection and as an allegorical figure. As Julia Borossa observes in her reading of the novel, various characters in the text may be understood to be not characters in the usual sense but as projections of aspects of the narrator (404–15). Accordingly, Awni could be read as representing the superego. At the same time, he could be considered as a symbol of the authoritarian state. A number of the very short stories that make up the novel centre on Uncle Awni, in which Alaidy gives the notion of agony uncle a darkly comic spin in that it quickly transpires that Awni is a sadist whose various therapeutic experiments are forms of torture that instead of alleviating phobias generate them. Very obliquely, it is implied that this is what the Mubarak generation, or father figures of the nation, do to their sons, that is, torture and humiliate them, producing neurotic, submissive subjects, cynically pretending that these measures are for the citizens' own good. Wael Ghonim writes of Mubarak's Egypt: 'The regime sought to plant fear in the hearts of Egyptians from an early age. Fear was embodied in local proverbs, such as "Walk quietly by the wall (where you cannot be noticed)," "Mind your own business and focus on your livelihood," and "Whosoever is afraid stays unharmed"' (3). While the tyrannical Awni counsels against fear, his legacy is nothing but all kinds of fear, as in this riff:

Decidophobia: fear of making decisions [...]
Epistomophobia: fear of knowledge [...]
Doxophobia: fear of expressing opinions or receiving praise [...]
Panophobia: fear of everything [...]
Phobophobia: fear of phobias [...]
Eleutherophobia: fear of freedom (66–7)

In addition to Awni, a female psychoanalyst, 'Blah-blah', is profiled in the narrative as a complicit maternal counterpart of this parental perversion. While Awni is a sadist, her persona is apparently more caring but experienced as abjectly intrusive, for instance: 'The transparent ball [a group therapy game] gives me the right to rummage and scramble about inside you' (56); 'Squeeze out your psychological pus' (57).

    While in *Taxi*, the therapeutic side of popular religion is engaged with in passing, in *Being Abbas El Abd* there is a certain reversal in that the psychotherapeutic discourse becomes an oblique means of parodying religious discourse. The philosophy at stake is presented as follows: 'Awni claims that there is a superego and a regular ego [...] And Awni asserts – based on what Freud said – that you are nothing but "I inside I inside I"' (65). It may be proposed that, distinct from the mystical loss of self in a greater whole, here there is a relentless singularization of subjectivity which could be paraphrased as: I trapped within I. Or, there is no outside to the 'I', no 'we', no collective sense and no human relationality. Hence the novel's assertion of an 'autistic' generation. How do you break out of this? This seems to be the question of the text, and its bleak answer is suicide. The text ends with the suicide of its narrator but it does not really end there. *Fight Club* ends with its timid protagonist killing his macho alter ego, a suicide that is also not one in that Tyler Durden is not real. Somewhat similarly, the suicide in *Being Abbas El Abd* may be read as an escape. It is as if the sense of historical paralysis can only be overcome through a shedding of the phobia-inducing superego, the cringing little ego, and the cynical bravado of the alter ego (Abbas). This is brilliantly set out in the graphic typography of the novel's ending, an elliptical version of which is:

[Ab (Awni) bas]

[Ab (Aw) bas]

[Abbas]

and...

I jump

The novel itself is like a parenthesis between its introduction and postscript in that the postscript returns us to the introduction in being a new version of it. The introductory scene takes place in Geneina Mall's Ladies Toilet where someone called Hind graffitis the message: CALL ME, with a phone number. The postscript scene takes place in Geneina Mall's Men's Toilet where someone called Abdullah graffitis the message: CALL ME, with the same phone number. This phone number that is being passed on in underground fashion as a call to connect amongst the youth could be read as the trickling beginning of a coming revolution, a youth-instigated revolution organized by means of Facebook and Blackberry. And, we can see in retrospect, that what has to be shed for this to take place is the stifling singularity of 'I inside I'.

'This is not a novel', the text asserts a third of the way through, in that its characters are but 'semidemihumans' with no great exploits to relate (51). Instead, the work is said to belong among 'the works that go along with the critics to the lavatory to assist them in the floating free of fat buttocks' (51). So, it is not a novel; it is a purgative: a way of getting rid of all the *pullshttt*, as such a text might write. In its unflinching resolve to reveal a dysfunctional society and in its accompanying candid, highly energized, linguistically playful and darkly funny satirical critique, *Being Abbas El Abd* is far from being *itself* a bleakly defeated, miserably self-absorbed postmodernist text. It offers us a certain ethics through its outrageousness and sense of outrage, as if it were protesting at, while laughing at, a pathetic impasse of social being. While it is free from any form of political correctness, the text could be seen to aim through a strategy of inversion or a negative dialectics at a kind of non-elevated moral purification: a 'floating free of fat buttocks'. What is effected by *Being Abbas El Abd* is nothing short of a parenthetical treatment of postmodernism: as if postmodernism could be bracketed off within a reassemblage of the ongoing relay of the satirical *maqāma* form.

Edward Said, in introducing Elias Khoury's *Little Mountain* (1977), writes the following:

> Khoury's ideas about literature and society are of a piece with the often bewilderingly fragmented realities of Lebanon in which, he says in one of his essays, the past is discredited, the future completely uncertain, the present unknowable. For him perhaps the finest strand of modern Arabic writing derives not from the stable and highly replicable forms native to the Arabic tradition (the qasidah) or imported from the West (the novel) but those works he calls formless [...] What Khoury finds in these formless works is precisely what Western theorists have called post-modern: the combinatorial amalgam of different elements, principally autobiography, story, fable, pastiche, and self-parody, the whole heightened by an insistent and eerie nostalgia. (xx)

The fact that Said has to resort to the term 'post-modern' here suggests a certain unfamiliarity with Arabic literary history, particularly if the alternative stark choice is between the qasidah, which is a genre of lyric poetry, often a panegyric, and the conventional Western novel. Stefan Meyer asserts that Said assumes 'that the relation between form and content in the Arabic novel is the same as in the Western novel', adding that 'Complexity and fragmentation of form are not, in themselves, a sign of postmodernity' (257). While this is the case, Meyer's assumptions are also problematic in that he says of Khoury: 'we are dealing not with postmodernism, but rather with modernism at a later stage' (257). Meyer makes a similar point about the work of Sonallah Ibrahim which he says 'only mimics the tone and style of postmodernism, or rather uses these to modernist ends' (247). Alaidy's work is in some ways comparable to that of Ibrahim, where he acknowledges, in the prefatory note to *Being Abbas El Abd*, the influence of not only Palahniuk but also Ibrahim (amongst other Egyptian writers).

What is questionable regarding the terms of the debate put forth above, especially from a postcolonial point of view, is the way in which Arab avant-garde prose writing has to be judged in terms of whether it measures up to the template of Western postmodernism, merely to be relegated to an earlier period of Western aesthetic history if there appears to be a misfit. Why do contemporary Arab novels need to be viewed from and through the perspectives of Western novels? Why not accept that other nations may have their own forms of avant-garde writing, their own forms of literary experimentation and literary modernity? What this reflects is the Western(ized) critic's viewpoint as one that but posits the other as object of a discourse rather than as subject of their own discourse.

It could be proposed that, instead of merely reading *Being Abbas El Abd* through a Western template, the novel itself invites us to read an American postmodernist text like *Fight Club* through Egyptian eyes, where postmodernism emerges as less something to be uncritically mimicked than as open to critique. Accordingly, I wish to suggest that Alaidy's text be considered as an experimental *maqāma*, as introduced in relation to *Taxi*, that may be here reprised as: an Arabic prose form of episodic or picaresque storytelling, allowing for composite forms, featuring virtuoso linguistic displays and roguish characters, and entailing social critique, parody and satire. This description is apt for Alaidy's *Being Abbas El Abd*, as well as incidentally for some of Khoury's experimental writings, called by Said 'formless'. In that the *maqāma* is a composite form that defies genre as a singularizing category, it has seemed apt to refer to the experimental *maqāma* as a short story novel whose form mediates the specifics of Arabic literary production. It may be further added that Sabry Hafez maintains that the short story is 'a popular and respected genre in Arabic literature', and a narrative form that occurs before that of the novel while contributing to the latter's development (9–14).

Being Abbas El Abd references postmodernism in the manner of quoting it and alluding to it, but just as it stages a suicide, it stages the shaking off of this American form in moving on to the newer oral/aural CALL ME popular cultural forms that make use of digital media to create new kinds of collective consciousness, especially as regards the popular imagination and political activism, a moving on from the alienated sadism of a *Fight Club*. Calling experimental Arabic prose writing 'postmodern' is tantamount to saying that the democratic movement in Egypt should be seen as reflecting an Arab desire to be cloned in the image of American late capitalist society: an obvious absurdity, even if such Orientalist perspectives exist. It could even be said that Tahrir Square makes postmodernist youth culture now look rather old-fashioned, where the Arab Spring has an epoch-making ability beyond its regional happening (see Mason 29–39). In the light of works by writers such as Alaidy, Al Khamissi, Al Aswany and Bassam, amongst others, this could turn out to be a case of how Arab cultures have evolved forms of collective consciousness missing from the old democracies, ones more resigned to capitalist complicity.

When I met with Alaidy in 2009 and 2010, he introduced me to his contemporary literary milieu at Merit's publishing house, located at the Tahrir Square end of Qasr El Nil. In spite of the then political state of authoritarianism, Merit's was anything but a depressed or 'autistic' environment. Writers and journalists swirled in and out, relaying stories, gossip, jokes, literary in-talk, political and cultural analysis, creating an environment of energetic currents: a sense of what was current and in motion, all happening, the sense of a vanguard. This experience made me feel that I was living in a novel. Interestingly, when Robert Fisk arrived in Egypt to report on the Egyptian revolution and found himself in a famous downtown literary café, he wrote the following:

> We took refuge in the old Café Riche off Telaat Harb Square, a tiny restaurant and bar of blue-robed waiters; and there, sipping

his coffee, was the great Egyptian writer Ibrahim Abdul Meguid, right in front of us. It was like bumping into Tolstoy taking lunch amid the Russian revolution. 'There has been no reaction from Mubarak!' he exalted. 'It is as if nothing has happened! But they will do it – the people will do it!' The guests sat choking from the gas. It was one of those memorable scenes that occur in movies rather than real life. (Fisk n.p.)

While I understand what Fisk means, I think a more precise wording is necessary. The vivid sense of living in a novel or in a film is not the feeling of inhabiting some dreamy alternative to 'real life'. Rather, it is the heightened feeling of 'real life' itself: great art as this. This point is being made for two reasons by way of conclusion. Firstly, while in *Fight Club* the young men can only feel alive through acts of violence, what they may be said to be really missing is the sense of collective awareness as that which constitutes the feeling of participating in history, democracy as this. It is *Being Abbas El Abd* that provides a kind of 'negative theology' of this understanding, while *Taxi* engages more directly with the collective attunements of sacred re-worldings. Secondly, while Bahaa Taher remarked in 2010, 'literature is democracy' (quoted Rooney 369), it would equally be possible to say that 'democracy is literature': the assemblies of Tahrir Square as avant-garde *maqāmat* or like a short story novel come to life?

Notes

1. Other works of relevance include Alaa Al Aswany, *The Yacoubian Building* (2007), *Chicago* and *Friendly Fire* (both 2009); Rehab Bassam, *Orz Belaban L'shaksheen* (2008); and Ahmed Khaled Towfik, *Utopia* (2011).
2. From an unpublished interview made with Khaled Al Khamissi in Cairo in 2010.
3. For instance, in the *London Review of Books* (2011), Žižek writes: 'Alain Badiou has argued that we live in a social space which is increasingly experienced as "worldless": in such a space, the only form protest can take is meaningless violence. Perhaps this is one of the main dangers of capitalism: although by virtue of being global it encompasses the whole world, it sustains a "worldless" ideological constellation in which people are deprived of their ways of locating meaning.'

Works cited

Alaidy, Ahmed. *Being Abbas El Abd*. Trans. Humphrey Davies. London: Arabia Books, 2008.

Al Aswany, Alaa. *On the State of Egypt: What Caused the Revolution*. London: Canongate, 2011.

Al Khamissi, Khaled. *Taxi*. Trans. Jonathan Wright. Wiltshire: Aflame Books, 2008.

Awadalla, Maggie. 'Generational Differences in Three Egyptian Women Writers: Finding a Common Ground.' *Journal of Postcolonial Writing* 47.4 (2011): 440–53.

Bassam, Rehab, 'In Less Than Five Years.' Interview by Caroline Rooney, Cairo, April 2010. *Journal of Postcolonial Writing* 47.4 (2011): 467–76.

Borossa, Julia. 'The Extensibility of Psychoanalysis in Ahmed Alaidy's *Being Abbas El Abd* and Bahaa Taher's *Love in Exile*.' *Journal of Postcolonial Writing* 47.4 (2011): 404–15.

El Général. 'Head of State.' http://www.youtube.com/watch?v=IeGlJ7OouR0

El Hamamsy, Walid. 'Blackberry or Big Brother: Digital Media and the Egyptian Revolution.' *Journal of Postcolonial Writing* 47.4 (2011): 453–66.

Fanon, Frantz. *The Wretched of the Earth*. Trans. Constance Farringdon. Harmondsworth: Penguin, 1970.

Fight Club, dir. David Fincher. Twentieth Century Fox, 1999.

Fisk, Robert. 'A People Defies its Dictator, and a Nation's Future is in the Balance.' *The Independent* (29 January 2011). http://www.independent.co.uk/news/world/africa/robert-fisk

Freud, Sigmund. 'Creative Writers and Day-Dreaming.' 1908. *The Standard Edition of the Complete Psychological Works of Sigmund Freud, Volume IX*. Trans. James Strachey. London: Hogarth Press, 1959. 141–53.

Hafez, Sabry. *The Quest for Identities: The Development of the Modern Arabic Short Story*. London: Saqi Books, 2007.

Hirschkind, Charles. *The Ethical Soundscape: Cassette Sermons and Islamic Counterpublics*. New York: Columbia University Press, 2006.

Jaquemond, Richard. *Conscience of the Nation: Writers, State and Society in Modern Egypt*. Trans. David Tresilian. Cairo: The American University in Cairo Press, 2008.

March-Russell, Paul. *The Short Story: An Introduction*. Edinburgh University Press, 2009.

Mason, Paul. *Why It's Kicking Off Everywhere: The New Global Revolutions*. London: Verso, 2012.

Meyer, Stefan G. *The Experimental Arabic Novel: Postcolonial Literary Modernism in the Levant*. New York: SUNY Press, 2001.

Palahniuk, Chuck. *Fight Club*. London: Vintage, 1997.

Rooney, Caroline. 'Egyptian Literary Culture and Egyptian Modernity: Introduction.' *Journal of Postcolonial Writing* 47.4 (2011): 369–76.

Said, Edward. Foreword to Elias Khoury, *Little Mountain*. Trans. Maia Tabet. Manchester: Carcanet, 1989.

Saint Shenouda Monastery. http://www.stshenoudamonastery.org.au/
modules/stshenouda4/
Stevenson, Robert Louis. *The Strange Case of Dr Jekyll and Mr Hyde and Other
Stories*. Harmondsworth: Penguin, 1979.
Žižek, Slavoj. 'Shoplifters of the World Unite.' *London Review of Books*
(19 August 2011). http://www.lrb.co.uk/2011/08/19/slavoj-zizek/shoplifters-
of-the-world-unite
—— *Welcome to the Desert of the Real*. London: Verso, 2002.

8
Topographies and Textual Negotiations: Arab Women's Short Fiction

Maggie Awadalla

> There are dimensions here, times and places, glacial
> or torrid zones never moderated, the entire exotic
> geography which characterizes a mode of thought
> as well as style of life. (Deleuze 128)

In the postcolonial world of diaspora and transnational cultural flow, attempts to map the world as a group of cultural regions or home-lands are confronted by a blurring of familiar lines between the 'here' and 'there', the centre and periphery, the colony and metropole, the private and public (Gupta and Ferguson 10). This blurring leads to a sense of displacement, ambivalence and ambiguity, or what Homi Bhabha describes as 'the uncanny of cultural difference' (72). In *The Wretched of the Earth* (1961), Frantz Fanon points out how the displacement of the colonized leads to an uprooting from their past, culture, traditions and history. Arab women's short fiction can be read in this context as an attempt to address the problematics of displacement and marginalization through their use of the fantastic, the mythic and at times the folktale (*hadouta*). These strategies grant them the means of reclaiming their oral traditions, as well as a means of freedom of speech under autocratic political regimes and an oppressive patriarchal society.

This chapter examines how displacement and marginalization are expressed in terms of issues posed by Gilles Deleuze and Félix Guattari in their book *Kafka: Toward a Minor Literature* (1975), which discusses how minority literatures attempt to deterritorialize and consequently reterritorialize the literary text. Although not all women's writing should be automatically categorized as a minor literature, a representative cross-section of Arab women's short stories can be positioned within a context of minority discourse due to the manner in which they position themselves within a marginalized context, both in terms of the textual dimension and through their use of language, form and characterization, all of which effectively contribute to the decentring of the literary constructions from which they are writing. Their short fiction has embarked on reclaiming its textual space, and, in some cases, these stories can be perceived as an attempt to rethink space, not only in terms of the imagined space but also in terms of its textual spaces. The deterritorialization of literary language and the negotiation of reclaiming the textual space is one of the primary quests that women writers embark on in the texts analysed in this chapter. According to Deleuze and Guattari, minor literature employs the tension of life lived on the edge to construct itself in relation to the dynamics of centres and margins – deterritorialization and reterritorialization. However, due to a lack of a comprehensive, cognitive non-Western discourse on the topic of marginalization and minor literatures, the challenge is to develop a discourse that examines non-Western women's writings in relation to the dynamics of centres and margins.

The Egyptian short story writer Alifa Rifaat addresses the polemics of displacement, ambivalence and ambiguity. In the story 'My World of the Unknown' (1983), a middle-class housewife, who is obliged to move house every time her husband is transferred, has an encounter with a snake in her new home. Having moved to a provincial town far from the metropolis, the protagonist takes solace in an 'excitingly dangerous' passionate preoccupation with this snake (70). The ambivalent feelings the protagonist experiences reflect an ambiguity within the text itself as to the true nature of the snake: 'Was the snake from the world of reptiles or from the djinn?' (71). The blurring of the lines between here and there, the real and the fantastic, is presented in this story as the protagonist seems to be constantly on the 'brink' or 'threshold' of something strange yet familiar (69). This state of in-between constantly challenges the reader's understanding of what is real and what is the figment of the narrator's imagination. Furthermore the encounters with the female snake are always when the protagonist finds herself in a state of hypnotic daze, or in a dream-like state of mind:

> The snake curled round on itself in a spiral ring, then tautened its body and moved forward. The sight gripped me; I felt terror turning my blood cold and freezing my limbs.
>
> My senses were numbed, my soul intoxicated with a strange elation at the exciting beauty of the snake. I was rooted to the spot, wavering between two thoughts that contended in my mind at one and the same time: should I snatch up some implement from the kitchen and kill the snake, or should I enjoy the rare moment of beauty that had been afforded me? (68)

In presenting the snake both as the possible 'daughter of the monarchs of the djinn' and as a reptile (70–1), Rifaat's work evokes elements of the fantastic genre as defined by Tzvetan Todorov in his work on the fantastic. The protagonist's hesitation between considering the extraordinary an element of belief or disbelief is a symptomatic trace of the supernatural in a world that no longer recognizes it.

In 'My World of the Unknown', the home – the place of encounter – is both part of the real world and the protagonist's other world. At the beginning of the story, as the protagonist travels by train to the new village, she sees 'images of a small white house' in her dreams. When she finally arrives, her 'dream' is actualized when she finds the very same house she dreamt of, old and abandoned on the edge of a broad canal (62–3). But the house – and its snake(s) inhabitants – remain an enigma throughout the story, a place of wonder. The story ends with the protagonist and her family forced to leave the house forever after the husband finds and kills a snake. Ferial Ghazoul argues that in the Arabic short fiction, the idea of home or homecoming is usually to a place that has become 'unhomely', where 'a sense of estrangement prevails characterizing the literature of the (post)colonial world in which the individual is excluded and deprived' (4). Ghazoul points out that other Arab critics such as Muhsin al-Musawi, Fadia Suyoufie and Mahmoud Kharbutli have also argued that the employment of the ambivalent and the uncanny allows writers to express themselves in an otherwise restricted ambiance, and therefore 'acquires a unique status as a mode of expression and existence' (Ghazoul 4).

Through the use of the uncanny or the 'unhomely', Arab writers are granted a considerable degree of freedom of expression. Here Rifaat is free to explore what is regarded as highly taboo subjects in the Arab world, namely female sexuality and desire, same-sex encounters and marital relationships on the whole. By presenting the snake as a mythic-folkloric creature and by blurring the boundaries between the world of the real and that of the mythic, she is able to explore the 'excitingly dangerous' passion between the protagonist and the female snake:

> There was no doubt but that the secret of my passion for her, my preoccupation with her, was due to the excitement that had aroused, through intense fear, desire within myself; and excitement that was sufficiently strong to drive the blood hotly through my veins whenever the memory of her came to me. (71)

However, as with most of Rifaat's stories, this story ends in the tormenting world of an unfulfilled and harsh reality when the husband kills a snake. This snake's appearance is far from the description of the mythical creature the protagonist encounters, and is described as an ugly two metres' long black snake lying dead at the husband's feet (76). Unlike the entrancing djinn-snake, this one brings the narrative back to the world of reality. In contrast to the biblical Adam and Eve story (where Eve is held responsible for the couple's exile), the male figure here is the one whose actions force the family out of the house. Through his act of aggression and cruelty, he unwittingly breaks 'the pact' between the inhabitants of the house and the snakes that share it with them and they are no longer safe. The djinn-snake appears before the protagonist and orders her out of the house: '"It is farewell," she said. "You have broken the pact and have betrayed one of my subjects, so you must both depart from this house, for only love lives in it"' (76).

The protagonist, through no fault of her own, is doomed to a life apart from her dream house of love and passion. The story ends with her yearning that one day she would be reunited with her lover. Rifaat presents this female relationship here as an ideal in contrast to that of the husband and wife. When the protagonist questions the djinn-snake, asking whether it would have been more 'natural' for the snake to be a man, the djinn-snake replies: '"Perfect beauty is to be found only in woman [...] so yield to me and I shall guide you to worlds possessed of such beauty as you have never imagined"' (75). When the djinn-snake and the protagonist embark on the most fantastic of journeys 'wandering together in worlds and living on horizons of daz-zling beauty', the narrative style becomes akin to that of folkloric tales and evokes the stories from *The Thousand and One Nights* (75). Given that discussing female sexuality and desire is taboo in Arab cultures, Rifaat expresses desire by evoking elements of the fantastic.

Throughout the collection, *Distant View of a Minaret and Other Stories* (1983), Rifaat's female protagonists fail to find companionship and fulfilment from their spouses. Rifaat explores what it means to be a woman living in a traditional Muslim society and questions many of the norms and attitudes relating to women and their place. The collection discusses women's sexuality, desires, dreams and dep-rivation in a predominantly patriarchal society. The title story por-trays the frustration a wife feels in a loveless relationship, in which both live in separate worlds. The opening paragraph begins:

> Through half-closed eyes she looked at her husband. Lying on his right side, his body intertwined with hers and his head bent over her right shoulder. As usual at such times she felt that he inhab-ited a world utterly different from hers, a world from which she had been excluded. (1)

After years of intentionally denying her sexual fulfilment, the husband suddenly dies in bed after intercourse and the wife cannot find any compassion to mourn his departure. However, the ultimate retribution for the husband lies in the fact that he died without purifying himself, an Islamic ritual that requests both parties to wash after intercourse.

The death of a husband is explored by the Iraqi short story writer 'Aliyah Mamduh in her story 'Al-Juththah' (The Corpse) (1977). As the female protagonist is left alone with the corpse of her husband and recalls their relationship, in an uncanny moment, a moment of madness, she decides to sleep with him, even though the corpse is already beginning to rot. Ghazoul argues that this 'intersection between life and death, desire and absence' in the story:

> presents a most uncanny scene of conjugal love. It is the repeti-tion of an erotic performance, and thus a familiar occurrence, and

yet because one of the partners is dead, the strangeness is over-
whelming. In this story of necromancy, the familiar is framed in
the unfamiliar. (9)

When exploring female sexuality and conjugal love, these two stories present the female individual at a moment of temporary loss of
sanity, a dislocation from reality and an alienation from the norm.

In *The Quest for Identities* (2007), Sabry Hafez argues that the short
story on the whole, and the Arabic short story in specific, is a genre
in which 'individuals express their innermost feelings and thoughts
and shape their sense of individual identity. Its focus is on the over-
looked individuals, the small fragments of the large fresco' (38). Two
key words he uses to describe the short story are 'differentiation'
and 'individuation' (38), where the individual and self-expression
are used as a means of resisting community hegemony and identity
politics. Hafez argues that a preoccupation with epistemological
themes in most of the authors selected for analysis in his book, 'is a
clear manifestation of the quest for objective knowledge of the "self",
or more precisely, the individual self' (39). Significantly, Hafez argues
that the short story has been used as a vehicle for expressing the 'tri-
als and tribulations of its individual characters [...] with their stock of
marginal and forlorn characters' and that the genre's popularity and
'overabundance' in the Arab world is a testament that 'their unhappy
histories and suffering may be taken as an indication of the absence
of happiness and security, of a problematic time' (40). However, the
question remains whether there are in fact differences in the quest
for identity characterized in men's writing (such as those analysed in
The Quest for Identities) in comparison with women's writing in the
Arab world today.

Rehab Bassam, a young Egyptian blogger and short story writer,
expresses how she sees her writing as an act of writing the history
of the individual and as an act of writing the lives of those who fall
outside history. In an interview with Caroline Rooney, she notes:

I think that, yes, in modern Arabic writing, I don't see myself so
what's wrong with a little bit of 'me, me, me' in Arabic literature!
(Laughter) Later on our lives will not be chronicled. It will seem
like we didn't exist. And there's a certain – when you read the
male writers, the ways in which they portray the women are not

that different from the older stereotypes. And even in the movies, it's rare that you see real characters so that you'd say 'this is somebody I know, this is somebody I could relate to'. Sometimes the women are portrayed as pure stereotypes. (473)

Bassam feels that her writing is a celebration of being 'different' and it is what her readers can relate to. There is a notable sense of cautious optimism in Bassam's attitude and writing, especially in regards to the political and social outlook for the future in Egypt. Bassam ends the interview hoping that, when looking back on the current situation, 'change' is possible (476).

In contrast to this, the earlier writings of Ahdaf Soueif and Hanan al-Shaykh demonstrate a sense of struggle in exploring their possibilities of reclaiming both public and private space in a predominantly patriarchal social system. Ahdaf Soueif's *Sandpiper* (1996) and Hanan al-Shaykh's *Women of Sand and Myrrh* (1989) explore how they use concepts of gender and confinement within a context of minority discourse. This is because they situate themselves within a marginalized context both in terms of the textual dimension and through their use of language and form, both of which effectively contribute to the decentring of the literary constructions from which they are writing. In addition, the authors have in many aspects imposed upon themselves a certain amount of distancing – and even exile – from the countries they are writing about. This lends itself to a reading of their work as an attempt to also reclaim the geographical space from which they write.

Notions of restriction, seclusion, imprisonment and prohibition are recurrent themes in both authors' works. One of the strategies they use to express these notions is through their choice of language. While al-Shaykh uses the Lebanese vernacular to express her breaking away from traditional Standard Modern Arabic, Soueif chooses to write in English. Soueif, an Egyptian-born writer, uses language to destabilize not only the Arabic literary canon, but also that of the English-speaking Western culture. The author's use of 'Arabo-English' has a dual function as it deterritorializes and consequently reterritorializes the author's discourse, and it also paves the way – not for a room of her own – but a cross-cultural, multinational arena of public discourse. Trabelsi argues that the production of this new discourse 'defies the constraints and taboos of the culture of origin (such as the "sacredness" of the Arabic language or the subaltern status of women) by putting it in dialogue with a different culture' (n.p.).

The two writers also use textual space to dramatize their protagonists' deep sense of confinement within a predominately vast surrounding. Both works write about women who live in the Gulf and are entrapped in their own psychological and geographical confines. Soueif and al-Shaykh depict women from both the West and the East and explore how each of them reacts to their lives in the Arab world and the Gulf region. In both works, the individual characters barely meet the other characters and are textually as well as physically separated. The authors use strategies that distinctly mirror the intense feeling of physiological and physical confinement. Soueif's *Sandpiper* is constructed as a collection of short stories of different women each confined to their own textual space, whereas al-Shaykh's novel, *Women of Sand and Myrrh*, is divided into four separate sections and each section is named according to one of the characters. Although presented as a novel, the construction of al-Shaykh's text shares many similarities with that of short fiction. Each character is confined not only physically to her separate space, but also is culturally and economically separated from the others.

Soueif constructs her fiction around conflicting cross-cultural encounters. In *Sandpiper*, she manipulates the surroundings to express the state of mind of the characters. On several occasions, Soueif juxtaposes the vastness of the surrounding space with the psychological entrapment of the characters. In the title story, for example, the protagonist, who is a foreigner married to an Egyptian man, significantly remains nameless throughout the story, and is portrayed as suffering from a dual confinement. This occurs on one level due to her status as a foreigner, and on another level she suffers from a deep sense of isolation as a woman whose husband has lost interest in her. She explains: 'My foreignness, which had been so charming, began to irritate him. My inability to remember names, to follow the minutiae of politics, my struggles with his language' (33). Her entrapment is complete within her own boundaries of culture and the language barriers she experiences. Soueif's characters in this collection tend to be marginal figures, and in 'Sandpiper' marginality is due to the character's foreignness. It is interesting to point out here that, as with Soueif, al-Shaykh's *Women of Sand and Myrrh* also dedicates one of its four sections to a Western woman named

Suzanne, who is living in the Gulf, and whose predicament is due to her inability to understand how the social system actually functions in the Gulf area. In both cases, the marginality of the characters is always associated with a dislocation and displacement of their public/private spaces.

In the story 'Sandpiper', this dislocation and displacement is dramatized by the author's skilful use of locale. As in many of Soueif's stories, physical walls play a significant role in the lives of the characters, and are used as a recurring motif to dramatize both the internal and the external state of confinement. The first paragraph demonstrates how the author manipulates external space to express the character's internal psychological boundaries. The story starts with a description of the protagonist's surroundings: 'Outside there is a path. A path of beaten white stone bordered by a white wall – low, but not low enough for me to see over it from here' (23). The path should serve to lead from one point to another, but here it is only portrayed as a tantalizing form of confinement where the protagonist is unable to 'see' beyond its walls. Later on, the protagonist leans against the wall of her room, and recounts her history with her estranged husband: 'twelve years ago I met him. Eight years ago, I married him. Six years ago, I gave birth to his child' (24). Her room rather than functioning as a sanctuary from the outside world is more of a confined space, where the protagonist spends her days counting. However, she is not calculating the days she has left to leave, but is recounting her past. Her past, as seen through her eyes, will not lead to new prospects. In this predicament, her entrapment is complete and final, since she has no expectations for her future.

Soueif uses the technique of continuous monologue to dramatize the protagonist's sense of complete entrapment. She adds, 'I should have gone. No longer a serrating thought but familiar and dull. I should have gone … knowing him as I did, I first sensed that he was pulling away from me, I should have gone' (27). Her inability to act is compounded with her inability to 'talk' to any one. In fact, the only single line of dialogue within this story is in the last paragraph, where she murmurs to her daughter as she kisses her: '"My Lucy, Lucia, *Lambah*" … Lucy. My treasure, my trap' (36). Significantly there is no answer. This juxtaposition of both the endless possibilities of freedom and entrapment is a theme that occurs in this collection. For example, the author starts the collection with an epigraph from Elizabeth Bishop's poem entitled 'Sandpiper' from where Soueif quotes the following: 'The world is a mist. And then the world is / minute and vast and clear. The tide is higher or lower. He couldn't tell you which.' This epigraph can be read as an overture for the entire collection where the world is portrayed as being full of contradictions: *both* minute *and* vast, misty *and* clear. Furthermore, the protagonist in the story entitled 'Sandpiper' can be compared to the bird mentioned in the epigraph. As she stands on the beach and looks out on the horizon upon the vastness of the sea, we might expect that she would experience a sense of openness and infinity. However, this is not the case. As she looks out to sea, she has the following insight. She says:

> Now I realise, I was trying to work out my co-ordinates I thought a lot about the water and the sand as I sat there watching them meet and flirt and touch. I tried to understand that I was on the edge, the very edge of Africa; that the vastness ahead was noth-ing compared to what lay behind me. But – even though I'd been there and seen for myself its *never-ending* dusty green interior, its mountains, the big sky, my mind could not grasp a world that was not present to my senses – I could see the beach, the waves, the blue beyond, and cradling them all, my baby. (26; my italics)

The beautiful imagery of a woman standing at the very edge of Africa, looking beyond her immediate visual horizon, is restricted by her ina-bility to see the infinity of the sea. Her own senses confine her because she is only able to conjecture the sea's boundaries: 'the other side'. The concept of the 'never-ending' which would normally denote infinity is here subverted to portray a restricting environment.

In the paragraph above, the protagonist displays her own sense of being trapped between two worlds, Africa and Europe, and even the sea is not large enough for her. The displacement the protagonist demonstrates is one that is woven throughout the collection, where the author takes metaphors traditionally used to suggest space and freedom, and skilfully reverses them to evoke a deep sense of close-ness and confinement. This technique used by Soueif to manipulate language is accomplished by destabilizing its conventional connota-tions and metaphors. In doing so, Soueif is using language to reorder and reclaim her own textual space.

In this process of reordering, the sandpiper, a bird which migrates south in winter, becomes, in this story, a metaphor for displacement and preoccupation, the bird is 'looking for something, something something. / Poor bird he is obsessed!' In this opening epigraph, the bird is portrayed not airborne in flight over continents, but restricted to its sandy surrounding, where it looks and pecks. Just as Soueif quotes George Eliot's *Middlemarch* (1871) at the beginning of her earlier novel *In the Eye of the Sun* (1992), here too the textual reference to the migrating bird is used to intersect, overlap and interconnect, in an attempt to unveil, what Spivak terms, 'unfamiliar conclusions' (xvii). Again, Soueif inserts the established familiar construction into an unfamiliar framework, thereby not only dismantling the coherence of the textual structure but also subverting the Western master-narrative, here, the poem.

In a similar strategy, al-Shaykh uses the technique of reversing traditional metaphors, so that the desert no longer comes to portray the vast and infinite, but on the contrary – through the eyes of Suha and Nur – comes to represent their deep sense of confinement. Thus, in *Women of Sand and Myrrh*, the desert, like Soueif's sea, becomes the very symbol of confinement and boundaries. The traditional geographical preconceptions of place are replaced, as al-Shaykh seeks to create her own space within the text. The setting in an unnamed Gulf country is portrayed as being both suffocating and constricting. The desert is what brings the four characters together, but it also keeps them captive. Here we find that the vastness of the desert is curtailed by the walls of the houses, which were high; Suha notes: 'the newer they were the higher'. Upon leaving the desert/city, Suha remarks: 'Do you know what amazed me the most … The walls, constricting everyone' (278). Upon leaving the desert, Suha feels whole again: no longer split between Suha of the desert and Suha the city dweller.

Through the manipulation of locale, both authors in very similar ways succeed in creating a dialectic of public and private space. Within this space, displacement and dislocation constantly fluctuate. According to Deleuze and Guattari, within this type of writing, 'the individual concern thus becomes all the more necessary, indispensable, magnified, because a whole other story is vibrating within it' (17). This 'whole other story', in the case of Soueif and al-Shaykh, is their attempt to rethink space in terms of imagined, psychological and textual spaces, in addition to those of the physical and geographical concepts. Furthermore, this 'other' story is enhanced by both authors' treatment of their characters. So far I have only pointed out the characters who suffer from the confines and limitations of their surroundings. However, some of the characters in al-Shaykh's work *Women of Sand and Myrrh* are deployed, in the words of Deleuze and Guattari, 'to express another possible community and to forge the means for another consciousness and another sensibility' (17). For example, Suha acts as a catalyst who brings together all the other characters. On another level, however, Suha literally brackets the content of the novel, where the novel starts with her story and ends with an epilogue of her leaving the desert forever.

Al-Shaykh effectively uses the respective houses of each protagonist to display the differences between the various characters: their cultural backgrounds, and their economic status within the desert society. The novelist, with great craft, portrays the life of each confined woman within her respective home, bringing the houses to life with colours and details, smells and atmosphere. But ultimately, even though each house is different, each and every one is effectively the protagonist's prison cell, be it large or small, tasteful or tatty. For example, Nur, who is the most superficial and the most negative of the four women in the novel, lives in an extended house with large grounds. Within the estate she has her own private house where she can drive a motorbike (which would be illegal for her as a woman to drive outside in public). Nonetheless, she is the character who suffers most from a deep sense of entrapment. Her public life beyond the walls of the family house is severely curtailed because she has to be chauffeured by a male driver whenever she wants to go out, while her passport has been confiscated by her estranged husband, making her imprisonment complete. For Nur, the only freedom she can visualize is the ability to walk down the street on her own two feet (248). In retaliation to this geographical and mental confinement, Nur resorts to having illicit sexual encounters both with the opposite sex and with her own, Suha being one of the many women she has sexual contact with. Nur 'admits to herself that [her] body was the outlet for [her] feelings' (264). Here the body and its physical boundaries become the focal point of freedom. Nur uses her body as a form of geographical and physical dialectic: a means to overcome the geographical confinements imposed on her by a rigid and severe patriarchal regime. This reminds us in some ways of how Alifa Rifaat uses the female body as a means of redefining cultural and physical boundaries. However, in this set of stories, al-Shaykh presents us with the antithesis to Nur's character, Tamr, who is portrayed as the only female protagonist who is able – and actually willing – to address her problems and try to solve them. Her one ambition is to become financially independent by opening her own business as a seamstress. Her brother throughout this episode is portrayed as the epitome of the patriarchal regime. He is against her project and is out to prevent it at all costs. Here Tamr, like Nur, has to use her body to attain what she wants. Tamr uses her body as a tactical weapon by abstaining from food until she is about to die, and only then does her brother agree half-heartedly to her opening her own business. Here al-Shaykh demonstrates how Tamr is finally able to achieve some sort of liberation through work and financial freedom.

However, within the mingled stories of these women, al-Shaykh offers very little in terms of hope or consolation. This is especially true of the English version. In the original Arabic version, the novel starts and ends with two positive characters; however, in the English translation, the chapter order is changed so that the novel begins and ends with two different sections which tell the stories of Suha and Nur. These two characters suffer most from the confinements of the desert life and have a very negative outlook on their surroundings. In its English translation, the novel begins with Suha, who is a dislocated protagonist who finally decides to leave the Gulf country and its suffocating city/desert life to go back to Lebanon. The story ends with Nur, who was born in the Gulf in a rich family, but who nevertheless suffers terribly from the confines of her meaningless life and dreams of being able to live as she had done in the past in a less restricted city. This bracketing of two dislocated protagonists is only in the English version of the novel. The original Arabic version, on the other hand, starts with Suha but ends on a more optimistic note with Tamr, a woman from the Gulf who has found her place, as it were, under the sun. This changing around of the chapters in the translated version considerably alters the tone of the novel, from a fundamentally positive note in the Arabic text, to a much more pessimistic view in the English translation.

On putting this question to the translator, she pointed out that in consecutive translations of other novels by al-Shaykh they mention at the beginning of the novels that the original text does not necessarily correspond to the translated text. This suggests an awareness of the respective English and Arabic audiences and that there is a definite amount of tailoring that occurs. Geoffrey Nash suggests that 'knowing the stereotypes of Arab gender relations favoured by Western readers, they may even play off these in the representations of Arab societies' (28). This obviously has some bearing on how the two versions can be read and interpreted. Despite this fact, even in the translated version, al-Shaykh does offer some respite to her characters on the textual level. First of all, the confinement of the characters is eased by their ability to narrate their own points of view in the first person. By giving her characters a voice within the text, al-Shaykh is creating an 'other' possibility. In addition, within the novel, the four main characters have met and have known each other, and despite the fact that their relationships are far from ideal, there is nonetheless some form of communication between them. Therefore, and in spite of the obvious dislocation the characters suffer, their lives are in some way affected by each other.

In Soueif's collection *Sandpiper*, the sense of dislocation is more severe, for the characters in each story never actually meet each other, and are textually separated by different sections, rendering their confinement complete within the textual space of the collection. Here, the characters are even visually bracketed within the pages of the collection and are separated by blank pages which enshroud the characters, each one in her own cocoon. Soueif, in an incredible display of language manipulation, dramatizes this deep and irrevocable sense of estrangement. In the first story, 'Melody', for example, Soueif uses various techniques to express the narrator's displacement within the life of a compound in a Gulf country. The boundaries of language and various cultural preconceptions and misconceptions of the other predominate its pages. The narrator (whom the reader can assume is from an English-speaking Western origin) demonstrates her limited understanding of different cultures through alarming and sweeping statements such as this: 'the way these Muslim women treat their husbands just makes me ill. They actually want to be slaves' (7). She develops a love/hate relationship with a Turkish family who also live within the compound. The narrator ridicules the way the Turkish housewife talks imperfect English: 'Ingie too is "very joyful person"' (7). The narrator and Ingie are both prisoners of their circumstances: the narrator is bored, cannot and will not attempt to understand her surroundings, and Ingie is entrapped by the tragic death of her daughter in a car accident and the consequent chain of events that unfolds. The narrator is entrapped by a continuous fascination and repulsion. Consequently the narrator's sentence structure suffers as her language becomes distorted, restrained and is confined between full stops: 'And she can dance. Arms and legs twirling. Neck side to side. Leaning backwards. The lot' (7).

In Deleuze and Guattari's summary of what constitutes a minor literature's utilization of language, they map a treatment of language very similar to that which Soueif is attempting in this story:

> Prepositions that assume all sorts of senses; prenominal or purely intensive verbs [...] conjunctions, exclamations, adverbs; and terms that connote pain [...] accents that are interior to words, their discordant function. (22)

Soueif, as an Egyptian novelist writing in English, is subverting the language twice, once for not using Arabic as her main discourse, and secondly by manipulating English to become a minor discourse within the major one. By doing this, she is moving her language 'towards its extremities or its limits' (23), and by doing so, is making herself a foreigner to her own language (25).

Soueif uses various techniques to create this 'continuous variation' to subvert the mainstream English language. One technique Soueif uses is the introduction of Arabic words like *inshallah*, without necessarily offering a translation or an explanation (85). Another more subtle manipulation of language can be seen in the short story 'The Water-Heater' where parts of the Egyptian vernacular are introduced into the text. The following sentence: 'Of course it was true that marriage was protection for a woman' is a good example, as it is a direct translation of '*al-gawaz sutra lil banat*' (72). The sentence in English makes sense, but for a reader with some knowledge of Arabic, it takes on another level of meaning and relates to (an)other set of connotations as it brings to the forefront a whole cultural heritage that would not necessarily be available for the reader who does not share the same cultural and social background. These sentences which are scattered throughout the text act in some manner as a private–public joke; where only some readers are able to appreciate the full allusions and share with the author its cultural meanings. For example, a cliché like '*al-gawaz sutra lil banat*' (marriage is protection for a woman) is widely used in the Arab media as a derogative comment on the status of women in society but also used within a questioning context where writers use the phrase to challenge and ridicule its connotations.

This suggestive use of another language is discussed in an introduction to the question of minority discourse in *Cultural Critique* by JanMohamed and Lloyd, where they problematize the use of Western languages as follows:

> Every time we speak or write in English, French, German [...] we pay homage to Western intellectual and political hegemony. Despite this, it would seem, Western humanism still considers us barbarians beyond the pale of civilization; we are forever consigned to play the role of the ontological, political, economical and cultural Other. (5)

The role of the 'ontological other' is an important theme in both Soueif and al-Shaykh's work. Through their writings, we are obliged to examine this claim presented by JanMohamed and Lloyd, in which they state that writing in a Western language is paying homage to the Western intellectual, who nevertheless perceives the Eastern intellectual as barbaric. Both authors have at least one predominant female character that comes from 'the cultural Other': the West.

Radwa 'Ashur describes how in Soueif's work English functions as a 'transparent veil' through which the Arabic language can be seen and the English follows 'the rhythm of Arabic in those places' (quoted in Massad 87). Soueif adds in her interview with Joseph Massad: 'I suppose I am writing in Arabic disguised as English!' (87). In another interview she adds:

> Writing in English definitely gives me more freedom because I can use English in literary terms better than I can use Arabic and so I can make the language do what I want with more ease. I suppose the question of language arises because there are passages in [my] book[s] which are sexually frank. (Quoted in Trabelsi n.p.)

But, as Soueif wonders: 'is it doable?' Deleuze, in an interview, argues that it is important to have a minor language, and suggests that:

> To be like a foreigner in one's own language [...] We must have a minor language inside our language, we must make a minor usage of our own language. (Bogue 175)

This use of language, 'to be like a foreigner in one's own language', is Soueif's endeavour to claim space in terms of language, by firstly deterritorializing the literary space and then reterritorializing it, in other words, 'to make it doable'. By reclaiming and redefining the old codes of the gendered body of the text, by expressing these forms of confinement through the act of writing, Arab women writers subvert these codings of patriarchal dominance, and, through this conflict, move the text from a state of entrapment to that of freedom.

Works cited

al-Shaykh, Hanan. *Women of Sand and Myrrh*. Trans. Catherine Cobham. London: Quartet, 1989.

Bassam, Rehab. 'In Less Than Five Years.' Interview by Caroline Rooney, Cairo, April 2010. *Journal of Postcolonial Writing* 47.4 (2011): 467–76.

Bhabha, Homi. 'Location, Intervention, Incommensurability: A Conversation with Homi Bhabha.' *Emergences* 1.1 (1989): 63–88.

Bogue, Ronald. *Deleuze and Guattari*. London: Routledge, 1989.

Deleuze, Gilles. *The Logic of Sense*. Ed. Constantin V. Boundas, trans. Mark Lester with Charles Stivale. London: Athlone Press, 1990.

Deleuze, Gilles and Félix Guattari. *Kafka: Toward a Minor Literature*. Trans. Dana Polan. Minneapolis: University of Minnesota Press, 1986.

Fanon, Frantz. *The Wretched of the Earth*. Trans. Constance Farrington. London: Penguin, 2001.

Ghazoul, Ferial. 'Iraqi Short Fiction: The Unhomely at Home and Abroad.' *Journal of Arabic Literature* 35.1 (2004): 1–24.

Ghonim, Wael. *Revolution 2.0*. London: Fourth Estate, 2012.

Gupta, Akhil and James Ferguson. 'Beyond "Culture": Space, Identity, and the Politics of Difference.' *Cultural Anthropology* 7.1 (1992): 6–23.

Hafez, Sabry. *The Quest for Identities: The Development of the Modern Arabic Short Story*. London: Saqi Books, 2007.

JanMohamed, Abdul R. and David Lloyd. 'The Nature and Context of Minor Literature.' *Cultural Critique* 7 (1987): 5–19.

Mamduh, 'Aliyah. 'Al-Juththah' ('The Corpse'). *Hawamish 'ila al-Sayyidah Ba'*. Beirut: Dar al-Adab, 1977.

Massad, Joseph. 'The Politics of Desire in the Writings of Ahdaf Soueif.' *Journal of Palestine Studies* 28.4 (1999): 74–90.

Nash, Geoffrey. 'Re-Sitting Religion and Creating Feminised Space in the Fiction of Ahdaf Soueif and Leila Aboulela.' *Wasafiri* 35 (2002): 28–31.

Rifaat, Alifa. *Distant View of a Minaret and Other Stories*. Trans. Denys Johnson-Davies. London: Quartet, 1983.

Soueif, Ahdaf. *Sandpiper*. London: Bloomsbury, 1996.

Spivak, Gayatri. Preface to Jacques Derrida, *Of Grammatology*. Baltimore: Johns Hopkins University Press, 1973.

Todorov, Tzvetan. *The Fantastic: A Structural Approach to a Literary Genre*. Trans. Richard Howard. Ithaca NY: Cornell University Press, 1976.

Trabelsi, Hechmi. 'Transcultural Writing: Ahdaf Soueif's Aisha as a Case Study.' 22 December 2012. http://english.chass.ncsu.edu/jouvert/v7i2/trabel.htm

9
At the Interstices of Diaspora: Queering the Long Story Short in Caribbean Literature by Women

M. Catherine Jonet

The appearance of gay and lesbian characters in Caribbean literature of the past 30 to 50 years has been a complicated affair. Timothy S. Chin offers that 'Caribbean literary production has traditionally maintained a conspicuous silence around issues of gay and lesbian sexuality' but 'there are more recent writers – emerging particularly within the last two decades – who have broken the taboo that has previously sur-rounded the question of gay and lesbian sexuality and homophobia in Caribbean culture' ('Bullers' 129). The entrance of transgender characters into contemporary Caribbean fiction has been no less com-plex. Rosamond S. King contends that transgender characters have a particular function in the service of normatively gendered characters that does not challenge dominant belief systems about queer peoples in Caribbean societies. She states, 'Trans people most often deliver these characters to safety, to a better understanding of themselves, and to their "true" destinies, feelings, or histories' (583). King continues:

> On the surface, portraying trans people as having special insight and abilities to help other people may seem positive and even pro-gressive because it places them in a position of power and shows them using their power to benefit others. But these portrayals are also problematic because Caribbean trans characters are also consistently kept on the margins of the texts and are deprived of their individuality. (583–4)

The breaking of silences around queer sexualities and gender identi-ties as well as their representation in popular media is not limited to long-form literature. For some authors, the short story is the place to openly confront difficult subjects that powerfully affect marginalized groups within a culture. In the case of many female writers – both queer and straight – the short story appears to be a central location for breaking taboos and analysing cultural ideas. With the appearance of Ismat Chugtai's controversial lesbian short story 'Lihaf (The Quilt)' (1941) to Mahasweta Devi's searing 'Breast-Giver' from her short story collection *Breast Stories* (translated into English by Gayatri Chakravorty Spivak in 1997), and a number of short story collections by and anthologies including female writers such as Edwidge Danticat, Kanchana Ugbabe and Pulitzer Prize-winning Jhumpa Lahiri, transnational female writers consider short fiction a significant medium. This impetus is no less imperative for queer female authors writing in the Caribbean diaspora.

This chapter explores short stories by Shani Mootoo and Makeda Silvera. Their short fiction is of particular interest because they use it to draw attention to the sexual subjectivity of queer women in the Caribbean diaspora living in Canada with strong ties to their homelands (Trinidad and Jamaica). These characters are often living in an in-between space and the events depicted in these stories demonstrate how female sexuality, especially female homosexuality, is deeply entangled with discourses of patriarchy, nationalism and the continued colonization of Caribbean bodies. For Mootoo and Silvera, female queer characters occupy the centre of their texts, and other identities inhabit the margins. This practice provides a glimpse into the workings of power in everyday lives for transnational queer women, and the compactness of the short story as a form makes the glimpse a commanding one.

Notes on the Caribbean context

Challenges from within different Caribbean cultures by self-identified gays, lesbians and trans people bring voices, identities and calls to end violence to the fore. However, since gay, lesbian and trans Caribbean peoples have been in the process of developing and claiming queer identities in the public sector, voices within national cultures, which are often supported by religion, law and homophobic groups, have attempted to force those identities back to the margins through violence and social sanctions. These attitudes have caused two separate responses. On the one hand, the already diasporic people of the Caribbean are undergoing another diaspora: queer peoples are leaving the Caribbean to articulate their identities elsewhere, often in supposedly more 'liberal' countries in the Global North. And on the other hand, the Caribbean is becoming marked as a particularly extreme homophobic space by Caribbean and non-Caribbean peoples alike.[1] The Caribbean becomes a kind of unofficial barometer against which other locales measure their own levels of homo- and trans-acceptance, and to present overinflated judgements regarding attitudes about queer peoples.

The perception that the Caribbean is one of the most homophobic spaces in the world has caused a great deal of stress for queer Caribbean peoples within and beyond the Caribbean: the very cultures that are marked as particularly homophobic are the cultures that produced them, their articulation of a queer identity, and are the cultures they love and belong to. In other words, one is queer *and* Caribbean or one is a *queer Caribbean*. One is not queer and *no longer Caribbean*. Makeda Silvera asks in regard to the tendency to separate a lesbian identity from Caribbean culture: 'What are we to assume from this? That Afro-Caribbean lesbians have no Caribbean culture? That they lose their community politics when they sleep with women? Or that Afro-Caribbean culture is a heterosexual commodity?' ('Man Royals' 531). Despite what anti-queer sentiments would like to assert, the Caribbean is not a monolithically heterosexual space; it too has queers, its 'battyboys' and 'zamies', to name only a few marginalized identities.

The Caribbean has its queer identities and spaces, and there are some in the queer Caribbean diaspora who not only chart these identities, but (re)claim them from invisibility imposed on them. The Caribbean editors of *Máka, Diasporic Juks: Contemporary Writing by Queers of African Descent* (1997), for example, state:

> It is often claimed that Jamaica is the most hostile of all Caribbean countries to queers. But no Caribbean country is hospitable to us, and, unlike Black North American, the Caribbean has had very few, if any, out queers. This does not mean that there are no lesbians, gays or bisexuals living in the Caribbean. We have always lived there, always lived quietly, on the fringes, in our own circles. Anyone with close ties to the Caribbean is well aware of the

contributions made by queers to every aspect of life: in the arts, in literature, in politics, in sports and in business. But they are forced to deny that they are homosexuals at home. (Douglass et al. xvi)

Part of these emerging, self-identified queer Caribbeans' work is to recover already existing queer identities, lives and spaces within the Caribbean's different cultures. As Rosamund Elwin offers in her introduction to *Tongues on Fire: Caribbean Lesbian Lives and Stories* (1998), 'there have always been lesbian lives [in the Caribbean], hidden but present' (7). Elwin eloquently asserts: 'We are there, we are here. And, like lesbians everywhere, we do find each other' (9). While queers in the Caribbean negotiate different networks and institutions than those in North American and European cultures, Elwin wants it to be clear that Caribbean lesbians exist, and even more so, that they locate each other and forge relationships with one another.

The belief that the Caribbean is an especially homophobic space and that those who are queer must leave it in order to 'live out' queer identities in other cultural locations is often accompanied by a sweeping away of identities. This erasure affects trans people and lesbians more than gay men. Many trans women, for example, are literally pushed to the edges of society as prostitutes and go unseen in city centres and during daytime. King states:

> Though popular and scholarly documentation and analysis of Caribbean unconventional genders is rare, it is not so difficult to hear about or see areas within or on the edges of urban areas where biological men who dress and/or live as women gather – often for prostitution (for instance in the Woodbrook area of Port-of-Spain, Trinidad). The presence of Caribbean trans persons in particular areas contributes to their perceived and enforced absence in the 'general' population. (583)

Though this statement can be applied to trans women in many countries, the point here is that it affects their viable presence in Caribbean culture and diasporic movements to other countries. Women are more greatly affected by erasure because of their continued associations with home, marriage and child-rearing. In fact, Makeda Silvera documents some of the forms female same-sex sexuality takes in the Caribbean in her 1992 essay 'Man Royals and

Sodomites: Some Thoughts on the Invisibility of Afro-Caribbean Lesbians.' Far from being 'invisible' as the essay's title suggests, it would seem that lesbians occupy the status of the 'open secret' in the Afro-Caribbean not only of Silvera's youth, but also the youths of her mother and grandmother.

Woman lovers, as Silvera calls them, were not invisible: people in the community knew who they were, knew their 'secret', and, according to Silvera, many in the community relished telling these women's stories to each other. Female same-sex sexuality existed as a public affair. The so-called invisibility of it brings to mind Douglas Crimp's observation in his essay from the seminal *Fear of a Queer Planet* that outing 'is not [...] the revelation of that [homosexual] secret, but the revelation that the secret was no secret at all' (307). In the case of female homosexuality, Silvera reveals that the invisible lesbians of Jamaica were not invisible. She suggests any revelation concerning the existence of female same-sex desire is that it is not really much of a disclosure to the community because it discloses what is already, in many ways, known. However, while it was there in the open, it was only allowed to remain so because it was not articulated in service of forming queer identities.[2] Silvera comments: 'So there were many of those kind of women around. But it wasn't broadcast. I remembered them [from my childhood]. Not as lesbians or sodomites or man royals, but as women that I liked. Women whom I admired. Strong women, some colorful, some quiet' ('Man Royals' 528).

Mootoo and Silvera

Since the period of Silvera's youth, many Caribbean cultures have undergone changes regarding mores fixed to women and female gender identity. But as Myriam Chancy argues, cultural transformations surrounding women's sexuality, especially women's same-sex sexuality, have been slower in coming. Chancy comments:

> Although Caribbean women of all racial backgrounds have been redefining traditionally gendered roles over the past several decades, sexuality presents the last frontier to pervasive, deep-reaching change. Indeed, in the Caribbean context, academic investigations of lesbian lives remain a startlingly incoherent area

of exploration despite advances in other areas of women's and feminist studies in the region generally. (51)

Perhaps due to the 'startlingly incoherent' exploration into female same-sex sexuality and other issues discussed above, many female writers from the Caribbean, especially those within a diasporic context, make sure to work political issues surrounding gender and sexuality into their works. For many of these writers, the short story serves a primary function because of the form's ability to circulate by publication in anthologies, internet outlets, teaching in classrooms – especially interested Women's Studies classrooms – and even magazines. Analysing the political underpinnings at work in Caribbean diasporic short fiction helps to render the study of queer women's lives coherent, and it helps to make plain those issues surrounding gender and female same-sex sexuality that travel from the region into new cultural locations.

Short stories by Shani Mootoo and Silvera do the cultural work of bringing political issues for queer Caribbean women to light through literature. Mootoo's 'Out on Main Street' (1993) and Silvera's 'Baby' (1994) recover lesbian identities and experiences and illustrate the effects of the Caribbean diaspora on these queer identities. Writers such as Mootoo and Silvera, who produce representations of queer Caribbean women, intervene in a process that would erase such identities from a Caribbean context and add to readers' understandings of complexities within the Caribbean diaspora.

'[A] gender dey forgot to classify': Mootoo's 'Out on Main Street'

Mootoo, an Indo-Caribbean from Trinidad living in Canada, received a great deal of attention for her first novel, *Cereus Blooms at Night* (1996). But her first short story collection, *Out on Main Street* (1993), garnered both attention and acclaim. Its title story was among the first in Mootoo's *oeuvre* to draw attention to the often overlapping hierarchies at work within multiple concurring diasporas and the destabilization of many of these hierarchies. Immigrants, such as those represented in Mootoo's short story, must deal with several diasporas at once: Caribbean, Indian and the movement of transnational queer identities from one location to another. Despite the difficulties those with direct ties to India and other colonized locations within the Indian diaspora can create for Indo-Trinidadians through the use of hierarchy, the characters in this story are 'out on main street' in more than one way. Alicia Menéndez Tarrazo notes, 'Ethnicity, however, is not the only issue here: as lesbians, their gender and sexuality intersect with their ethnic origin, adding to their marginalization from an urban space which has been constructed as predominately heteronormative' (104).

'Out on Main Street' focuses on an unnamed narrator visiting an Indian restaurant to eat sweets with her girlfriend Janet. The story takes place in Vancouver and involves the ways the narrator of the piece and her girlfriend are 'watered down Indians' because they are Indo-Trinidadian in an often shifting cultural space (45). They are not what she calls 'good grade A Indians' because her family and other Indo-Caribbean families like hers do not maintain nor keep up with Indian practices, customs or ways of being that occur in the ancestral country (45). However, Indian culture in Trinidad maintains certain practices, such as the preparation and consuming of the sweets that brings the characters to the restaurant. But, years of distance have created a cultural rift: Indo-Trinidadian culture no longer calls the sweets by common names used in India. This becomes a major point in the narrative because the server at the restaurant uses this alternative naming as a way to humiliate the protagonist. The narrator asserts that she and other Indo-Trinidadians are 'watered down Indians' (45). She describes her own family's detachment from India: 'We skin brown, is true, but we doh even think 'bout India unless something happen over dere and it come on de news. Mih family remain Hindu ever since mih ancestors leave India behind, but nowadays dey doh believe in praying unles things real bad' (45). The narrator describes a situation where maintaining links with India does not exist as a special priority due to race. Her family gets information about events in India in much the same ways that many others do: they get it from the news. Moreover, while the family remains Hindu, they are not religious and pray only in moments of trouble.

The narrator's girlfriend, however, comes from a family that converted to Christianity, and they rank among the Indian families that were converted by Canadian missionaries in the Presbyterian Church in Trinidad. The narrator states: 'And Janet great-grandparents is one a de first South families dat exchange over from Indian to Presbyterian. Dat was a long time ago' (46). Interestingly, the narrator says that Janet's family 'exchanged' over from Indian to Presbyterian. The fact that she equates 'Indian' rather than 'Hindu' to Presbyterian Christianity suggests a link between cultural identity and religious practice. To change religions, especially to change from Hinduism to Western Christianity, is to 'exchange over' from one kind of life to another. However, even families such as the narrator's who do not convert still lose bonds with the homeland through change in location and cultural practice. Once they are in the new space of the Caribbean, a loss is further compounded with immigration to Canada. Interestingly, the narrator notes the cultural dis/connection in the case of Janet's family name:

> Is only recentish I realize Mahase is a Hindu last name. In de ole days every Mahase in de country turn Presbyterian and now de name doh have no association with Hindu or Indian whatsoever. I used to think of it as a Presbyterian Church name until some days ago when we meet a Hindu fella fresh from India name Yogdesh Mahase who never even hear of Presbyterian. (47)

Names as well as their associations change in the diaspora. And, the diaspora continues because many straight and queer Indo-Caribbeans also leave Trinidad to go to places like Canada. In fact, it is in Vancouver that the narrator sees 'dem gay fellas dat [...] more femme dan even Janet' (50). However, to be 'Indian-in-skin-colour-only' does not make the narrator and Janet non-Indian nor does it make them fully Trinidadian (51). The narrator states: 'Chinese people, Black people, White people. Syrian. Lebanese. I looking forward to de day I find out dat place inside me where I am nothing else but Trinidadian, whatever dat could turn out to be' (52).

While the narrator and Janet refer to Indian foods in the ways that their home communities do, the 'Indian Indians' employ the 'correct' or 'proper' terms and names for the different foods. This aspect of the narrative becomes linked to gender performance and sexuality because the narrator and Janet are a butch/femme couple. The narrator, a masculine lesbian sporting jackboots and a crewcut, has 'a gender dey forget to classify' (48). While Indian foods have terms and names that Indo-Caribbean culture has lost or renamed, the narrator's butch gender performance is one that 'real flesh and blood

Indian[s] from India' do not have a language for (47). However, classification is the language of European imperialism, not Indian history. Janet, on the other hand, is so feminine that she is hyper-feminine. The narrator describes her as 'so femme dat she redundant' (48). Interestingly, the unnamed narrator's gender is outside of classi-fication while Janet's is in excess. One is outside taxonomy, the other dismantles categorization through surfeit. Both characters queer gender as much as they queer Indian- and Trinidadianness.

The narrator associates Indo-Trinidadian cultural authenticity with excess, '[W]e like we meethai and sweetrice too much and it remain overly authentic, like de day Naana and Naani step off de boat in Port of Spain harbor over a hundred and sixty years ago. Check out dese hips here nah, dey is pure sugar and condensed milk, pure sweetness!' (45–6). Since there is no language to classify who they are as Canadian Indo-Caribbean lesbians, the narrator comes up with her own term. She tells Janet they are 'cultural bastards' (52). She continues: 'De thing is: all a we in Trinidad is cultural bastards, Janet, all a we. *Toutes bagailles!*' (52). In a sense, all of Trinidad is queer space because of its histories of colonialization, mixes of different cultures and its continued globalization. There is always a sense of excess and the refusal of easy classification.

While the main characters must face ostracism by others in the res-taurant because of their differences, this difference is briefly removed when two white Canadian men enter the space to drunkenly belit-tle the staff who had been hassling the narrator just prior to this moment. Unlike other women in the restaurant, the narrator does not wholly sympathize with the staff. Mootoo demonstrates that the humiliation of the male staff by the two white men is tied to mas-culine gender performance and heteronormativity. One of the other Indian women near the main characters' table states: 'I can't stand to see our men humiliated by them' (53). The emphasis on 'our men' speaks on several levels. It notes the existence of a racialized group where all members' fates are in some way in common, but it also speaks to a particular gender performance where Indian men need to be able to behave in a certain way to uphold the 'naturalness' of heterosexuality.

However, not long after the two white men leave, several young Indian women enter and are immediately sexually pounced on by the staff, a group of brothers. When the female customers immediately

reject their advances, the brothers then become undesirably flirta-
tious with other female customers. One of the female customers tells
the narrator:

> Whoever does he think he is! Calling me dear and touching me
> like that! Why do these men always think that they have permis-
> sion to touch whatever and wherever they want! And you can't
> make a fuss about it in public, because it is exactly what those
> people out there want to hear about so that they can say how
> sexist and uncivilized our culture is. (55)

This statement speaks of gender privilege, but it also contains and
addresses race and colonialist legacies. The speaker directs 'our culture' at the narrator, who views herself as outside of Indian culture
because of her Trinidadianness and sexuality. The main character
also stands apart in this moment because she is not sexualized by
the brothers. The narrator asserts: 'I ain't remotely interested in having a squeak of a flirtation with a man, it doh hurt a ego to have a
man notice yuh once in a very long while' (50). Although Janet is
a target of their inappropriate advances, the narrator discusses how
she herself feels invisible to most heterosexual men due to her gender
insubordination.[3]

Mootoo's 'Out on Main Street' is a layered piece that locates Indo-
Caribbean lesbian representation within Caribbean, Indian and
queer space. In fact, at the end of the story, Janet and the narrator
are joined coincidentally by two other lesbians in the restaurant
also in search of sweets. The narrator states about the arrival of the
other lesbian couple: 'Well, all cover blown. If it was even remotely
possible dat I wasn't noticeable before, now Janet and I were over-
exposed' (57). Her sense of being 'over-exposed' brings to mind those
other moments in the texts that trouble categories through excess or
inability to classify. At this point, it is lesbian identity that becomes
troubled through superfluousness. The story leaves the reader with
the dissolution of the bond between the narrator and the woman
who spoke out against the brothers' unwanted advances because of
the definitive revelation of her sexuality when joined by the other
couple. She says, 'I turn to acknowledge Giraffebai [the woman],
but instead a any recognition of our buddiness against the fresh
brothers, I get a face dat look like it was in de presence of a very foul

smell' (57). Solidarities are transitory and effortlessly disengaged in a space where the 'over-authenticity' of the main characters meets the 'hypothermia' of the restaurant (57).

Silvera's Afro-Caribbean: not invisible

Silvera's work has maintained a consistent focus on bringing attention to the lives and identities of lesbians in the Caribbean. Her piece, 'Man Royals and Sodomites', is anthologized in texts concerning race, feminism, lesbianism and postcoloniality. Silvera's interest in revealing the existence of female homosexuals in the Afro-Caribbean as well as in immigrant communities in Canada has played a role in her two short story collections, *Remembering G and Other Stories* (1991) and *Her Head: A Village and Other Stories* (1994), as well as her first novel, *The Heart Does Not Bend* (2003). This novel, like many of Silvera's other works, shows that Caribbean lesbians not only face Caribbean culture's view of them while in the Caribbean: they must also face Caribbean cultural ideas in the diaspora. Contrary to ideas that circulate about queer peoples leaving inhospitable environments for more welcoming ones in other countries, Silvera's writing demonstrates that one does not really leave. One can emigrate from one country to another, but one does not emigrate from the cultural ideas used to raise a person. Moreover, one must make the decision to completely cut oneself off from members of one's community or continue to live 'closeted' in one sense or another in diasporic spaces by continuing cultural times with community.

Silvera's theoretical text about 'man royals' and 'sodomites' shares concerns with *The Heart Does Not Bend* and with the short story examined here, 'Baby', because these stories explore the continuation of the ideas of 'home culture' in new cultural spaces. Silvera points out in the essay that names such as 'man royal' and 'sodomite' are 'dred words' (522). They are 'so dred that women dare not use these words to name themselves' (522). She sees them as names used by men and as after-effects of a system that would want women to create hierarchies to compete with each other by keeping women 'in their places' (531). Staying in and breaking with a woman's proper place as a lesbian is an important feature of 'Baby'. While Silvera's work reveals the presence of 'silenced' Afro-Caribbean lesbians, it also illustrates how systems of power work within Jamaican culture and through gendered identities. Silvera states in her essay in regard to Afro-Caribbean lesbians: 'There is more at risk for us than for white women' (529). She continues:

> We [Afro-Caribbean lesbians] have no race privilege and very, very few of us have class privilege. The one privilege within our group is heterosexual [...] It is inconceivable, almost frightening, that one could turn her back on credibility in our community and the society at large by being lesbian. (531)

'Baby' resituates these concerns from Jamaica to Toronto, Canada. The story demonstrates how heterosexuality offers 'one' privilege within their culturally marginalized group, and the ways, if two women choose not to be heterosexual, certain individuals within their community feel both compelled and justified to attempt to forcefully push them into the location of heterosexual 'privilege'.

'Baby' juxtaposes intimate conversation between two Caribbean lesbians in the bedroom of the home they share with the thoughts of another Caribbean immigrant, standing outside their bedroom door, who has broken into their house and plans to rape and kill the two of them because 'women like these, his own people' should not be 'stooping to this [lesbianism]' (237). The narrative couples this imminent threat, unknown to the two women, with one of the women, Asha, describing her fear and inability to come out – even though they now live in Toronto and that she would be coming out to non-Caribbean communities. While Asha fears retribution for her visibility, her lover, Baby, refuses a life in the closet. She states, 'I can't stop my life because some people hate Blacks. And I am bloody well not going to stop living my life because another group hates lesbians' (235). Feeling as though she is caught between discourses of racism and homophobia, Baby refuses to capitulate to either while Asha is hyper-aware of not only the presence but the effects of those discourses in her life. Unlike Baby, Asha does not put race and sexuality on a par. She sees their intersections, but fears losing her job as a teacher because of the discovery of her sexuality. She says, 'I love my work. I am a good teacher, and the Black students need that model. They need to see us in positive roles. They need to see more than the pimps-prostitutes-junkies' (235). Her comment is directed at racial stereotyping, but could be extended to sexuality. Asha is unaware of exactly how her students 'see' her. Her job as a teacher places her in situations where she can potentially confront cultural prejudices, just as Baby seeks to do through demonstrations and other political actions. Their different approaches to bigotry, however, overlook the ways cultural ideas about women and same-sex sexuality from their homeland affect their lives in Canada, too.

While Asha has difficulty in publicly affirming her sexuality, Baby claims she is not afraid of the 'dred' words. She states: 'I know what I am [...] I'm a lesbian. A zami. A sodomite. A black-skinned woman' (234). However, the sections of the story that concentrate on the man who has broken into their house demonstrate something beyond Asha's fears of losing her job. His entrance into the narrative reflects the importance of cultural ideas of a homeland in diasporic communities, and also demonstrates the impotence of male patriarchal authority. Masculine cultural dictates about women's sexuality is rendered as impotent. The man might feel called upon to physically enforce cultural beliefs, but it does not mean that these cultural beliefs will be followed or accepted.

Silvera describes how the man notices them and feels compelled to enter their home to brutalize them until they 'agree' to be heterosexual. While Asha's fears of the two being discovered as a couple prevent her from going out with Baby in any space that could be interpreted as romantic, she does not account for the local restaurant where members of the Caribbean community would go, and would notice the two women always together, never apart or with a man. This restaurant, the Hot Spot, comes to represent the community space for Jamaican people in Toronto. It is where people gather to eat Caribbean food and buy products that are common to Caribbean peoples. The men in the Hot Spot notice Asha and Baby and say, 'Bwoy, dem girls different. Dem need a good fuck. Can't understand how nice Black woman like dem get influence in dis lesbian business' (236). The voices also say: 'Nastiness man, nastiness. Satan work' (236). This 'nastiness' and 'Satan work' becomes connected to them through their emigration to Canada from the Caribbean. The men in the Hot Spot and the man who breaks into their house do not want to believe that the women are Jamaican lesbians, or that lesbians exist in the Caribbean.

The man feels justified about completing his plans to rape and kill them because he believes 'they come to Canada and they adopt foreign ways' (236). He views his extreme acts of aggression against them as a way to bring them to their senses. He feels it is his duty as a Caribbean man to perform these acts. He thinks to himself: 'Tonight he was going to put a stop to all this nastiness. He'd try to help them, and if they didn't listen, then they'd have to face the consequences' (237). However, the man does not act on his desires beyond breaking into their home and standing outside their bedroom door to masturbate. This act is the extent of his power over them. His sexualization of them, related but not identical to physical violence, offers him a form of power over them that they cannot surmount since it is connected to other discourses on female sexuality. But Silvera very carefully links the eroticization of lesbian sexuality by straight male culture with the potency of the phallus: the man masturbates while he decides on the right moment to attack them as he waits outside their room. 'He could hear it all through the closed door. The gun was getting warm and sticky in his hand. The front of his shorts jumped like a trapped crab' (237). His masturbation is as connected to his desire to force the women into heterosexuality as it is to force a particular set of cultural ideas on them. The man becomes as excited by his role as representative of dominant, correct Jamaican culture as he does as voyeur. Once the man ejaculates, he feels his cultural potency leave him and regrets not acting while he still had an erection, 'He was getting impatient. Too much arguing. He wished he had kicked the door in earlier. He should have done it when the crab was awake. He'd never wake it now' (238). Silvera reduces the cultural authority empowering him to little more than an erect penis that loses its power when it becomes flaccid. While the two women remain unaware of the threat when the man decides to leave their home, Silvera leaves the reader with the idea that these threats are always present for Afro-Caribbean lesbians. They do not go away, and they are not limited to the Caribbean. Baby and Asha do not have to go out or risk Asha's role at a demonstration to hazard danger; it can break into their home.

Locales and interstices

In an article by Timothy Chin on Caribbean writer Patricia Powell, Chin notes how Powell's novels 'break the silence surrounding issues of gay/lesbian/non-normative sexuality and her subsequent "queering" of the Caribbean subject depends on her ability to exploit the disjunctions between various locales, to work the interstices, in other words, of the diasporic border zones' (536). Working the interstices and disjunctions of diasporic border zones in order to break silences and challenge the status quo are also important features of short fiction by Mootoo and Silvera. The shifting hierarchies, allegiances and disciplining impulses come into view. This allows Mootoo and Silvera to confront erasures and threats to women's bodies that can materialize when they step outside cultural ideas. In the case of 'Baby', these can crawl back through the same kitchen window through which they entered. For 'Out on Main Street' they can shift identifications and allegiances in a space in a matter of time. The cross-cultural subject crosses and is often crossed, but making the female same-sex sexuality of a number of these subjects visible is an important part of determining crossings.

Notes

1. In a 2006 *Time* article, Tim Padgett writes, 'Jamaica may be the worst offender, but much of the rest of the Caribbean also has a long history of intense homophobia' ('Most Homophobic'). A 2010 survey conducted in Jamaica by the University of the West Indies 'found that 89 percent of respondents were homophobic' (Acosta). Psychologist Gloria Careaga notes, 'the English-speaking Caribbean seems to be unable to shake off the influence of Victorian morality, and not only maintains laws that criminalize gays and lesbians, but also argues the case for homophobia' (quoted in Acosta).
2. This brings to mind Michel Foucault's famous discussion of confession and relations of power in *The History of Sexuality* (1977) as well as Eve Kosofsky Sedgwick's *Epistemology of the Closet* (1990). Debates about the easy applicability of Western notions of the closet as it pertains to homosexuality are complicated by a number of postcolonial theorists. However, the short stories discussed in this essay are diasporic and incorporate the trope of the closet into their prose.
3. The brothers are clearly 'aggressing on woman, woman warding off a herd a man who just had dey pride publicly cut up a couple times in just a few minutes' (55). But, the narrator does not see that her mere presence as an openly lesbian woman is acted upon by some heterosexual women as an advance in itself. She thinks: 'And de women dem embarrass fuh so to watch me in mih eye, like dey fraid I will jump up and try to kiss dem, or make pass at dem. Yuh know, sometimes I wonder if I ain't made enough to do it just for a little bacchanal, nah' (48).

Works cited

Acosta, Dalia. 'Homophobia in the Caribbean Varies Widely.' *IPS Inter Press Service News*. 16 May 2011. Web. 14 March 2012.

Chancy, Myriam J.A. 'Subversive Sexualities Revolutionizing Gendered Identities.' *Frontiers: A Journal of Women Studies* 29.1 (2008): 51–74.

Chin, Timothy S. '"Bullers" and "Battymen": Contesting Homophobia in Black Popular Culture and Contemporary Caribbean Literature.' *Callaloo* 20.1 (1997): 127–41.

—— 'The Novels of Patricia Powell: Negotiating Gender and Sexuality Across the Disjunctures of the Caribbean Diaspora.' *Callaloo* 30.2 (2007): 533–45.

Crimp, Douglas. 'Right On, Girlfriend!' *Fear of a Queer Planet: Queer Politics and Social Theory*. Ed. Michael Warner. Minneapolis: University of Minnesota Press, 1993. 300–21.

Douglass, Debbie et al., eds. Introduction to *Máka, Diasporic Juks: Contemporary Writing by Queers of African Descent*. Toronto: Sister Vision Press, 1997.

Elwin, Rosamund. 'Tongues on Fire: Speakin' Zami Desire.' *Tongues on Fire: Caribbean Lesbian Lives and Stories*. Ed. Rosamund Elwin. Toronto: Women's Press, 1997. 7–12.

King, Rosamond S. 'Re/Presenting Self and Other: Trans Deliverance in Caribbean Texts.' *Callaloo* 31.2 (2008): 581–99.

Mootoo, Shani. *Out on Main Street and Other Stories*. Vancouver: Press Gang Publishers, 1993.

Padgett, Tim. 'The Most Homophobic Place on Earth?' *Time*. 12 April 2006. Web. 15 March 2012.

Silvera, Makeda. 'Baby.' *Tongues on Fire: Caribbean Lesbian Lives and Stories*. Ed. Rosamund Elwin. Toronto: Women's Press, 1997. 231–8.

—— 'Man Royals and Sodomites: Some Thoughts on the Invisibility of Afro-Caribbean Lesbians.' *Feminist Studies* 18.3 (Fall 1992): 521–32.

Tarrazo, Alicia Menéndez. 'Bridge Indians and Cultural Bastards: Narratives of Urban Exclusion in the World's "Most Liveable" City.' *Atlantis: Journal of the Spanish Association of Anglo-American Studies* 31.2 (2009): 95–109.

10

'They can fly': The Postcolonial Black Body in Nalo Hopkinson's Speculative Short Fiction

Lee Skallerup Bessette

Caribbean-Canadian writer Nalo Hopkinson prefaces one of her short stories in the collection *Skin Folk* (2001) with the following lines of poetry, written by her father, artist Slade Hopkinson: 'These are the latitudes of ex-colonized, of degradation still unmollified' (183). Hopkinson, using the flexibility afforded by speculative fiction, symbolizes this degradation physically through her characters' bodies in her short stories. Each of her protagonists must overcome their perceived or real physical imperfections in order to achieve some sort of internal balance and happiness, or as Hopkinson puts it in the preface, 'whatever burdens their skins bear, once they remove them [...] they can fly' (1). In each case, the degradation and physical deformity can be traced back to injuries caused by their postcolonial condition. Using the story 'A Habit of Waste' as a central basis of the analysis, this essay will outline the different ways Hopkinson interrogates and problematizes the postcolonial condition through the body.

Nalo Hopkinson was born in Jamaica but, growing up, lived all over the Caribbean. When she was 16, her family relocated permanently to Toronto, Canada, where she has lived ever since. Her father was a well-known writer and actor and her mother worked in libraries, and thus Hopkinson grew up surrounded by literature and other forms of art. Her influences include Caribbean folktales, Western mythology, hard science fiction, and fantasy. For Hopkinson, the merging of these different genres in her writing represents an opportunity to be 'perverse and subversive and oppositional and revolutionary [creating] a wonderful literature for radical and marginalized communities' (Burwell and Johnston 45). In linking science fiction and fantasy with traditional Caribbean folktales, Hopkinson hopes to insert a 'worldview [that] is not one that the genre experiences often' (Wolff 27). Hopkinson has been asked in the past if the 'massa's tools will never dismantle massa's house' (Hopkinson 7), to which she replies, in the introduction to the anthology *So Long Been Dreaming* (2004), 'In my hands, massa's tools don't dismantle massa's house – and in fact, I don't want to destroy it so much as I want to undertake massive renovations – they build me a house of my own' (8). As put by Ruby S. Ramraj, 'Very much a postcolonialist, Hopkinson reveals in her texts her abhorrence of the ideology of imperial oppression towards both men and women, towards the disenfranchised and towards the subaltern' (136).

Hopkinson is very aware of the role the physical body plays in the history of colonialism and the oppression still physically being carried around by its victims:

> It's pretty clear for the past 500 years or so, the fortunes of the European nations were built on the backs of black and other racialized bodies. That has repercussions into the present day, because the work hasn't been done to even the imbalance in any big way [...] For that to change, something fundamental about the nature of humans or human understanding has to change. That's one of the places where science fiction and fantasy can be really exciting, where they can envision how that change might come about. (Glave 153)

Being black, both physically and metaphorically, represents a clear physical marker of difference and oppression, to be seen as *less than*. But, as Hopkinson points out:

> However, in fantastical fiction, I can directly manipulate the metaphorical structure of the story. I can create a science fictional world in which relative fatness or slimness has about the same significance as eye color, but only persons under five feet, five inches are considered beautiful. I can show people desperately trying not to grow taller and taking pills intended to cure them of the 'disease' of tallness, which is considered to be epidemic in their society. I can show people who develop emotional disorders related to

being tall. Another thing I might do is to create a fantastical world in which my fat protagonist magically becomes thinner in order that she can convince people to ignore her, so at the moment when she finally would be considered beautiful, she disappears […] In other words, one of the things I can do is to intervene in the readers' assumptions by creating a world in which standards are different. (Nelson 100–1)

Hopkinson, however, does not limit herself to questioning the traditional physically manifested black/white, fat/thin, old/young, poor/rich binaries, but also uses the very physical (and often taboo) nature of bodies to disrupt and subvert, yet again intervening on the readers' assumptions, but in a different way. Menstruation becomes the stuff of magic, eating becomes more than simply consumption but a sacred act, sex and the exchange of bodily fluids literally produces supernatural energy. Rejecting the 'systematic ordering' of the body that takes place within our society (which often punishes black and female bodies more severely), Hopkinson embraces the bodies' 'permeable, leaky boundaries [representing] the ultimate transgression' (Gething 269). The stories in *Skin Folk* are the result of Hopkinson's efforts to be 'perverse and subversive and oppositional and revolutionary', in particular with the body.

Black bodies despised

Cynthia, the main character in 'A Habit of Waste', is confronted with the unexpected one day on her way home from work; she sees another woman wearing her old body: 'It was my original body, the body I had replaced two years before, same full, tarty-looking lips; same fat thighs, rubbing together with every step; same narrow torso that seemed grafted onto a lower body a good three sizes bigger, as though God had glued left-over parts together' (183). Cynthia had saved up her salary in order to buy a new body from 'Mediperfection', a place that can only exist (for now) in science fiction, but a place that we can believe would exist if the technology were available. Cynthia, it should be noted, was black, the daughter of first-generation Caribbean immigrants to Canada. She chose to reject her physical Caribbean heritage, choosing to become a 'Diana' with 'their lithe muscles and small, firm breasts' (184). Although not explicitly mentioned immediately, her new body is revealed to be white (185).

But why does Cynthia save her money in order to buy a new, improved, white body? Cynthia loathes her former body, describing it thus:

> I studied my former body carefully as it made its way down the center of the streetcar. I hated what she'd done to the hair – let it go natural, for Christ's sake, sectioned it off, and coiled black thread tightly around each section, with a puff of hair on the end of every stalk. Man, I hated that back-to-Africa nostalgia shit. She looked like a Doctor Seuss character. There's no excuse for that nappy-headed nonsense. She had a lot of nerve, too, wrapping that behind in a flower-print sarong miniskirt. Sort of like making your ass into a billboard. When it was my body, I always covered its butt in long skirts or loose pants [...] All the seats on the streetcar were taken. Good. Let the bitch stand. I hoped my fallen arches were giving her hell. (184–5)

She judges the wearer of her old body the way she, perhaps, felt judged herself as a black woman, living in Toronto. In *Black Bodies, White Gazes* (2008), George Yancy investigates the different ways 'the black body [...] is torn asunder through the internalization of the white gaze' (xxiii), the white gaze that 'install[s] the Black body as inferior, a "thing" fit for comedy, hypersexuality, and animal-like' (xxiii). One can see the parallels between a character like Cynthia and one like Pecola Breedlove from Toni Morrison's *The Bluest Eye* (1972). Cynthia physically rejects her blackness and instead 'undergoes a psychological split so massive that she comes to image that she in fact *has* the bluest eyes' (183). Cynthia would seem to have completely assimilated and incorporated the white gaze in her new white body, only able to see 'the Black self as ugly, bestial, dirty, and worthless' (191).

Cynthia is not the only character in the collection who has internalized the white gaze and thus attempt to discipline and despise their black selves. In the story 'Something to Hitch Meat To', the protagonist Artho works for an online porn site modifying explicit pictures for the tastes and sensibilities of their subscribers, a 'virtual fluffer' (32). He is confronted daily with the realities of being black in a predominantly white city: the cashier takes great pains to check his money to make sure it isn't counterfeit; taxis that won't stop for him; businessmen approaching him to ask him if he can sell them drugs; darkening a light-brown black man (and extending his penis) in order that he fit more readily into the 'Banjee Boys' section of the porn site. His own mother, much like Cynthia, tries to distance herself from appearing black, 'with her stiff, dead, pressed hair and the pale pink lipstick blanching her full brown lips' (33). Artho is miserable and swallows his anger, especially when confronted by his boss, Charlie:

> 'Make that guy blacker. Looks like a dago.' Charlie turned away. Stopped. Turned back and peer at the screen. Guffawed. 'Jesus, Arth! He's darker than you! Well, whaddya know 'bout that? Betcha his dick's no match for yours, though. Eh? Eh?' Charlie cackled and elbowed Artho in the ribs, then shaking his head and chuckling at his own wit, stumped his way out of the office [...]
>
> Artho sighed and got to work again with his mouse, sticking cocoa-colored pigment to the man like tar on the Tar Baby. He ignored the feeling of his ears burning. IT went away eventually. (35)

Artho, late one Friday night at work, is confronted by a little girl, who asks him, 'Do you like people making *you* be not real?' (37). It turns out that the little girl is Anansi, the trickster, who grants Artho the power to 'peel off [people's] fake skins' and reveal what is really inside of them. And as one woman clutches her purse tighter as he walks by at the close of the story, Artho wonders: 'Maybe he should work that nkyin nkyin thing on himself; it was in him, after all. He wondered what she would see then' (43). The ability to have people see a black body as it really is inside, instead of how the white gaze perceives it to be is an important disruption not only for those look-ing, but, more importantly, for those who are victims of the gaze.

Two other male characters, Samuel in 'The Glass Bottle Trick' and Cleve in 'Ganger (Ball Lightening)', also experience this sort of trauma stemming from the white gaze. Cleve is unable to fulfil him-self or his partner sexually, and the tension, anger and resentment manifest themselves as a ball of energy that threatens to kill them both. Cleve tells his lover Issy that 'I 'fraid to use harsh words, Issy, you know that. Look at the size of me, the blackness of me. You know it is to see people cringe for fear when you shout?' (245). Samuel, on the other hand, is dark-skinned, but behaves 'white': 'He had been abroad, talked of exotic sports: ice hockey, downhill skiing. He took her to fancy restaurants she'd only heard of [...] Samuel had polish' (91). He also disliked it when his lighter-skinned wife went out into the sun, and rebuked her when she called him 'Black Beauty': 'Never call me that, please, Beatrice [...] You don't have to draw attention to my colour. I'm not a handsome man, and I know it. Black and ugly as my mother made me' (94). Beatrice, now four months pregnant, remembers Samuel telling her, 'no woman should have to give birth to his ugly black babies' (96). She discovers that Samuel killed his previous two wives when they were pregnant, and inadvertently sets their duppies (spirits) free to seek revenge.

  These four stories, taken together, show the real danger of the white gaze as it is experienced by the black body. George Yancy calls it 'the elevator effect', a 'microcosm of some of the dynamic processes of a larger, systemic form of colonial invasion within which its undesired incursions, pernicious acts of usurpation, and regulatory processes of white normativity are played out on the body of the colonized' (16). These black bodies that Hopkinson creates react in different ways, sometimes dangerous, sometimes destructive, but always in reaction to the experience of colonization. Unfortunately, one of the ways that these bodies may come to terms with their identities as black bodies is through age and wisdom, elements that are often seen as deformities and weaknesses, and thus also rejected.

Deformed and disconnected black bodies

By rejecting 'blackness', Hopkinson's characters are also rejecting parts (or all) of their history and heritage. Although many of the short stories in *Skin Folk* take place in Toronto, the characters' bodies are still suffering oppression, both internal and external, and renegotiating what it means to be 'home', or, as put by Anindyo Roy, there is a 'complex affiliation with postcolonial politics of transnationality, whose profile in the aftermath of decolonization and neocolonialism is increasingly being circumscribed (and also reified) by the new identification of "home" and "location"' (101). Physically being separated from a birthplace or remnants of ancestry represent an important area that Hopkinson explores, as well as how the postcolonial condition of disenfranchisement and oppression is continued in a new place. 'Home' for many of her characters is neither here nor there; Canada is not welcoming, the home of their parents completely foreign. How, then, does that conflict inscribe itself physically onto the bodies of the postcolonial subject?

Western popular culture has long celebrated youth as a sign of beauty. The aged body, as put by Sander L. Gilman, is 'unaesthetic, unerotic and pathological' (295). Plastic surgeries 'promise the illusion that decay can be "treated" [...] With breasts made perky again, faces lifted, eyelids pulled, tummies tightened, we can cure the disease of aging' (Askew 24). This ideal of youth and impossible thinness causes women to construct 'a self that is distorted and divided against itself, self-policing and self-destructive' (Valentine 113). Cynthia not only embraces the ideal of whiteness, she also embraces the ideal of physical youth. She points out the allure of changing bodies frequently: 'I wondered if I should start saving for another switch. It's really a rich people's thing. I couldn't afford to keep doing it every few years, like some kind of vid queen' (Hopkinson 188).

Choosing the name 'Diana' for the body Cynthia replaces her own with does not appear to be an accident on Hopkinson's part, either. Princess Diana was, for an entire generation of women living in the Commonwealth (and beyond), the picture of beauty, grace and elegance; a fairy tale come to life. For a young girl, longing to belong in Canada, she could choose no better a symbol for her fumbled attempt at assimilation and Canadian identity. Diana, as British Royalty, reminds the reader of the connection to the problematic history of colonization, slavery and domination. But Princess Diana also revealed that her life was not a fairy tale, but a nightmare of oppression and manipulation; her figure was artificially maintained through bulimia and her husband was in love with another woman. The reality of Cynthia's fairy tale is no less disappointing: 'And weren't those crow's-feet around my eyes? Shit. White people aged so quickly' (185). Age, it would seem, is also the enemy, representing physical deformity as well as an important source and connection to the past, a past that makes it difficult to maintain a static postcolonial identity.

Later in the story, Cynthia admonishes her parents to herself: 'And I really wished they'd drop the Banana Boat accents. They'd come to Canada five years before I was even *born*, for Christ's sake, and I was now twenty-eight' (188). Her father reveals that Cynthia gets her figure from her mother, further severing the bond between parent and child, heritage and herself. For Cynthia, there is no room for reminders from home, for the language, customs (her father is attracted by her mother's full figure) or traditions, nor of old age and the wisdom that may come from it. Although Cynthia may no longer carry her heritage with her physically, she still carries the pain, exhibited in the negative assessment, not only of her old body, but the inherent judgement of the woman who now inhabits it. She longs for the Diana fairy tale (which is problematic and false) and disconnects herself from those other parts of her identity. Who is she?

Cynthia's stable (if unhealthy) identity, and her binary way of understanding it, is disrupted by Old Man Morris, who frequents the food bank where she works. Cynthia judges Old Man Morris simply by the way he looks and his material condition: 'He looked to be in his sixties, but he was probably younger; hard life wears a person down. Tallish, with a brown, wrinkled face and tightly curled salt-and-pepper hair, he had a strong, upright walk for someone in his circumstances [...] At least he seemed clean' (187). Her co-worker suggests that Cynthia take his food for Thanksgiving over herself and provide some company for the old man who was also from the Caribbean. When he invites her to stay for dinner, 'with an old man from back home', Cynthia thinks to herself, 'I'm not from back home' (192). This again represents the disconnect she feels to her parents and her heritage. Her preference for the evening would be to spend it by herself, at a movie theatre, consuming the pop culture of her new home over the potential of connecting with the old culture of her parents.

Over Thanksgiving dinner, however, Cynthia is presented with a different way to look at her identity. It is revealed that Old Man Morris scavenges for food in Toronto, collecting flowering kale from the front of buildings, killing rabbits and growing his own herbs. After his wife died and facing slow starvation, Old Man Morris remembers how he would never go hungry back home in Trinidad and decides to learn about the native edible flora and fauna in Toronto: 'They squirrels-them always looking fat and happy; they mus' be eatin' something! And the Indian people-them-self too; they

must be did eat something else besides corn before the white people
come and take over the place!' (198). Old Man Morris learns to survive and thrive in his adoptive home by combining the knowledge
and skills he learned in his youth in Trinidad with a willingness to
learn and adapt to the realities of Toronto. This marriage of old and
new knowledge is accentuated with his ability to hunt and kill wild
rabbit with his slingshot: 'But I still think the slingshot was a master
stroke. Nobody ain't expect an ol' black man to be hunting with a
slingshot down in the ravine!' (199). He presents Cynthia with an
alternative way to adapt and adopt, but also shows her how not to
fear aging as a deformity or trial, but to embrace it as a source of
power and wisdom.

Ancestral knowledge and age, and the next generation's rejection
of both, are also linked in the story 'Greedy Choke Puppy'. Jacky, in
'Greedy Choke Puppy', is a young girl who is currently writing her
PhD entitled 'Magic in the Real: The Role of Folklore in Everyday
Caribbean Life'. Ironically, she has little time for her Granny's stories
about the spirits. Instead, she finds her information about Caribbean
folklore in the library, focusing on the 'Soucouyant': 'an old evil-
tempered woman who removes her skin at night, hides it, and then
changes into a ball of fire. She flies through the air, searching for
homes in which there are babies' (174). She looks for the babies so
she may steal their life force. In the story, there is a soucouyant who
comes out at night and in fact kills one of Jacky's friend's babies.
As readers, we are led to believe (or we allow ourselves to believe)
that the soucouyant is in fact Granny. But, it is revealed that Jacky
is the one who takes off her skin to steal the life force of the young:
'When we live empty lives, the hunger does turn to blood hunger.
But it have plenty of other kinds of loving, Jacky. Ain't I been telling
you so? Love your work. Love people close to you. Love your life [...]
I try to tell you, like I try to tell you mother: Don't be greedy' (180).
Here, the youth could have benefited from the wisdom of the older,
wiser, grandmother, but instead Jacky chooses modern, Western
values, formalized sources of knowledge and material wealth, but
also a traditional view of femininity, marriage and the nuclear family. Her grandmother offers an alternative, a way to 'cool we down';
note how she talks about loving her work, loving her life, in a
non-traditional way. Like Old Man Morris, Granny offers wisdom to
survive in modern times.

Deprived and disciplined

Symbolically, Cynthia, in her new body, can no longer enjoy the one part of her cultural heritage she still seemed to value and enjoy, the food. As Old Man Morris describes his cooking for Cynthia, her mind wanders back to her childhood and her mother's cooking:

> Salted cod and cabbage. Flavoured with French thyme and hot pepper. My mother made that on Sunday mornings too, with big fried flour dumplings on the side and huge mugs of cocoa. Not the cocoa powder from the tin, either; she bought the raw chocolate in the chestnut-sized lumps from the Jamaican store, and grated it into boiling water, with vanilla, cinnamon, and condensed milk. Sitting in Mr Morris's living room, even with the remains of dinner on the table, I could almost smell that pure chocolate aroma. Full of fat, too. I didn't let my mom serve it to me anymore when I visited. I'd spent too much money on my tight little butt. (195)

Depriving herself of what she loves, and, by extension, her heritage, Cynthia prioritizes the perceived values of her adoptive country. Both the monetary and symbolic capital she has invested in her 'Canadian' identity is too much for Cynthia to squander on indulgences. She has been fully colonized, but her assimilation is so precarious that it cannot even sustain a deviation from the prescribed diet.

But, Cynthia quickly realizes, her new identity, her discipline and her ability to deprive herself cannot protect her. As Cynthia is leaving Mr Morris's apartment, she is attacked. She is unable to defend herself and is alone, terrified of what might happen to her. What initially saves her is the jar of preserves Mr Morris gave her; dropping it startles the attacker and the glass wounds his leg. This delay allows Mr Morris to drive away the attacker with his slingshot from his apartment window. Her traditional food and community save Cynthia, not the police or people she more closely aligns herself with. What we eat, and, more importantly, who we eat with, matter more than the 'skin' we wear. After the attack, Cynthia attends her family's Thanksgiving dinner, where her 'plan is to [...] eat everything you put on my plate. If I get too fat, I'm just going to have to start walking to work. You've got to work with what you've got, after all' (201). Cynthia even allows herself to lick the bottom of the pot of cocoa, not wanting it to go to waste. This can be read as a highly transgressive act because, as put by Veronica Thompson, it is a 'rejection of the confining limits imposed on female behavior and desire in male-dominated culture' as well as an 'apt expression of colonial or post-colonial opposition to imperialism' (quoted in Gething 274). Reconnected with what she has and rejecting the limits imposed on her, Cynthia is able to reconnect with her family, her heritage and her true self.

Blaise in the story 'Slow Cold Chick' also deprives herself of what she needs to eat in order to come to terms with herself. The story opens with Blaise trying to remember her mother's cornbread recipe, but unable to call because the phone has been disconnected. When she finds an egg in her fridge and tries to incorporate it into the mixture, it's rotten, and a strange thing happens: a creature is born, a 'cold-grown chick' (107). Blaise is Jamaican, but living now in Toronto, and she is, herself, a 'cold-grown chick', displaced in her new city. As she watches her 'Venus-built' neighbour tend her garden, she wonders, 'how did the tropical tree flourish in this northern climate?' (104). This is the question that plagues Blaise, feeds her bitterness and feeds the bitterness of the creature hatched in a moment of anger, frustration and despair.

The Venus-built lady is described in stark contrast to Blaise; Venus-built lady (later revealed to be named Sharon) has 'gingered brown hair [...] crinkled in dreadlocks down her back. Blaise had chemically straightened all the kinks out of her own hair' and 'Blaise looked down at her own dull brown hands. The Venus-built lady's skin had the glow of full-fat chocolate' (104). Sharon does something strange, however; she eats the flowers that she grows. Her male partner, Johnny (who is white), however, eats the earth: 'Johnny likes to take earth into himself. Soil and rock and iron' (113) while Sharon eats the flowers because 'It bears, and feeds my soul. Is a flavour from home' (112). But when asked what she eats to nourish her, Blaise has no answer, unable to reconcile herself with her new home and come to terms with what she needs. Instead, Blaise recoils at the thought of what might be missing: 'The bird birthed of the heat of Blaise's anger had eaten as it pleased, and it had turned into a monster' (114).

When the trio confront the monster bird, full of fire and bile, Blaise is posed the question, 'You want to kill your every desire dead?' (115). When Blaise finally articulates her desires, to be able to be honest in her feelings, for better or for worse, what she needs in order to flourish, the bird climbs down her throat. After that, she feels 'strong, sure of herself' (117). Blaise finally is able to eat, to consume what she needed in order to be fully herself. Blaise, much like Cynthia, is unable or unwilling to accept who she really is, worried about how she will be perceived in her new homeland. Blaise straightened her hair, behaved in a meek and passive–aggressive way, in order to fit within a certain picture of what an immigrant, minority woman should be, what a 'good Canadian' is. Johnny, he of earth and ore, is in part a stereotype of the West, the Industrial Revolution and colonial expansion, but he is honest and open about his needs, allowing for his 'true essence', so to speak, to serve as a positive. His relationship with Sharon signifies the potential of the Old World (Europe) and New World (in this case, the Caribbean) to live together if each is willing to be honest about who they are and what they need.

Desolate bodies

One thing that all of the characters mentioned in this chapter (and those who are not) share is their precarious economic status. Cynthia lives from paycheck to paycheck while Mr Morris lives in one of the worst parts of town. Blaise's phone is disconnected, one would imagine, due to non-payment. Beatrice marries Samuel in no small part because he is in a much more stable socio-economic position. Artho worries about money and reflects on how little he is paid, despite working in a high-tech position at a company in a high-profit area (porn). These bodies are economically exploited, which becomes as much a part of their second-skins as any other pathology caused by neo-colonial attitudes towards skin colour, weight or age. It is yet another skin they need to shed in order to 'fly' free.

Identity and economic class are important issues to consider for the Caribbean diaspora living in Canada. According to Chaim I. Waxman, 'the stigma of poverty is a special type of stigma which attributes to the poor a status of being "less than human"' (69). One only has to look at Cynthia's assumptions about Mr Morris based on his material status; she wrongly assumes that he scavenges 'half-smoked cigarette butts' and 'pop cans he would return for deposit money' (187). Cynthia sees Mr Morris, others who come to the food bank and even her co-workers as less-than, internalizing the stigma of being poor. This is a common trope in building a national identity, according to Roxanne Rimstead: 'When a society and its national dream admire the rich because they acquire wealth and power that allows them to stand outside of the community [...] the same community must denounce the other polarity, those who do not succeed in the national dream' (5). This leads to the poor being located 'outside the imagined community on the fringes as fragments of nation' (7). This idea of fragmentation, of existing on the fringes but longing to be a part of the centre, is an important theme for Hopkinson. Her characters in one way or another are unable to assimilate into the dominant culture through economic mobility, and thus are left with a fragmented identity of being from neither here nor from 'back home'.

There is, in fact, 'a direct correlation between cultural identity [for Caribbean-Canadians] and social class. The middle class experiences a sense of greater incorporation into Canadian culture than the lower class; consequently, cultural identity constituted by race and the sense of "back home" is most under erasure for the black middle-class' (Woodall 121–2). Anton L. Allahar calls this population 'event-specific Caribbean people, whose recollections of their pasts are heavily informed by a nostalgic sense of "home," who are educationally, occupationally, financially, residentially, and culturally well on the way to being assimilated' (67). What many of the characters in Hopkinson's stories get backwards is the rejection of their home culture before they are economically stable enough to be accepted as mainstream Canadians. Characters like Cynthia, or Artho's mother, look to reject the stigma of race and cultural heritage, but cannot escape the stigma of being poor. Through a character like Mr Morris, Hopkinson shows how being poor does not have to mean being stigmatized, at least not according to the cultural values of their adopted home. By embracing both cultures, the postcolonial black body can transcend the stigmas, nourishing themselves culturally within a society that refuses to nourish them materially.

These are just a few examples of how Nalo Hopkinson uses black, postcolonial bodies to symbolize the oppression still faced by those who were victims of colonization. But, as Cynthia learns, skin is just something we wear; what matters is making the best with what we have. While she does not go back to her old body (it would seem that that is an impossibility, even in a world where one can buy a new body), she finds a way to be herself in her new body, finds a way to be Caribbean and Canadian, something new, something more true to herself. One element that all Hopkinson's stories share is hopefulness; that the characters being able to come to terms with themselves and their reality are the first steps to a better life. As put by Cristina Bacchilega, Hopkinson's stories are 'stories of change, even liberation, then, where the ordinary and the extraordinary mingle to positive ends' (203).

Works cited

Allahar, Anton L. 'The Political Economy of "Race" and Class in Canada's Caribbean Diaspora.' *American Review of Political Economy* 8.2 (2010): 54–86.

Askew, Emily. '*Extreme Makeover* and the Classical Logic of Transformation.' *You've Come a Long Way, Baby: Women, Politics, and Popular Culture*. Ed. Lilly J. Coren. Lexington: University Press of Kentucky, 2009. 15–34.

Bacchilega, Cristina. 'Reflections on Recent English-Language Fairy-Tale Fiction by Women: Extrapolating from Nalo Hopkinson's *Skin Folk*.' *Fabula* 47.3–4 (2006): 201–10.

Burwell, Jennifer and Nancy Johnston, eds. 'A Dialogue on SF and Utopian Fiction, between Nalo Hopkinson and Elizabeth Vonarburg.' *Foundation* 81 (2001): 40–7.

Gething, Anna. 'Menstrual Metamorphosis and the "foreign country of femaleness": Kate Grenville and Jamaica Kincaid.' *Rites of Passage in Postcolonial Women's Writing*. Ed. Pauline Dodgson-Katiyo. Amsterdam and New York: Rodopi, 2010. 267–82.

Gilman, Sander. *Making the Body Beautiful: A Cultural History of Aesthetic Surgery*. Princeton University Press, 1999.

Glave, Dianne D. 'An Interview with Nalo Hopkinson.' *Callaloo* 26.1 (2003): 146–59.

Hopkinson, Nalo. *Skin Folk*. New York: Warner Books, 2001.

Hopkinson, Nalo and Uppinder Mehan, eds. *So Long Been Dreaming: Postcolonial Science Fiction and Fantasy*. Vancouver: Arsenal Pulp Press, 2004.

Nelson, Alondra. 'Making the Impossible Possible: An Interview with Nalo Hopkinson.' *Social Text* 20.2 (2002): 97–113.

Ramraj, Ruby S. 'Nalo Hopkinson: Transcending Genre Boundaries.' *Beyond the Canebrakes: Caribbean Women Writers in Canada*. Ed. Emily Allen Williams. Trenton NJ: Africa World Press, 2008. 135–54.

Rimstead, Roxanne. *Remnants of Nation: On Poverty Narratives by Women*. University of Toronto Press, 2001.

Roy, Anindyo. 'Postcoloniality and the Politics of Identity in the Diaspora: Figuring "Home," Locating Histories.' *Postcolonial Discourse and Changing*

Cultural Contexts: Theory and Criticism. Ed. Gita Rajan and Radhika Mohanram. Westport CT: Greenwood Press, 1995. 101–15.

Valentine, Catherine G. 'Female Bodily Perfection and the Divided Self.' *Ideals of Feminine Beauty: Philosophical, Social, and Cultural Dimensions.* Ed. Karen Callaghan. Westport CT: Greenwood Press, 1994. 113–23.

Waxman, Chaim I. *The Stigma of Poverty: A Critique of Poverty Theories and Policies.* New York: Pergamon Press, 1977.

Wolff, Christian. 'An Interview with Nalo Hopkinson.' *MaComere* 4 (2001): 26–36.

Woodall, Richardine. '(Re)Thinking my "-Ness": Diaspora Caribbean Blacks in the Canadian Context.' *Shibboleths: A Journal of Comparative Theory* 1.2 (2007): 120–6.

Yancy, George. *Black Bodies, White Gazes.* Lanham MD: Rowman and Littlefield, 2008.

11
Threshold People: Liminal Subjectivity in Etienne van Heerden, J.M. Coetzee and Nadine Gordimer

Barbara Cooke

In *Mad Dog and Other Stories* (1992), Afrikaans writer Etienne van Heerden meditates on the damage apartheid wreaks on normative understandings of human subjectivity. In this chapter, I will be focusing on the ways in which two stories from the collection, 'White Monkey' and 'My Afrikaner', constitute a vicious cycle whereby the racist and hierarchical understanding of human subjectivity posited by apartheid is predicated upon, and becomes the occasion for, physical and epistemic violence. Experience of that violence further damages the subjectivity of victim and perpetrator alike. This preoccupation with the psychic and physical effects of an apartheid mentality aligns the *Mad Dog* narratives with works from two canonical South African writers: J.M. Coetzee's *Waiting for the Barbarians* (1980), written during the latter years of apartheid, and Nadine Gordimer's *The House Gun* (1999), set in the new South African state. Like van Heerden's narratives, *Barbarians* and *The House Gun* ask what sort of subjectivity, or potential for human reciprocity, apartheid and its associated outrages leave in their wake.

Before going further, I should explain exactly what is meant here by 'normative understandings of human subjectivity'. Essentially, this is an understanding of the self as a human being in relationship with other human beings and the material world. Full subjectivity entails an understanding of one's self as socialized and able to act upon both other people and the wider world. Selfhood, then, is forged within *encounters* with other beings and things. It cannot exist in isolation. This understanding has influenced an existentialist tradition that develops and challenges G.W.F. Hegel's master–slave dialectic, and has negative as well as positive applications. In Jean-Paul Sartre's appropriation of the dialectic, the subject's ability to act is always at the expense of another who is acted upon (Bauer 104–35). While the subject is defined by activity, its opposite is reduced to a role of passivity and is, within the existentialist idiom, an object. If the subject is the self then the object becomes not another, which might connote equality, but the Other. Sartre's appropriation of the Hegelian master–slave dialectic is particularly pertinent to the postcolonial context as it informs 'The Negro and Recognition' in Frantz Fanon's *Black Skin, White Masks* (1952). Like Sartre, Fanon denies the possibility of 'absolute reciprocity' that concludes the Hegelian dialectic (217).

The two key encounters dealt with in this chapter – those occurring in van Heerden's 'My Afrikaner' and 'My Cuban' – feature 'masters' who are compelled, rather than straightforwardly wish, to dominate their 'slaves' by historical precedent and the immediate conditions of their encounter. As such, they occupy a liminal space between the asymmetrical dominance of the Sartrean–Fanonian master–slave dialectic and the phenomenon of horizontal violence Sartre delineates in the preface to Fanon's *The Wretched of the Earth* (1965). While horizontal violence refers to the fury of the oppressed who, having internalized the brutality of their oppressors, have no outlet but to unleash it on one another (Sartre Preface 16), the violence encountered in these late apartheid narratives is a shared horror for both master and slave (Fanon *Wretched* 143). Their individual positions are dictated by a racist state apparatus that seeks to define itself by destroying the Other.

Within apartheid psychopathology the conflict between self and Other is almost parodically clear: the self, or state, is white while the Other is black. White society equates to a white skin. 'I' and 'we' correspond to white, while 'not-I' and 'not-we' correspond to black. This visceral, negative identification aligns apartheid Othering not only with Sartrean–Fanonian existentialism but also Julia Kristeva's ground-breaking theory of the abject (1–8). For Matthew P. Fitzpatrick, Kristeva's category of the abject confounds the binarism of the master–slave dialectic as it hovers uncertainly between subject and object, self and other (479); 'Not me. Not that. But not nothing, either' (Kristeva 2). For Anne McClintock, the abject is 'that liminal state that hovers on the threshold of the body and the body politic' (72);

here, the realization that the white and black skins apartheid psycho-pathology fetishize, demonize and hold apart are in fact no bounda-ries at all is one way in which the 'grand border' of apartheid itself reveals itself to be an anxious site, haunted by the uneasy awareness of its own fiction: 'How can I be', asks Kristeva, 'without a border?' (4).

The Sartrean–Fanonian master–slave dialectic and Kristeva's theory of abjection constitute an epistemological backdrop against which apart-heid violence towards black South Africans is meted out. As Sartrean Others, the state views their subjectivity as less than full, less than human. Consequently, full subjects are not required to treat Others as human beings. In language that echoes the Sartrean encounter, *The House Gun* reflects upon this logic as 'a rejection of all that is human [...] a deliberate cultivation of cruel unfeeling, whether to endure blows inflicted upon oneself, or to inflict them on others' (Gordimer 142).

Why, however, is violence desirable – as Gordimer suggests it is – in this context? Why must blows be inflicted upon the Other, once they have been assigned that inferior status? The answer is because, whether the Other is identified as object or abject – it still challenges the self. The abject threatens the subject by refusing to separate its (not-)self from it. Thus, while the subject gives birth to itself by expelling the abject, the abject remains 'something rejected from which one does not part' (Kristeva 4). The frustration and distress this causes for the subject results in violence directed at the abject, which necessarily is violence also directed at the subject (5).

The objectified Other, by contrast distinct from the self, remains a danger because it aspires to full selfhood. This is only achievable at the expense of the subject. Consequently, the subject must fight to contain the Other in its subordination. Nancy Bauer refers to this struggle as the 'fight to the death' (118). Presumably, force is not only necessary but also desirable in this context, confirming the inflictor as an active and therefore full being.

For Fanon, even the abolition of slavery preserved these condi-tions. As freedom was *given to* the slaves by their masters, slaves were not the agents of their own liberation. They remained *acted upon* rather than being full actors. Abolition, and particularly the white population's self-congratulation for their benevolence, there-fore became another means of ensuring that former literal slaves remained enslaved conceptually. The former slave rejects this false equality, and thus the fight continues (*Masks* 220–2).

Apartheid South Africa inflicts epistemological, self-destructive violence on its black population by denying it full subjectivity. In *The House Gun*, the physical violence unleashed by this mass Othering cannot be limited to white-on-black aggression. It takes on a life of its own, 'blindly roving' and 'living on' after the system that engendered it has been dismantled. In Gordimer's novel the father of a murderer wonders if the experience of living under a regime founded on the debasement of some human lives has given 'licence to a young man to pick up a gun that's to hand and shoot in the head a lover' (142); Harald Lindgard's son Duncan has killed Carl Jespersen in an ostensibly apolitical crime of passion. Apprehension of his son's act forces Harald to conclude that 'violence is the common hell of all who are associated with it' (143).

Etienne van Heerden's short stories take place within that 'common hell'. The narratives under discussion here feature encounters that bear a relationship to both the mechanics of the master–slave dialectic and its manifestation within the apartheid state. 'White Monkey' and 'My Afrikaner' are narrated by characters who visit violence on their eponymous victims and, as should be obvious from the stories' titles, neither of these victims are a black South African. Narrators and victims remain nameless. The diversity of the characters coupled with this deliberate non-specificity testifies to the boundless nature of apartheid-sanctioned violence and underscores the fact that it is not possible to attack an individual subject, or subjects, without calling human subjectivity itself into question.

'My Afrikaner' is set during what Gordimer has called the '"interregnum", the brutal days and years of apartheid's spasmodic demise' (Gordimer cited in Lazarus 621) and charts the fate of a Boer soldier captured by a group of freedom fighters. The soldier is imprisoned and his interrogator, the narrator, launches an 'onslaught' on the Afrikaner's body 'three times a day' (85) with fire-irons, hooks and hoses (88–9). The physical pain of this torture is inextricably linked to the narrator's attempts to dismantle the Afrikaner's sense of his own selfhood. The methods used in this individual encounter are also associated with the overarching aims of totalitarian states:

> The totalitarian assault on human nature is an attempt to create something closer to nature than human beings ought to be, and to destroy the specifically human qualities that distinguish

human beings from animals, namely their capacity to initiate
action and thought. (Margaret Canovan cited in Rothberg 47–8)

In Canovan's summary, which recalls Fanon's description of slaves as
'machine-animal men' (*Masks* 220), the 'animal' occupies the place
of Other; that is, as something against which human subjectivity
can define itself. Human beings are set apart from animals by their
'capacity to initiate action and thought', and Elaine Scarry and John
Berger have suggested that language is the principal means by which
this capacity is realized. To speak is to act and, usually, speaking is an
action which communicates thought.

A consideration of language also underscores an understanding
of human subjectivity as shaped by encounter, for communication
requires that there be someone else to communicate *to*. Berger isolates the capacity for language as *the* facilitator of human encounter:

> Even if the encounter [between two men] is hostile and no words
> are used (even if the two speak different languages), the *existence*
> of language allows that one of them, if not both mutually, is con-
> firmed by the other. (3)

Crucially, it is not the fact that two men can understand one
another's speech that allows for mutual confirmation, but an appreciation of the potential for a shared language that exists between
them. What happens to human subjectivity, then, when that potential is deliberately closed down?

The narrator of 'My Afrikaner' insists that he and his captive 'speak
two different languages' (van Heerden 92). However, unlike Berger,
this observation points to radical divergence rather than reciprocity.
The torturer proclaims to be educated, having studied at 'university
overseas' (90). He is aware that his behaviour is the product of that
violent history that requires one either 'to endure blows inflicted
upon oneself, or to inflict them on others'. Here, however, the difference between the positions of *inflicting* or *enduring* those blows
results in a profound schism of experience that precludes empathy.
After noting his similarity to his captive in superficial matters such
as age and build, the captor reflects that

> When I was born in a hut with a candle and I lay beside my bleed-
> ing mother and a goat bleated outside (it was in a 'reserve' as you

called it), you most likely slid out into the soft white cloth held by a clever doctor to catch you, and then straight into an incubator. And when you learnt to write in a clean white exercise book [...] I and three others tried to scratch on a slate all at the same time with grubby fingers.

And for this reason, my Afrikaner, we speak two different languages. (92)

The material conditions created by apartheid, let alone the immediate physical situation, prevent the Afrikaner and his captor from relating to one another as full human subjects. The narrator categorically refuses the shared understanding, the shared subjectivity, the ability to speak represents:

I know [your] language, yes, and I hear how sweetly it sits on your broken tongue. It opens up memories for me [...] But, all the same you know: I do not understand it. (88)

By denying his captive's capacity for language, the narrator effectively silences his victim: 'your words no longer exist', he says, 'because we do not understand' (90). In her seminal study *The Body in Pain*, Elaine Scarry argues that this denial of voice forms one of the primary means by which torture victims are unmoored from their worlds. By refusing the Afrikaner's language, the narrator refuses his 'capacity to initiate action', derailing his captive's words on their transition from bodily noise to coherent self-expression. The Afrikaner's body has become just that, a body. In terms of the master–slave dialectic, it has become radically objectified, wholly passive. It can no longer be used to register, through speech, the presence of a subject in the world that surrounds it. Through his refusal to understand, the narrator detaches the Afrikaner's words from their referents and ensures that everything he thought he knew about the world evaporates. He thereby not only shuts down the Afrikaner's ability to act on the world but also breaks the connection that speech forges between the self and the world. The physical world may as well now disappear altogether: 'Never ask me again – as you did the day before yesterday – which way is south [...] South no longer exists – it is just a direction of the wind' (90). The 10-rand notes which the Afrikaner uses to make patterns on the floor of his cage are a symbol of this vanished order. They 'no longer exist, because [they] can't buy anything' (90); like the Afrikaner himself, they have no purchase. For Scarry this denial of a victim's relationship to the material world constitutes the initial purpose of torture, whereby a sufferer's universe is reduced first to the torture chamber or prison and then to the body. The sparse setting of 'My Afrikaner' is receptive to this analysis, as the only solid objects in a deliberately vague and generalized bush landscape are the captive's cage and the interrogation hut.

In 'My Afrikaner', the violent encounter between the torturer and his victim is framed as an inevitable consequence of what Harald Lindgard characterizes as 'the inhumanity of the old regime's assault upon body and mind' (Gordimer 142). The old regime necessitated the 'fearsome' revolution of which 'My Afrikaner' is a fictionalized sliver, and the fallout from both is mooted as the ultimate cause of Duncan Lindgard's killing of his lover. A loaded gun would never have been 'to hand', lying casually on a coffee table in a shared house, were it not for the historical context of apartheid. *Waiting for the Barbarians*, written earlier than either *Mad Dog* or *The House Gun*, offers an allegory of the systematic violence meted out by the apartheid regime itself. The structural similarities between the torture of the Afrikaner and J.M. Coetzee's protagonist reinforce the sense that the behaviour of both van Heerden's and Gordimer's violent characters is in accordance with a brutal psychopathology.

The narrator of *Barbarians*, again unnamed and known only as the Magistrate, lives on a frontier of 'the Empire' (6ff). Beyond the frontier live the barbarians who, the Empire's citizens believe, periodically gather to attack them; the barbarians represent the threatening Other to the Empire's self. Defining the Magistrate by his official position foregrounds the expectation that he will embody the laws and values of the Empire, but as the narrative progresses he develops sympathy for the barbarians and contempt for the Empire he is supposed to serve. He is then accused of 'treasonously consorting with the enemy' and punished by torture (Coetzee 85, 132). Like the Afrikaner, the Magistrate's torturers seek to damage his status as a rational being by dismantling the semantic power of his language:

He slips the noose from my neck and knots it around the cord that binds my wrists. 'Pull him up.'

> [...] as my feet leave the ground I feel a terrible tearing in my
> shoulders as though whole sheets of muscle are giving way. From
> my throat comes the first mournful dry bellow, like the pouring of
> gravel [...] I bellow again and again, there is nothing I can do to
> stop it, the noise comes out of a body that knows itself damaged
> perhaps beyond repair and roars its fright [...] 'He is calling his
> barbarian friends,' someone observes. 'That is barbarian language
> you hear.' There is laughter. (132)

His dry bellowing, like the tearing of his back muscles, issues from
the Magistrate's body without his consent. His bellowing does have
a limited ability to convey meaning, as it signifies that his body is
damaged and frightened. However, even involuntary expression that
bypasses rationality is denied him as his yell is recast as 'barbarian
language'. The Magistrate's tormentors will translate his utterances,
voluntary and involuntary, to the laughing audience. They will
decide what, if anything, they mean.

For Scarry, treatment such as that inflicted on the Magistrate and
the Afrikaner ensures that a once socialized being for whom the
world outside the boundaries of his or her own body once held
meaning, and whose words and deeds affected that world, becomes
to him or herself nothing more than a suffering body for whom no
stimuli exist beyond their own pain (27–58). Silencing, and the isolation it engenders, reduces the Afrikaner and the Magistrate to a state
of radical Otherness. This, it will be recalled, is what Scarry considers
to be the primary aim of torture: a desecration of human subjectivity
through combined mental and physical abuse. Within the Sartrean
master–slave dialectic, this destruction is carried out in order that
the subject (torturer) may attain full subjectivity. Scarry's arguments
regarding the ultimate aims of torture also follow this pattern.

Here, language remains the torturer's greatest weapon. Scarry
rejects the claim that, through torture, interrogators are in pursuit
of valuable, previously unknown information. Instead, she sees
the interrogation process as the means by which a victim is forced
to acknowledge the authority of his or her torturer and the world-
view they represent. The world of the victim is destroyed in order
that the world of his or her oppressor may expand to dominate the
vacated space (36–7). She cites an example from the slogans of South
Vietnamese torturers: 'if they are not guilty, beat them until they

are' (41). This is the attitude of the camp's political commissar in 'My Afrikaner', who counsels the narrator to '[b]urn' the Afrikaner until 'he calls you a kaffir and then we will take him over' (95). In *Barbarians*, too, Colonel Joll describes the 'certain tone' that 'enters the voice of a man who is telling the truth':

> I am speaking of a situation in which I am probing for the truth, in which I have to exert pressure to find it. First I get lies, you see [...] then pressure, then more lies, then more pressure, then the break, then more pressure, then the truth. (5)

The Magistrate's torture follows his refusal to say what his interrogators want to hear. He will not 'confess' to fraternizing with the barbarians and only insists that 'no one deserves to die': 'That', he is told, 'isn't enough' (130).

If interrogation is successful, then a victim's language is transformed from a positive act that communicates thought into a conduit for another's understanding of the world. One human subjectivity is crushed so another may reign supreme. However, neither of the interrogations examined here quite conform to Scarry's structure. Colonel Joll's interrogators 'pressure' the Magistrate but never get their 'break'. He is reduced to 'something closer to human nature than human beings ought to be' – he sleeps rough and becomes obsessed with procuring food (141) – but the descent is temporary. Eventually, 'word gets round' the town that 'the old Magistrate has taken his knocks and come through' (139). While it would be an oversimplification to say that everything goes 'back to normal' for the Magistrate, he does return to his old apartment when Joll's men leave and is surprised to find it 'as familiar as ever' (156).

Seemingly, the Magistrate is able to maintain his own sense of self because of his own tenacity, his active refusal to let the forces of the Empire overwhelm him. This plays into the hands of an old assumption regarding interrogation that Scarry is anxious to dispel. A victim who 'breaks' under pressure and tells the interrogator what they want to hear has not made a conscious decision to do so. Considerations such as loyalty or politics no longer apply as, for Scarry, during the experience of extreme violence 'all the psychological and mental content that constitutes both one's self and one's world, and that gives rise to and is in turn made possible by language, ceases to exist'

(30). Consequently, the question asked of the victim 'will matter so little to the prisoner [...] that he will give the answer' (29).

In 'My Afrikaner', it is the interrogator who prevents the political commissar's world-view from being channelled through the silenced Afrikaner. He does not wish, it seems, to 'take over' his victim to that extent and instead carries out his interrogations in silence, claiming that 'You would not answer the kind of questions that the commissar orders' (87). Rather than seeking to consolidate his own authority, the narrator brings the Afrikaner to the limits of degradation as an end in itself. He does not raise himself up above his victim but seeks to share with the Afrikaner an appreciation of their mutual nothingness: 'You are naked and you are nothing,' he says, 'as I am' (87).

'My Afrikaner' thus offers a nihilistic way out of the Sartrean master–slave dialectic. Instead of seeking full subjectivity at the expense of the other, the dominant party in an encounter foregoes his mastery and joins his adversary in a state of abject Otherness. Indeed, Berger's statement regarding mutual confirmation implies that this is the only possible outcome when one half of a human encounter has been so Othered. If the narrator refuses to recognize the Afrikaner as a linguistic being then he has declared him to be something less than fully human. 'You become my dog' (85), the narrator tells the Afrikaner; according to Berger, 'No animal confirms man, either positively or negatively' (3).

Any inquiry, then, into the effect of violence on human subjectivity must take into account both parties to the encounter. Whether one denotes the being that opposes the subject as object or abject, it is impossible to damage or destroy the subjectivity of the Other without simultaneously destroying one's own selfhood. This claim might appear to echo Sigmund Freud's observations regarding the doppelganger, separated by a hair's breadth from the abject, in which the double is the 'uncanny harbinger of death' (357). According to Nicholas Royle, one 'may want one's double dead' because it represents a suppressed aspect of the self but, because of this, 'the death of the double will always also be the death of oneself' (191). This idea has a rich legacy in postcolonial thought, most notably in references to Mrs Rochester as Jane Eyre's suppressed, colonial Other (Said 73).

While there is a strong argument for reading 'White Monkey' in particular through the prism of Freud's construction of the doppelganger, my own interpretation of the self's self-destructive destruction of the Other stems more directly from Kristeva and, subsequently, from Michael Rothberg's reassessment of Hannah Arendt's 'Boomerang Violence' and Aimé Cesaire's *un choc en retour* (Rothberg 23). Rothberg's discussion also concerns the return of the repressed. It develops and diversifies Arendt's and Cesaire's contemporaneous theories of violence and chimes with Sartre's subsequent verdict that 'violence is thrown back upon us as when our reflection comes forward to meet us when we go towards a mirror' (15). Throughout the first section of *Multidirectional Memory*, Rothberg explains that the effects of violence cannot be limited to its victims but are also revisited at the origin of that violence. This means that both immediate perpetrators, and the original site of the perpetration, will be damaged along with the victims of a violent encounter (see especially 68–9).

In both *Waiting for the Barbarians* and *The House Gun*, that 'original site' is revealed to be the totalitarian and contradictory worldview promoted by the apartheid state. The short story form of 'My Afrikaner' and 'White Monkey' provides the ideal environment in which to interrogate these general psychopathological conditions through contained, staged encounters between one protagonist and one antagonist. Van Heerden's ascetic language and minimal indicators of physical setting isolate his central characters, and use of the first person presents 'My Afrikaner' and 'White Monkey' as monologues or, perhaps, confessions. The remainder of this chapter explores van Heerden's particular vision of the master–slave dialectic and attempts to discover if any potential for reciprocity is left open in the *Mad Dog* encounters. It concludes by asking if Gordimer's text, the only narrative written after 1994, offers any way forward to a post-apartheid mode of being.

In *Mad Dog*, the boundary commonly held to exist between human and animal breaks down. This is unsettling, for it challenges the human perception of ourselves as essentially 'civilized' beings, intrinsically superior to non-human animals. The predicament of the Afrikaner as he cowers naked in his cage is a literal imagining of what respondents to the Nazi Holocaust have called 'bare life' (Giorgio Agamben cited in Rothberg 45):

The greatest danger to the 'new kind of human beings' created in the camps is that all markers of culture and civilisation have been stripped away from them, leaving them naked and vulnerable. (Rothberg 46)

Denial of language and removal from civilization has consigned the Afrikaner to a liminal state between human and non-human animal, just as for Sartre the colonial native was 'neither man nor animal' (Preface 14). Elsewhere in *Mad Dog*, the obverse occurs and animals take on 'human' characteristics. In 'Fences' (104–11), this partial metamorphosis emphasizes bestial aspects of Afrikaner settler culture such as the fetishization of virile masculinity and breeding. Here, the heir to a seventh-generation family farm's rape of a housemaid is implied through a dream that imagines the rapist as the stud's 'patriarch ram' (110). The story takes place as the housemaid, whom the reader assumes is black, goes into labour. The rapist's father and cousin wait 'to see if the baby would have blue eyes or not' (111).

'White Monkey' forms a useful parallel to 'My Afrikaner' as it follows the same structure of violent encounter between subject and object. Here, however, the Other within that encounter is physically rather than existentially non-human, and his trajectory is at odds with the Afrikaner's: through his suffering the monkey becomes more, not less, human to the narrator, the subject of the encounter. There is a subtle difference in the latter's position too for, while he does end by killing his Other, the monkey's cruellest treatment is at the hands of characters extraneous to this central relationship.

'White Monkey' is narrated by a young white farmer, a 'kleinbaas' (68). A troop of monkeys has been plundering the farm's crops. In order to stop them, one monkey is captured, shaved and painted white:

> I walked with Pa. 'It will keep the troop away for ever. It's a bit cruel, but with all the damage to the mealies and peaches we've got no choice …'
> 'Will his hair … grow again, Pa?' I asked carefully.
> 'Usually – ' Pa was hesitating, I could hear – 'usually, I believe, the monkey pines to death. The troop flees from him because he's white but he can't understand why they run away from him.' Pa was silent for a moment. 'In the end, yes, he pines away.' (70)

The kleinbaas does not let this happen. He witnesses the monkey's rejection by his troop and, once the other animals have 'melted into the trees', he shoots the creature in the face (73).

The means of execution is significant as the encounter begins when the narrator meets the monkey's eyes: 'With his glance', he says, 'the monkey had become human for me' (68). Though the monkey is categorically incapable of language, the kleinbaas recognizes something human in his glance; something that in turn recognizes the kleinbaas and demands a response from him. The monkey makes a moral claim on the narrator as his gaze implores him to act in his defence. The kleinbaas' sense of duty is compounded by the fact that the monkey appears not just as a human but as a human child ('he sat just like a child by a rock in his cage' (67); 'that little face' (69): innocent, endangered and entitled to the protection of those stronger than him.

In one sense, the narrator does protect the monkey. He spares him a drawn-out and lonely death. This rescue however is deeply ambivalent, and is achieved by literally and symbolically destroying the gaze that formed the connection between them. The centrality of eye contact to 'White Monkey' engages with the Sartrean concept of 'The Look' (Bauer 84), which explains how the self relies on the Other to confirm his subjectivity. Bauer holds that within the Sartrean master–slave dialectic 'the desire for recognition is a wish for another human being to reflect back to you a fixed image of yourself, an image reduced to what you take to be your most flattering aspect' (120).

By describing the function of the Other thus, Bauer reveals the continuity between Sartre's 'Look' and psychoanalyst Jacques Lacan's mirror stage. In the mirror stage, the human infant recognizes its own reflection in a mirror for the first time. At this stage in their development, infants' 'physical ambitions outstrip their motor capacity, with the result that their recognition of themselves is joyous in that they imagine their mirror image to be more complete, more perfect than they experience in their own body' (Mulvey 17). The infant believes its mirror image to be in control of itself, possessed of perfect agency. It gazes upon its 'ego ideal' in narcissistic delight (Lacan 2). The force and longevity of Lacan's argument has been such that the concept of the gaze is ubiquitous across psychoanalytic and postcolonial analysis, coded as a controlling look that projects onto the other the qualities the self wishes to see (Mulvey 17ff; Suleri 16; Rothberg 154).

For Sartre, the objectified other takes the place of Lacan's mirror and reflects back an ego ideal to the self. Only a wholly idealized other could do this as it has been reduced to parroting the world-view of the subject and is no longer capable of independent thought. However, any thinking consciousness will reflect the would-be sub-ject back to himself not as he wishes to be seen but as the Other sees him; Sartre explores this scenario in the play *Huis Clos* (1947). Consequently, the 'Look of the Other', or the disastrous moment when the object returns the subject's gaze, has the power 'to deter-mine and reveal the truth of who you are' (Bauer 121).

Perhaps the monkey's human gaze is destroyed because it revealed something to the kleinbaas about himself that he cannot bear to confront, such as his inability or, worse, his unwillingness to act upon a moral imperative; whilst the narrator saves the monkey from pining away, he makes no attempt to prevent his being shaved and painted. Instead, he hurries away from 'the click-click of the shears' when the monkey begins 'chattering in distress' (70). He appears like Pa to have no choice in the unfolding events and even imagines 'a bullet striking that little face' (69) long before he pulls the trigger. He knows what will happen, and that it is wrong. He does the best he can with the situation he is given, but makes no attempt to change that situation. His actions, along with those of Afrikaner's interroga-tor and Duncan Lindgard, are framed as inevitable.

The narrator of 'My Afrikaner' articulates the circumstances which have brought him and his captive to the cage and the interrogation hut. He is aware that their situation is engineered but seems unable or unwilling to break out of the cycle laid down by the apartheid state. He claims that their polarized experiences preclude him from understanding the Afrikaner, and hence from recognizing him as a fellow human being. This refusal condemns both to a limbo of abject Otherness and, although this appears to be the narrator's aim, he is not able to wholly shut down the urge towards some sort of reciproc-ity in either him or his captive. The Afrikaner asks his interrogator to help him escape, even as 'I was slipping the waterpipe carefully down your throat' (88) and 'although I fasten your tongue with a wire [...] you still ask me: do you have a wife?' (89). The Afrikaner holds out his words to the interrogator and his useless 10-rand notes 'to the commander every day' (95), hoping that one or the other will be accepted. Although the narrator cannot allow this to happen,

'You won't break me open, not with your words, my Afrikaner' (88), he does wish circumstances were different. He performs silent inter-rogations not because he believes there is nothing to say but because 'I know you know what the answers are that I seek. We are past questions and answers, I believe' (89).

In the penultimate sentence of 'My Afrikaner', the narrator looks beyond the deadlock of his encounter with the Afrikaner to remark that 'Perhaps in our dreams we may find one another, in a quiet country where we can say everything that is to be said.' Any hope for reciprocity and full subjectivity is thereby consigned to an imagined world beyond the text. If there were any doubt of this, the narrator of 'My Afrikaner' confirms it in his final invitation to his captive: 'Come, my beloved Afrikaner, the fire-irons await us' (95).

The House Gun is set in that world beyond the text. It is Gordimer's first novel to take place in the post-apartheid era (Lazarus 621), and she has spoken of the immense political and social value of the fact that, with the election of Nelson Mandela in 1994, 'there are now no overlords or underlings in the eyes of the law' (Gordimer cited in Lazarus 622). South Africa will no longer be organized as a nation-wide exercise in the Sartrean master–slave dialectic. However, the events of *The House Gun*, not to mention Fanon's damning assess-ment of post-abolition subjectivity, warn that the legal enshrine-ment of equality is not enough to bring it into being. As Neil Lazarus points out, in order that social life may

> unfold not as it was before, it is obviously necessary for the mate-rial conditions of existence to change in South Africa. But it is also necessary for the damaged forms that subjectivity has assumed to change and, even more important [...] for the damaged forms that *intersubjectivity* has assumed to change. (622)

One might take Carl Jespersen's murder as evidence that subjectiv-ity is as damaged as ever; moreover, by not only dominating but permanently effacing his Other, Duncan Lindgard has foregone his own chance for full selfhood. Duncan slips out of the narrative, the murder calling his very existence into question. The narrative asks 'Why is Duncan not in the story?' and answers 'His act has made him a vacuum; a vacuum is the antithesis of life' (151). Once again, however, the new South African order prevents this situation from reaching one possible logical conclusion: the Death Penalty is declared unconstitutional just after Duncan is sentenced to imprisonment (284). He is not obliged to become the literal 'antithesis of life', and wonders if 'you can break the repetition just by not perpetrating violence on yourself', by not turning 'the gun on your own head'. Duncan chooses to try and rescue his own subjectivity and the novel closes with his observation that 'I've had to find a way to bring life and death together' (294).

Duncan, spared death by both the state and himself, seeks a new mode of 'intersubjectivity' by imagining a reciprocity for himself and Carl Jespersen which murder has rendered impossible. Although this is arguably an improvement on the limbo of 'My Afrikaner', the solution is unsatisfying as 'there can be no recompense for the one whose life is taken' (103). Ultimately, Duncan's imagined reciprocity can only benefit his own subjectivity. It is debatable whether one *can* work out one's own salvation in these circumstances, and a residual selfishness is evidenced in Duncan's misinterpretation of a note sent to him by a mutual friend: 'UNGEKE UDLIWE UMZWANGEDWA SISEKHONA' (249). Duncan thinks this means 'Something like, you will never be alone because we are alone without you' (250). Anthony O'Brien offers a more accurate translation, not explained in the text but surely known to Gordimer: 'You are not consumed by sorrow, we are still here' (261).

Both interpretations of the Zulu saying speak to the master–slave dialectic, but only the second hints at a subjectivity that may lie beyond it. While the first expresses a narcissistic need for the other ('I need you, because I need you to recognize me'), the second offers the services of the self to save the Other from being consumed and bring him or her to a fuller subjectivity. This offer is not quite taken up in *The House Gun*, but, crucially, the novel presents 'the psychic and ideological conditions of possibility' (Lazarus 623). The Lindgards stand on the threshold of a subjectivity that breaks out of Sartre's fight to the death, and *The House Gun* extends a hope not available to *Barbarians* or *Mad Dog* that the constitutional renunciation of apartheid might, in the end, prove the death knell for its epistemic legacy.

Works cited

Bauer, Nancy. *Simone de Beauvoir, Philosophy, and Feminism*. New York: Columbia University Press, 2001.

Berger, John. *About Looking*. London: Writers and Readers, 1980.

Coetzee, J.M. *Waiting for the Barbarians*. 1980. London: Vintage, 2004.

Fanon, Frantz. *Black Skin, White Masks*. 1952. London: Pluto Press, 1986.

—— *The Wretched of the Earth*. Trans. Constance Farrington. 1965. London: Penguin, 2001.

Fitzpatrick, Matthew P. 'The Pre-History of the Holocaust? The *Sonderweg* and *Historikerstreit* Debates and the Abject Colonial Past.' *Central European History* 41 (2008): 477–503.

Freud, Sigmund. 'The Uncanny.' 1919. *Pelican Freud Library, 14*. Trans. James Strachey. Harmondsworth: Penguin, 1985. 335–76.

Gordimer, Nadine. *The House Gun*. London: Bloomsbury, 1999.

Heerden, Etienne van. *Mad Dog and Other Stories*. Trans. Catherine Knox. London: Allison & Busby, 1995.

Kristeva, Julia. *Powers of Horror: An Essay on Abjection*. Trans. Leon S. Roudiez. New York: Columbia University Press, 1982.

Lacan, Jacques. 'The Mirror Stage as Formative of the Function of the I as Revealed in Psychoanalytic Experience.' *Ecrits: A Selection*. 1949. Trans. Alan Sheridan. London: Tavistock, 1977. 1–7.

Lazarus, Neil. 'The South African Ideology: The Myth of Exceptionalism, the Idea of Renaissance.' *South Atlantic Quarterly* 103.4 (2004): 607–28.

McClintock, Anne. *Imperial Leather: Race, Gender and Sexuality in the Colonial Contest*. London: Routledge, 1995.

Mulvey, Laura. *Visual and Other Pleasures*. Basingstoke: Macmillan, 1989.

O'Brien, Anthony. *Against Normalization: Writing Radical Democracy in South Africa*. London: Duke University Press, 2001.

Rothberg, Michael. *Multidirectional Memory: Remembering the Holocaust in the Age of Decolonization*. Stanford University Press, 2009.

Royle, Nicholas. *The Uncanny*. Manchester University Press, 2003.

Said, Edward. *Culture and Imperialism*. London: Chatto & Windus, 1993.

Sartre, Jean-Paul. *No Exit and Three Other Plays*. New York: Vintage, 1989.

—— Preface. Frantz Fanon, *The Wretched of the Earth*. 7–26.

Scarry, Elaine. *The Body in Pain*. Oxford University Press, 1985.

Suleri, Sara. *The Rhetoric of English India*. Chicago University Press, 1992.

12
African Short Stories and the Online Writing Space

Shola Adenekan and Helen Cousins

For many young African writers access to new media technology, with its faster and more advanced means of communication, marks the beginning of a new wave of writing and an exchange of ideas. While they are using the traditional media for longer outputs, such as novels, the web provides the space for more immediate and shorter productions. Arguably, publishing online allows African writers to break away from the politics of postcolonial literary production which expects them to adopt certain styles, treat themes in particular ways and publish books to certain markets. In the online space, authors can choose to side-step the judgements of publishers and journal editors. For example, some young African writers are forming online publishing collectives such as *Storymoja*, *Kwani?* and *Saraba*, probably to avoid the old postcolonially framed distribution and publishing networks, thus writing in new voices to new audiences alike. There are also numerous 'unguarded' outlets in the form of blogs and social networking sites, like Facebook and Twitter. This last platform has encouraged the growth of African flash fiction – very short stories fitting into two SMS (Short Message Service) or two tweets. Following the spirit of innovation of these writers, we have taken a broad definition of short fiction, assuming, like Clare Hanson, that it has 'no inherent, determining characteristics' (5). Hence, our discussion is illustrated by a range of formats and platforms for publication. Karin Barber has made a case for the study of all genres, arguing that the traditional obsession with 'canonical texts has blocked our view of the real historical processes at work in the emergence and spread of literary forms' (40). Barber suggests that all literary forms deserve our attention, including those that are just emerging. We want, here, to explore the ways in which the online medium is shaping an emergent African writing marked by innovative reading practices through interaction between writers and readers, which signify a break from Western valorizations of individual authorship.

The 'internetting' of African literature arguably started in the 1990s when writers seeking to draw attention to their printed work started posting poems and short stories on emailing lists such as Krazitivity and Ederi, and other similar listservs hosted by the likes of Yahoo. Some of these works also appeared on African-owned websites such as Nigeria.com, Africanwriters.com, African-writing.com, Chimunrenga.com, odili.net and Nigeriavillagesquare.com. By the turn of this century, some of the established literary magazines in and outside of Africa, not wanting to be left out of the internet race, started asking for short stories, essays and poems that would appeal to a growing online reading public. At the same time, many writers, seeking to take more control of their work, started publishing creative writing on personal blogs, and joining online writer collectives.

In Kenyan literature, for example, Binyavanga Wainaina's rise to critical acclaim arguably started when his online autobiographical fiction *Discovering Home* won the 2002 Caine Prize for African Writing; from this, the same year he launched an online literary magazine *Kwani?* In an interview with Rob Spillman, Wainaina recounted the role that the digital space is playing in African literature:

> You have all these young writers in Nigeria who know writers in Kenya because they met on Facebook and so-and-so's workshop. You start to get the sense of this piling up of power and production, which is now larger than the sum of any parts you can see. That certainly has meant more to writing out of the continent than any other thing. (Spillman para. 42)

Wainaina concedes that there is still a place for the print medium; however, in his view, ultimately, 'We've all got to go digital. There's no question about it anymore. Print has to die' (para. 44). In part, this is because of the difficulty of accessing print copies within and outside of their countries of production, but equally, Wainaina appears to be suggesting that the freedom associated with writing online accrues power to the writers and not to the publishers as in print production.

Additionally, it is cheaper and faster to publish creative writing on the internet, and this work will potentially reach a wider audience, fuelled by a rapid uptake of internet and mobile phone technology within Africa. Out of the needs to find an alternative to mainstream ideologies and new forms of expression, this generation of African writers have found the internet an ideal platform to present their versions of self and society. The recent successes of some of the leading members of new African voices such as Wainaina, Chimamanda Ngozi Adichie and Uwem Akpan, coupled with this new mode of publishing, has fuelled interest in literary careers among several educated young Africans, leading to an upsurge in creative writing published in the digital space. Justin Reich argues that the cheap cost of online publishing 'leads to qualitatively different behaviour by web users [...] Because cheaper communication allows new communication media and practices, we have a whole new set of shared cultural texts created and distributed outside of the traditional, hierarchical publication network' (3). That is, that arguments relating to the 'quality' of this proliferating output are irrelevant when attention is paid to the consumption of this writing.

Reich's view is shared by writers who either self-publish on the internet or use the internet to promote their self-published works. The Kenyan writer Rasna Warah, in an email discussion on 'Kenyan Writers' listserv, asserts that:

> self-publishing, if I may defend it [...] offers several advantages that NGO-funded books or books published by other publishers don't. You retain control over the product, for one, and in my case, you have access to the global market, which local publishers do not provide [...] so I am not complaining. (n.p.)

Praise for online platforms is reiterated by Nigerian writer Myne Whitman, who insists that she owes her self-publishing success to the internet:

> I will always be grateful for the vehicle the internet provides to a writer and published author like me to get my book out there. Setting up an active blog and publishing my book has served a double purpose for me; finding out the target audience for my kind of writing and building a platform too. If not for the social

networking channels, *A Heart to Mend* would never have gone viral the way it did [...] I put up chapter one of the book on a free reading website and it became a massive hit. ('Writing' 6)

A Google search of Whitman's novel shows a network of material relating to her writing: copies of the novel are available in print and as a download from Amazon; as a pdf copy, hosted by Free-online-novels.com; as well as a related Facebook site, a website and the blog. Free-online-novels.com, in particular, bills itself as 'helping to meet the desires of writers and readers' (screen 2), and Whitman's comments highlight the synergy between readers and writers in the online space.

The title of this chapter, in identifying 'African' short stories, intentionally insists upon cyberspace as diasporic in the 'romantic' sense defined by Yogita Goyal: 'a form that can harmonize seemingly irreconcilable opposites [...] collapse distances of time and space [...] imply[ing] a certain wholeness of vision that refuses to accommodate any sense of difference at all (spatial, temporal [...] or geographical)' (9). Arguably, in the conventions surrounding the online writing space, a writer is more intimately connected not only with other writers, but also with readers who might be from other parts of Africa or from the diaspora. As Wainaina excitedly comments: 'There are 19-year-olds who've read all your work and they're based in Zimbabwe' (Spillman para. 42). Many readers of African fiction online are 'friends' of the writers on Facebook and follow them on Twitter, and the writers are also 'friends' of those African readers. Readers and writers are able to see each other's personal life in pictures and on video, with some writers regularly sharing family photos, day-to-day activities, political thoughts and fashion tips with their readers on social media sites, alongside short stories and poetry. Equally, readers can leave comments on many of these sites relating to the author's writing, at times instigating a dialogue about the work, providing extra-textual material that alters and shapes that work. The nature of texts within the new media landscape is altered by the close interaction between the writer and her or his readers. It removes the tenets by which distinctions and value judgements are traditionally made about what is 'good' versus that which is 'popular', generally based on the reputation of the publishing house and on individual authorship. In this process, both writers and readers are starting to embrace different values regarding literature, as cyberspace abruptly frees up notions of literature for experimentation, collaboration and disconnection from specifics of place, politics and culture.

Writers of particular African ethnicities and nationalities are not limited to readers of specific ethnicities or nationalities in this space, nor restricted to the subject matter deemed appropriate to that identity by often foreign or Western publishers. In this way, the stories fit with Roger Berger's analysis of African short stories which 'tend to assume place, marking it with signifiers of the "African" rather than with lengthy ethnographic or topographical passages' (73). He suggests that by doing this, writers are deliberately addressing 'an African reading and listening audience' (78) and not a 'foreign reader' attracted to a 'sense of the exotic [...] *and* an overt manifestation of the great anticolonial theme' (78). Short stories online, literally dis-placed into a cyberspace adrift from the material world, participate in the diaspora through a detachment from the continent, and simultaneously become marked by 'Africa'. In turn, as suggested above, being written under the sign of 'Africa', ensures that the stories are ideologically differentiated from earlier, print-based writings – often novels – where place, and its associated political and cultural specificities, predominated.

For a new generation of Africans and global readers, popular modes of communication such as Facebook posts, Twitter tweets and text messages invite more abbreviations and less rigidity in written convention. Brevity is encouraged by readers' attention spans, notoriously limited when reading online. However, short story theory suggests that the form also has a political attraction for African writers. For Hanson, it is 'a marginal form' (5) which has 'offered itself to losers and loners, exiles, women, blacks – writers who for one reason or another have not been part of the ruling "narrative" or epistemological/experiential framework of their society' (2). Thus it becomes:

> a vehicle for different *kinds* of knowledge, knowledge which may be in some way at odds with the 'story' of dominant culture. The formal properties of the short story – disjunction, inconclusiveness, obliquity – connect with its ideological marginality and with the fact that the form may be used to express something suppressed / repressed in mainstream literature. (6)

In similar ways, Paul March-Russell suggests that 'the postcolonial short story is potentially a more dissident form than the major genres, especially with regards to rethinking the postcolonial' (247). It appears that online short fiction written by African authors tends towards controversy, perhaps because of the perceived freedom of expression available on the internet where cyberspace represents an escape from the constriction of the physical space and its associations with a colonial past; thus the online authors can circumvent the assumptions of a previous generation of African writers that a break from the past is impossible. In cyberspaces, writers feel more at liberty to set their own ideological agendas, and so are bringing fresh perspectives on issues such as homosexuality, prostitution and class. The form of short fiction, as Hanson suggests, is a key enabler in this. Additionally, Adrian Hunter notes how 'one repeatedly encounters the idea that the short story is somehow "up to speed" with the realities of modern life' (3).

However, it is Gilles Deleuze and Félix Guattari's notion of minor literature that most usefully describes postcolonial short fiction. Used by both Hunter and March-Russell, for our purposes Deleuze and Guattari's term '"deterritorialization"': whereby language is displaced and contorted by the pressures of colonization' (March-Russell 248) is particularly pertinent as English increasingly becomes the lingua franca of the internet, slipping away into proliferating ownerships and expression, no longer bound to its national roots. Equally relevant is their 'emphasis upon fragmentation' (March-Russell 248), which is apt for online short fiction. Text online is impermanent, intertextual, with adverts, images, hyperlinks and even sound; blogs in particular are structured to be episodic and ongoing, a far cry from Edgar Allan Poe's definition of short stories as requiring a 'unity of impression'. On a technical level, the text itself is compiled of pixillated fragments bringing a new, literal meaning to R.C. Feddersen's description of postmodern short stories where 'experience is fragmented into collage or a mosaic of reality' (xxx). Thus, even if various examples of what is currently being published online by African writers reads like, or looks like, something that could have been published in print, it is essentially different. As Raine Koskimaa notes in relation to online fiction:

> Even if certain contemporary works look exactly like older literary pieces in their formal, structural and semiotic aspects, they are

nevertheless written and read in a new context. Writing and read-ing strategies as well as our cognitive-emotional engagement with literature are quite different today than during previous periods of history. (5)

Koskimaa suggests here that the interpretation or reading of online literature is not distinct from its writing, returning us to the synergy between readers and writers in online African fiction through which we can begin to appreciate the way in which many young people across Africa (like their counterparts from around the world) read texts and comprehend life through their engagement with digital technologies. In turn, these new forms of reading practices affect literature in the way plots, characters and texts are constructed, dis-played and consumed.

Thus, African online fiction is particularly well described by Nadine Gordimer's notion of short stories as written by a 'flash' of experience:

> all the time [the novelist's] characters have the reader by the hand, there is a consistency of relationship throughout the experience that cannot and does not convey the quality of human life, where contact is more like the flash of fireflies, in and out, now here, now there, in darkness. Short-story writers see by the light of the flash; theirs is the art of the only thing one can be sure of – the present moment. (Gordimer 264)

Gordimer's views might well have been shaped by her experiences of apartheid South Africa where the repressive, military regime made human relationships precarious and liable to disruption. However, African short fiction online continues to work within this 'flash', expressed in social networking which encourages a broad spread of acquaintances with whom one has brief, intermittent and possibly disjointed interactions. As Whitman notes:

> The beauty of the internet was that I could remain in my work room with just my laptop and a connection, and meet up with these dozens of interviewers [...] I continued networking with other writers and self-published authors and as I shared what I had learnt, I picked up some good nuggets from them too. I set up a

Twitter page and opened up my Facebook profile for use with my pen name [...] I learnt how to interconnect these media, how to set up scheduled tweets or how to update Facebook via RSS feeds. ('Writing' 6)

This type of authorial operation encodes short fiction as an extension of the social exchanges of Twitter, Facebook and other social networking sites.

One effect of online social networking on writing is that, in the online writing space, African literature appears to reflect the news cycles, building on academic and journalistic investigations. In fact, there is often no clear separation between fiction writers, reporters and social commentators, roles that are frequently embodied in a single online persona. Take, for example, the writings of Chika Unigwe. In her short story 'Dreams' (2004) the female character, Uche, is forced into prostitution to care for her children after the death of her husband. Although the medical cause of death is heart failure, Uche's mother-in-law, Mama Obi, consults a 'prophet' who explains the unexpected demise in spiritual terms, placing blame on the 'evil' wife. This allows Mama Obi to invoke traditional practices to take her young grandson to raise, and to evict Uche from her home along with her twin daughters. Comments on the *Nigerian Village Square* website make links between this story, social reality and the need for social change to protect women:

With cases as such very popular (happened to someone I know [...]), I think it'd be such a great idea if the Government made laws (and enforced them) that protects the Uches from the hands of Mama Obis who try to separate them from that which is rightfully theirs. Such women should not have to have to prostitute [*sic*] to make ends meet. (Anike n.p.)

Unigwe regularly gives interviews in new media forums such as *The Guardian* (UK), *The Independent* (UK), *The New York Times* (USA) as well as several African online forums, where she discusses some of the characters in her fictional narratives and how these characters represent real-life women that she came across when she was doing background research for her creative work, reiterating those connections between reality and fiction.

A story like 'Dreams' deviates ideologically from much of the earlier creative work that came out of Africa which considered the negative effect of modernity on young women in particular, and which regularly considered how women, corrupted by the urban environment, needed to be redeemed through a return to traditional roles or to rural locations. (For example, Cyprian Ekwensi's trilogy on the fictional character of Jagua Nana.) African short stories that are being published in the new media space are equally preoccupied with the life of female urban dwellers but position themselves differently in ideological terms. Online writers explore the social and cultural circumstances which shape women's experiences in the city, and much of this explores how women's sexuality is exploited, as in 'Dreams', or, in a slightly different way, in Sefi Atta's online fiction 'Glory' (African Writing Online Vol. 4 – no date). Here the narrator describes desperate young Nigerian women hanging out in Lagos hotels looking for a way out to Europe:

> The hotel was full of prostitutes, packed with them, and they were dressed in western attire. They could easily pass for proper elite. What gave them away were the crooked-legged walks they acquired from parading up and down the diplomatic district. Glory called them *va bene*, not *ashawo*, as everyone else called them. So many of them ended up in Rome. (Atta para. 11)

Atta references not only the uses to which women's bodies are put, but also the risks of human trafficking faced by African women desperate to improve their circumstances. Chimamanda Ngozi Adichie's story 'Birdsong' (2010) takes a different part of the continuum by writing about a young woman whose lover is a married man. This relationship is akin to prostitution in its expectations of exchange – the woman gets gifts from the man in exchange for sex. Adichie's story attracted many comments which debated the sexual theme of the story: some suggested that she was sex-obsessed, or trivializing sex, but one commentator took a feminist position to suggest that Adichie 'describes sex and sexuality from a unique, dignified and wholly female perspective' (Adichie comment 17). Adichie does not condemn her female character, nor pity her, but shows her gradual recognition that she is in a relationship where only her body is valued. Her status is clear to the wider society, as when she visits a restaurant with the lover:

> 'Good evening, sah,' the waiter said when we were seated. 'You are welcome, sah.'
> 'Have you noticed that they never greet me?' I asked my lover.
> 'Well ...' he said, and adjusted his glasses.
> The waiter came back [...] and I waited until he had opened the bottle of red wine before I asked, 'Why don't you greet me?'
> The waiter glanced at my lover, as though seeking guidance, and this infuriated me even more. 'Am I invisible?' (Adichie paras 66–70)

Her new awareness that her sex defines her spills into her workplace too when she questions why it is always her, or her female co-worker, who have to cut up and distribute the birthday cakes the men bring in. Using fiction to highlight social inequality is not new, but because this is published online, the story's debate is carried into its reading in overt ways through readers' comments. If reader-response theories that insist meaning lies with the reader are correct, here is a practical manifestation of that process enabled by the publishing platforms on the internet.

In another example from the same theme, the short story 'Ashewos Anonymous' (2009) posted on Facebook by the Nigerian writer Terfa Tilley-Gyado, shows that some texts in the digital space can serve to perpetuate the accepted decorum on intimacy. In 'Ashewos Anonymous', the narrator tells the story of six socially mobile Lagos women who meet regularly as a self-help group intended to 'cure' their nymphomania (para. 1). One reader comments on the content and style of the piece:

> It is so true, it hurts!! Sadly the biz of 'Ashewo' has been 'rebranded.' They drive the posh cars, live in big houses, they are the bigz [sic] gals, the movers and shakers of the big cities, they even get political appointments!! Sad, very sad. God help us. Nice piece, very humorous too, I didn't want it to stop. (Tilley-Gyado comment 18)

The social commentary, then, does not have to be in a didactic style; the stories retain their purpose to entertain, but the reader maintains a right to moralize about the women's actions. In 'Her Friend's Father' (2010) by the young Kenyan writer Pauline Odhiambo, similar sentiments are expressed by readers commenting on the narrative about a 20-year-old Nairobi woman, who is having an affair with her best friend's father, using the money the man is giving her to buy mobile phones and mobile phone accessories. One reader relates the text to his own experiences and also offers advice on the topics that the writer should tackle:

> The introduction of this story is very catchy. It's creatively written. Your story is real. It happens every day, and brings to light the strange behaviors [*sic*] of Kenyan men. I am one of them, and for sure we Kenyan Men don't know what we want. And hence, we end up being manipulated ... It's sad. Pauline, I would advise you to come up with a book, exposing how Kenyan men are being exploited by college girls [...] Men, when will we begin identifying what we want? Lets [*sic*] be ourselves. (Odhiambo comment 7)

The reader's final appeal speaks out to the other male readers of this story and replicates the comments of other readers of online short stories who comment on fiction by relating their personal experience of intimacy to the fictional events. By instigating discussions on these fictional characters, the online writing space becomes a site for defining gendered performances. D.O. Adebayo et al. argue that not only does the society and culture influence intimacy, but sexual behaviour in Africa is also impacted upon by technology (745). At the beginning of the last century, the printing press helped define the modern African girl as sexualized and corrupt; now at the start of a digital age, some of the new online fictions are suggesting that this stereotype remains tenacious, but by providing immediate ways in which to debate female sexuality, the internet can allow the writer and his or her readers to interact in challenging the stereotypes. Readers and writers can comment and respond rapidly, and publicly, so that a debate or even an online community can form quickly out of these discussions in a way that was not possible in the print age. For example, the interactive discussions on the writer Tolulope Popoola's creative writing blog led to the formation of *Favouredgirl Writes* – a Facebook fans page with about four thousand members, dedicated to both fictional and real-life discussions on sexual intimacy and romance in Nigeria and Africa. The blog *Myne Whitman Writes*, which used to describe itself as 'authoring romantic fiction and sharing thoughts on life, love, books and Nigeria' (n.p.), eventually translated into a Facebook page with the same focus as the blog. Unlike the canons of printed works, the internet space is less gender-weighted towards men and represents more equally the voices of male and female readers and writers.

One further feature of minor literature is its 'social and political function; that fosters collective rather than individual utterances' (Bogue 116). In this view of writing, 'there are no possibilities for an individuated enunciation that would belong to this or that "master" and that could be separated from a collective enunciation' (Deleuze and Guattari 57). Deleuze and Guattari insist that the revolutionary potential of literature comes not from its ideological stances but 'because the literary machine alone is determined to fulfil the conditions of a collective enunciation that is lacking elsewhere in this milieu: *literature is the people's concern*' (57; italics in original). Nowhere in African writing is this more apparent than in online fiction, always deterritorialized, and always in dialogue. The comments quoted above are not merely add-ons to the stories 'proper' but are part of the fictional narrative which becomes collective. However, this notion of minor literature is not the only challenge to Western-based ideas of individual authorship. Whilst Deleuze and Guattari present a philosophical challenge, the internet provides a practical one in its capacity to obliterate a 'real' writer entirely.

Blogs represent one of the more experimental forms of online African literature. Some, like *iBhuku: Free Poetry and Short Fiction PDFs from Southern Africa*, operate much like an ezine, but other writers blog directly to the online community. The episodic and open-ended structure of blogs refuse conventional definitions of short fiction, making them reflect 'a sense that life can only be rendered in fragments and compressed subjective episodes which stimulate instead of drugging the mind' (Shaw 43). However, more significant and radical is the slippage between fiction and life writing exposed by an uncertainty over authorship. The example that will be discussed here, *Nairobi Nights*, has generated much extra-textual comment on its own pages and on other blogs, particularly in relation to the veracity of 'Sue', the identified author who claims to 'practice along

Koinange Street, Nairobi' (Sue 'About Me') as a prostitute. Fellow bloggers question the truthfulness of this claim. Obruni, on *Onamba Forum*, notes:

> This blog [...] *supposedly* belongs to [a] hooker in Nairobi with stories about the life and adventures of a working girl in Nairobi.
>   Judging from the writing the girl must have at an [*sic*] university education, both when it comes to style and 'philosophy' in the *short stories*.
>   On the other hand *it might come from a journalist* (or maybe a ghost-writer) bit [*sic*] the stories are both entertaining and might make one think a bit. (comment 1; my italics)

Posts left on the *Nairobi Nights* blog by readers who are considering its authorship are divided but generally doubts are coupled with appreciation of the writing, content and style. After the chapter where Sue discusses the debates over her identity, one commentator notes: 'if it is fiction, then you're a genius' and 'I don't care if its [*sic*] fiction or not the thing is you are a very good and talented writer' (Sue 'Of Coming Out of the Closet' comment 2). Doubts such as these arise from the generally suspect nature of authorship online where anonymity or pseudonyms are more easily maintained than in more traditional interactions. One notorious case was the *Gay Girl in Damascus* blog, apparently written by a Syrian lesbian, which turned out to be the work of a 40-year-old, male postgraduate student, creating outrage from those who had subscribed to its authenticity ('Syria Gay Girl'). In Sue's case, one commentator claims: 'Guys this is not who you think it is. It is actually not even a woman. It is a guy who is a journalist in one of the papers' (Sue 'Of Coming Out of the Closet' comment 7). But generally, our interest – and that of Sue's readers – is not in discovering Sue's true identity but in how this uncertainty shifts the putative 'life writing' into a short story. Exposing Sue as a fictitious creation, then, would only serve to reinforce the blog's designation as fiction and the comments on the blog suggest that it would not be so much of an issue for a readership which already accepts the blog's 'authenticity' in describing recognizably the life of an African street prostitute. Through this manoeuvre, a different type of collective voice is formed through the lacuna where individual authorship traditionally appears. As in the case of Kafka's K which 'no longer designates a narrator or a character but an assemblage' (Deleuze and Guattari 58), Sue is also a 'collective', a 'persona', rather than a subject.

Roger Berger claims that the 'Anglophone African short story [...] provides a model for a new kind of postcolonial text' (78). In these stories 'readers are introduced to Africa mainly on its own terms. For this reason, the African short story may well displace – indeed, has always already displaced – the novel as *the* postcolonial genre' (78). We concur, and add that the widespread adoption of internet publishing by African writers and readers is instrumental in and necessary for sustaining this new fiction which 'heralds a confident, decolonized, truly postcolonial mode of fiction' (Berger 73) arising from Africa, typified by a collective voice.

Works cited

Adebayo, D.O. et al. 'Gender, Internet Use, and Sexual Behavior Orientation Among Young Nigerians.' *CyberPsychology and Behaviour* 9.6 (2006): 742–52.

Adichie, Chimamanda Ngozi. 'Birdsong.' *The New Yorker*, 20 September 2010. http://www.newyorker.com/fiction/features/2010/09/20/100920fi_fiction_adichie

Anika. 'Re: Short Story by Chika Unigwe.' *Thread: Short Story by Chika Unigwe*. 8 October 2006. http://www.nigeriavillagesquare.com/forum/books-creative-writing/5486-short-story-chika-unigwe.html

Atta, Sefi. 'Glory.' *African Writing Online*. 4.1 2008. http://www.african-writing.com/four/sefiattah.htm

Barber, Karin. *The Anthropology of Texts, Persons and Publics: Oral and Written Culture in Africa and Beyond*. Cambridge University Press, 2007.

Berger, Roger. 'The Place of (and Place in) the Anglophone African Short Story.' *The Tales We Tell: Perspectives on the Short Story*. Ed. Barbara Lounsberry et al. Westport CT and London: Greenwood Press, 1998. 73–81.

Bogue, Ronald. *Deleuze and Guattari*. London and New York: Routledge, 1989.

Deleuze, Gilles and Félix Guattari. 'What is a Minor Literature?' *Poetry and Cultural Studies: A Reader*. Ed. Maria Damon and Ira Livingston. Chicago: University of Illinois Press, 2009. 56–60.

Feddersen, R.C. 'Introduction: A Glance at the History of the Short Story in English.' *A Reader's Introduction to the Short Story in English*. Ed. Erik Fallon et al. London and Chicago: Fitzroy Dearborn, 2001. xiii–xxxiv.

Free-online-novels.com. 2011. http://free-online-novels.com/index.html

Gordimer, Nadine. 'The Flash of Fireflies.' *The New Short Story Theories*. Ed. Charles E. May. Athens: Ohio University Press, 1994. 262–7.

Goyal, Yogita. *Romance, Diaspora, and Black Atlantic Literature*. Cambridge University Press, 2010.

Hanson, Clare. 'Introduction.' *Re-reading the Short Story*. Ed. Clare Hanson. Basingstoke and London: Macmillan, 1989. 1–9.

Hunter, Adrian. *The Cambridge Introduction to the Short Story in English*. Cambridge University Press, 2007.

iBhuku: Free Poetry and Short Fiction PDFs from Southern Africa. http://ibhuku. blogspot.com/

Koskimaa, Raine. 'The Challenge of Cybertext: Teaching Literature in the Digital World.' *Uoc.edu. Papers: e-journal on the Knowledge Society*. March 2007. http://www.uoc.edu/uocpapers/4/dt/eng/koskimaa.html

March-Russell, Paul. *The Short Story: An Introduction*. Edinburgh University Press, 2009.

Obruni. 'Hooker's Blog: Nairobi Nights.' *Onamba Forum*. 16 January 2011. http://www.omanbaforum.com/showthread.php?1333-Hooker-s-blog-Nairobi-Nights

Odhiambo, Pauline. 'Her Friend's Father.' *Storymoja Blog*. 25 October 2010. http://storymojaafrica.co.ke/main/2010/10/editors-pick-her-friend% E2%80%99s-father-by-pauline-odhiambo/

Popoola, Tolulope. *Favouredgirl Writes*. 20 March 2011. https://www.facebook. com/favouredgirl

—— *Favoured Girl's Blog*. 5 December 2011. http://favouredgirl.blogspot.com/

Reich, Justin. 'Reworking the Web, Reworking the World: How Web 2.0 is Changing Our Society.' *Beyond Current Horizons*. December 2008. http:// www.beyondcurrenthorizons.org.uk/wpcontent/uploads/final_reich_ reworkingtheweb_20081201_jb.pdf

Shaw, Valerie. *The Short Story: A Critical Introduction*. London: Longman, 1983.

Spillman, Rob. 'Binyavanga Wainaina.' *Bomb Magazine* 116. Summer 2011. http://bombsite.com/articles/5107

Sue. 'About Me.' *Nairobi Nights: A Kenyan Prostitute Building a Brand*. 2011. http://www.nairobinights.info/p/about-me.html

—— 'Of Coming Out of the Closet.' *Nairobi Nights: A Kenyan Prostitute Building a Brand*. 21 January 2011. http://www.nairobinights.info/2011/01/episode-11-of-coming-out-of-closet.html

'Syria Gay Girl in Damascus Blog a Hoax by US Man.' *BBC News*. 13 June 2011. http://www.bbc.co.uk/news/world-middle-east-13744980

Tilley-Gyado, Terfa. 'Ashewos Anonymous.' *Facebook Note*. 15 June 2009. https://www.facebook.com/note.php?note_id=101111261372

Unigwe, Chika. 'Dreams.' *Eclectica Magazine*. January/February 2004. http:// www.eclectica.org/v8n1/unigwe_dreams.html

Wainaina, Binyavanga. 'Discovering Home.' *G21 Africa*. 2002. http:// generator21.net/g21archive/africa29.html

Warah, Rasna. Email communication on 'Kenyan Writers' listserv. 4 November 2009.

Whitman, Myne. 'Myne Whitman Writes.' 11 March 2011. http://www. blogher.com/frame.php?url= http://www.mynewhitmanwrites.com

—— 'Writing and Publishing in the Age of Social Media.' *Saraba 7: The Tech Issues*. November–December 2010: 5–6. http://sarabamag.com/featured/saraba-7/

Bibliography

Primary sources

Alaidy, Ahmed. *Being Abbas El Abd*. Trans. Humphrey Davies. London: Arabia Books, 2008.

Alfian Sa'at. *Corridor: 12 Short Stories*. Singapore: SNP, 1999.

Al Khamissi, Khaled. *Taxi*. Trans. Jonathan Wright. Wiltshire: Aflame Books, 2008.

al-Shaykh, Hanan. *Women of Sand and Myrrh*. Trans. Catherine Cobham. London: Quartet, 1989.

Atta, Sefi. 'Glory.' *African Writing Online*. 4 January 2008. http://www.african-writing.com/four/sefiattah.htm

Coetzee, J.M. *Waiting for the Barbarians*. London: Vintage, 2004.

Douglass, Debbie et al., eds. *Máka, Diasporic Juks: Contemporary Writing by Queers of African Descent*. Toronto: Sister Vision Press, 1997.

Elwin, Rosamund, ed. *Tongues on Fire: Caribbean Lesbian Lives and Stories*. Toronto: Women's Press, 1997.

Gordimer, Nadine. *The House Gun*. London: Bloomsbury, 1999.

Grace, Patricia. *Collected Stories*. Auckland: Penguin, 1994.

—— *Small Holes in the Silence*. Auckland: Penguin, 2006.

Heerden, Etienne van. *Mad Dog and Other Stories*. Trans. Catherine Knox. London: Allison & Busby, 1995.

Hopkinson, Nalo. *Skin Folk*. New York: Warner Books, 2001.

Hopkinson, Nalo and Uppinder Mehan, eds. *So Long Been Dreaming: Postcolonial Science Fiction and Fantasy*. Vancouver: Arsenal Pulp Press, 2004.

Ihimaera, Witi. *Dear Miss Mansfield: A Tribute to Kathleen Mansfield Beauchamp*. Auckland: Viking, 1989.

—— *Kingfisher Come Home: The Complete Maori Stories*. Auckland: Secker & Warburg, 1995.

——, ed. *Where's Waari: A History of the Maori through the Short Story*. Auckland: Reed, 2000.

Islam, Syed Manzurul. *The Mapmakers of Spitalfields*. Leeds: Peepal Tree Press, 1997.

Kumar, Sukrita Paul and Muhammad Ali Siddiqui, eds. *Mapping Memories: Urdu Stories from India and Pakistan*. New Delhi: Katha, 1998.

Lahiri, Jhumpa. *Interpreter of Maladies*. London: Flamingo, 2000.

—— *Unaccustomed Earth*. London: Bloomsbury, 2008.

Lee, Nancy. *Dead Girls*. London: Faber & Faber, 2003.

Lim, Suchen Christine. *The Lies that Build a Marriage: Stories of the Unsung, Unsaid and Uncelebrated in Singapore*. Singapore: Monsoon, 2007.

Memon, Muhammad Umar, ed. *An Epic Unwritten: The Penguin Book of Partitions Stories from Urdu*. New Delhi: Penguin, 1998.
—— *Fear and Desire: An Anthology of Urdu Stories*. Oxford University Press, 1994.
—— *The Tale of the Old Fisherman: Contemporary Urdu Short Stories*. Washington: Three Continents Press, 1991.
Mootoo, Shani. *Out on Main Street and Other Stories*. Vancouver: Press Gang Publishers, 1993.
Munro, Alice. *The Beggar Maid*. London: Allen Lane, 1980.
—— *Hateship, Friendship, Courtship, Loveship, Marriage*. London: Chatto & Windus, 2001.
—— *The Love of a Good Woman*. London: Chatto & Windus, 1998.
—— *Runaway*. London: Chatto & Windus, 2005.
—— *Something I've Been Meaning to Tell You*. London: Penguin, 2006.
Odhiambo, Pauline. 'Her Friend's Father.' *Storymoja Blog*. 25 October 2010. http://storymojaafrica.co.ke/main/2010/10/editors-pick-her-friend%E2%80%99s-father-by-pauline-odhiambo/
Poon, Wena. *The Proper Care of Foxes*. Singapore: Ethos Books, 2009.
Rifaat, Alifa. *Distant View of a Minaret and Other Stories*. Trans. Denys Johnson-Davies. London: Quartet, 1983.
Sheikh, Moazzam, ed. *A Letter from India: Contemporary Short Stories from Pakistan*. New Delhi: Penguin, 2004.
Sinclair, Iain. *Downriver*. London: Vintage, 1995.
—— 'The Griffin's Egg.' *It's Dark in London*. Ed. Oscar Zarate. London: Serpent's Tail, 1996. 43–52.
Soueif, Ahdaf. *Sandpiper*. London: Bloomsbury, 1996.
Sue. 'About Me.' *Nairobi Nights: A Kenyan Prostitute Building a Brand*. 2011. http://www.nairobinights.info/p/about-me.html
—— 'Of Coming Out of the Closet.' *Nairobi Nights: A Kenyan Prostitute Building a Brand*. 21 January 2011. http://www.nairobinights.info/2011/01/episode-11-of-coming-out-of-closet.html
Tawhai, Alice. *Festival of Miracles*. Wellington: Huia, 2005.
Te Awekotuku, Ngahuia. *Ruahine: Mythic Women*. Wellington: Huia, 2003.
Tilley-Gyado, Terfa. 'Ashewos Anonymous.' *Facebook Note*. 15 June 2009. https://www.facebook.com/note.php?note_id=101111261372
Unigwe, Chika. 'Dreams.' *Eclectica Magazine*. January/February 2004. http://www.eclectica.org/v8n1/unigwe_dreams.html
Wainaina, Binyavanga. 'Discovering Home.' *G21 Africa*. 2002. http://generator21.net/g21archive/africa29.html

Secondary sources

On individual authors
Anika. 'Re: Short Story by Chika Unigwe.' *Thread: Short Story by Chika Unigwe*. 8 October 2006. http://www.nigeriavillagesquare.com/forum/books-creative-writing/5486-short-story-chika-unigwe.html

Bacchilega, Cristina. 'Reflections on Recent English-Language Fairy-Tale Fiction by Women: Extrapolating from Nalo Hopkinson's *Skin Folk*.' *Fabula* 47.3–4 (2006): 201–10.

Baker, Brian. *Iain Sinclair*. Manchester University Press, 2007.

Bentley, Nick, ed. *British Fiction of the 1990s*. Abingdon: Routledge, 2005.

Bond, Robert. *Iain Sinclair*. Cambridge: Salt Publishing, 2005.

Borossa, Julia. 'The Extensibility of Psychoanalysis in Ahmed Alaidy's *Being Abbas El Abd* and Bahaa Taher's *Love in Exile*.' *Journal of Postcolonial Writing* 47.4 (2011): 404–15.

Burwell, Jennifer and Nancy Johnston, eds. 'A Dialogue on SF and Utopian Fiction, between Nalo Hopkinson and Elizabeth Vonarburg.' *Foundation* 81 (2001): 40–7.

Chotiner, Isaac. 'Jhumpa Lahiri.' *The Atlantic* (March 2008). http://www.theatlantic.com/doc/200802u/jhumpa-lahiri

Ciuraru, Carmela and Tamara Frankfort. 'A Personal Matter: An Interview with Jhumpa Lahiri.' *Real Simple* (June 2001): 130–3.

Du Plessis, Rosemary, ed. *Feminist Voices: Women's Studies Texts for Aotearoa/ New Zealand*. Oxford University Press, 1992.

Glave, Dianne D. 'An Interview with Nalo Hopkinson.' *Callaloo* 26.1 (2003): 146–59.

Grace, Patricia. 'Influences on Writing.' *Inside Out: Literature, Cultural Politics, and Identity in the New Pacific*. Ed. Vilsoni Hereniko and Rob Wilson. Lanham and Boulder: Rowman and Littlefield, 1999. 65–73.

—— 'The Maori in Literature.' *Tihe Mauri Ora: Aspects of Maoritanga*. Ed. Michael King. Hong Kong: Methuen, 1978. 80–3.

Groes, Sebastian. *The Making of London: London in Contemporary Literature*. Basingstoke: Palgrave Macmillan, 2011.

Howells, Coral Ann. *Alice Munro*. Manchester University Press, 1998.

Hunter, Adrian. 'Story into History: Alice Munro's Minor Literature.' *English* 207 (2004): 219–38.

Ihimaera, Witi. 'A Maori Perspective.' *Journal of New Zealand Literature* 9 (1991): 53–4.

Islam, Syed Manzurul. *The Ethics of Travel: From Marco Polo to Kafka*. Manchester University Press, 1996.

Jackson, Kevin. 'Psychogeography: Will Self and Iain Sinclair in Conversation.' Transcribed Karian Schuitema, ed. Steven Barfield. *Literary London* 6.1 (2008). http://www.literarylondon.org/london-journal/march2008/sinclair-self.html

Kabir, Ekram. 'Manzu Islam: Creator of the First Literary Map for Brick Lane.' (2008). http://www.scribd.com/ekram.kabir/d/3503550-Manzu-Islam-Creator-of-the-first-literary-map-for-Brick-Lane

Lane, Richard J. et al. *Contemporary British Fiction*. Cambridge: Polity Press, 2003.

Laskin, David. 'Alice Munro's Vancouver', *The New York Times*, 2006. http://travel.nytimes.com/2006/06/11/travel/11footsteps.html

Massad, Joseph. 'The Politics of Desire in the Writings of Ahdaf Soueif.' *Journal of Palestine Studies* 28.4 (1999): 74–90.

Mitra, Madhuparna. 'Lahiri's "Mrs. Sen's".' *The Explicator* 64.3 (2006): 193–6.

Munro, Alice. 'A Conversation with Alice Munro.' 2008. http://reading-group-center.knopfdoubleday.com/2010/01/08/alice-munro-interview/

Murray, Alex. *Recalling London: Literature and History in the Work of Peter Ackroyd and Iain Sinclair.* London: Continuum, 2007.

Nash, Geoffrey. 'Re-Sitting Religion and Creating Feminised Space in the Fiction of Ahdaf Soueif and Leila Aboulela.' *Wasafiri* 35 (2002): 28–31.

Nelson, Alondra. 'Making the Impossible Possible: An Interview with Nalo Hopkinson.' *Social Text* 20.2 (2002): 97–113.

Obruni. 'Hooker's Blog: Nairobi Nights.' *Onamba Forum.* 16 January 2011. http://www.onambaforum.com/showthread.php?1333-Hooker-s-blog-Nairobi-Nights

Perril, Simon. 'A Cartography of Absence: The Work of Iain Sinclair.' *Comparative Criticism* 19 (1997): 309–39.

Poon, Angelia. 'Mining the Archive: Historical Fiction, Counter-modernities, and Suchen Christine Lim's *A Bit of Earth*.' *The Journal of Commonwealth Literature* 43.3 (2008): 25–42.

Sheppard, Robert. *Iain Sinclair.* Tavistock: Northcote House, 2007.

Silvera, Makeda. 'Man Royals and Sodomites: Some Thoughts on the Invisibility of Afro-Caribbean Lesbians.' *Feminist Studies* 18.3 (1992): 521–32.

Sinclair, Iain. *Hackney, That Rose-Red Empire.* London: Penguin, 2009.

—— *Lights Out for the Territory.* London: Granta, 1997.

—— *London Orbital.* London: Penguin, 2003.

Spillman, Rob. 'Binyavanga Wainaina.' *Bomb Magazine* 116. Summer 2011. http://bombsite.com/articles/5107

Tausky, Thomas E. '"Stories That Show Them Who They Are": An Interview with Patricia Grace.' *Australian & New Zealand Studies in Canada* 6 (1991): 90–102.

Trabelsi, Hechmi. 'Transcultural Writing: Ahdaf Soueif's Aisha as a Case Study.' 22 December 2012. http://english.chass.ncsu.edu/jouvert/v7i2/trabel.htm

Wigston, Nancy. 'Dead Girls: Lament for those Lost and Forgotten – Interview with Nancy Lee.' http://www.booksincanada.com/article_view.asp?id=1973. 2002.

Williams, Laura Anh. 'Foodways and Subjectivity in Jhumpa Lahiri's *Interpreter of Maladies*.' *MELUS* 32.4 (2007): 69–78.

Wolff, Christian. 'An Interview with Nalo Hopkinson.' *MaComere* 4 (2001): 26–36.

On the short story

Burgess, Anthony. 'On the Short Story.' *Journal of the Short Story in English* 2 (1984): 31–47.

Daymond, Margaret J. 'Complementary Oral and Written Narrative Conventions: Sindiwe Magona's Autobiography and Short Story Sequence.' *Journal of Southern African Studies* 28.2 (2002): 331–46.

Fallon, Erik et al., eds. *A Reader's Introduction to the Short Story in English.* London and Chicago: Fitzroy Dearborn, 2001.

Ghazoul, Ferial. 'Iraqi Short Fiction: The Unhomely at Home and Abroad.' *Journal of Arabic Literature* 35.1 (2004): 1–24.

Hafez, Sabry. *The Quest for Identities: The Development of the Modern Arabic Short Story.* London: Saqi Books, 2007.

Hanson, Clare, ed. *Re-Reading the Short Story.* London: Macmillan, 1989.

Head, Dominic. *The Modernist Short Story: A Study in Theory and Practice.* Cambridge University Press, 2009.

Hunter, Adrian. *The Cambridge Introduction to the Short Story in English.* Cambridge University Press, 2007.

Lewis, Bernard. *Land of Enchanters: Egyptian Short Stories from the Earliest Times to the Present Day.* London: Harvill, 1948.

Lounsberry, Barbara et al., eds. *The Tales We Tell: Perspectives on the Short Story.* Westport CT and London: Greenwood Press, 1998.

March-Russell, Paul. *The Short Story: An Introduction.* Edinburgh University Press, 2009.

May, Charles E., ed. *The New Short Story Theories.* Athens: Ohio University Press, 1994.

Memon, Muhammad Umar. 'Partition Literature: A Study of Intizar Husain.' *Modern Asian Studies* 14.3 (1980): 377–410.

O'Brien, Edward J. *The Advance of the American Short Story.* New York: Dodd, Meal, 1931.

O'Connor, Frank. *The Lonely Voice: A Study of the Short Story.* New York: Harper & Row, 1985.

Padamsee, Alex. 'Uncertain Partitions: Undecidability and the Urdu Short Story.' *Wasafiri* 53.1 (2008): 1–5.

Pattee, F.L. *The Development of the American Short Story.* New York: Biblo and Tannen, 1975.

Shaw, Valerie. *The Short Story: A Critical Introduction.* London: Longman, 1983.

Winther, Pers et al., eds. *The Art of Brevity: Excursions in Short Fiction Theory and Analysis.* Columbia: University of South Carolina Press, 2004.

On postcolonial literature and theory

Awadalla, Maggie. 'Generational Differences in Three Egyptian Women Writers: Finding a Common Ground.' *Journal of Postcolonial Writing* 47.4 (2011): 440–53.

Barber, Karin. *The Anthropology of Texts, Persons and Publics: Oral and Written Culture in Africa and Beyond.* Cambridge University Press, 2007.

Bhabha, Homi. 'Location, Intervention, Incommensurability: A Conversation with Homi Bhabha.' *Emergences* 1.1 (1989): 63–88.

Brah, Avtar. *Cartographies of Diaspora: Contesting Identities.* London: Routledge, 1996.

Chin, Timothy S. '"Bullers" and "Battymen": Contesting Homophobia in Black Popular Culture and Contemporary Caribbean Literature.' *Callaloo* 20.1 (1997): 127–41.

—— 'The Novels of Patricia Powell: Negotiating Gender and Sexuality Across the Disjunctures of the Caribbean Diaspora.' *Callaloo* 30.2 (2007): 533–45.

Deer, Glenn. 'Remapping Vancouver: Composing Urban Spaces in Contemporary Asian Canadian Writing.' *Canadian Literature* 199 (2008): 118–44.

Dodgson-Katiyo, Pauline, ed. *Rites of Passage in Postcolonial Women's Writing.* Amsterdam and New York: Rodopi, 2010.

Donnell, Alison. *Twentieth-Century Caribbean Literature.* London: Routledge, 2006.

Fanon, Frantz. *Black Skin, White Masks.* London: Pluto Press, 1986.

—— *The Wretched of the Earth.* Trans. Constance Farrington. London: Penguin, 2001.

Gopinath, Gayatri. *Impossible Desires: Queer Diasporas and South Asian Public Cultures.* Durham NC: Duke University Press, 2005.

Goyal, Yogita. *Romance, Diaspora, and Black Atlantic Literature.* Cambridge University Press, 2010.

Gupta, Akhil and James Ferguson. 'Beyond "Culture": Space, Identity, and the Politics of Difference.' *Cultural Anthropology* 7.1 (1992): 6–23.

Herrero, Dolores and Sonia Baelo-Allue, eds. *The Splintered Glass: Facets of Trauma in the Post-Colony and Beyond.* Amsterdam: Rodopi, 2011.

Hirschkind, Charles. *The Ethical Soundscape: Cassette Sermons and Islamic Counterpublics.* New York: Columbia University Press, 2006.

Jameson, Fredric. 'Third-World Literature in the Era of Multinational Capitalism.' *Social Text* 15 (1986): 65–88.

Jaquemond, Richard. *Conscience of the Nation: Writers, State and Society in Modern Egypt.* Trans. David Tresilian. Cairo: The American University in Cairo Press, 2008.

Keown, Michelle. *Pacific Islands Writing: The Postcolonial Literatures of Aotearoa/ New Zealand and the Pacific.* Oxford University Press, 2007.

King, Rosamond S. 'Re/Presenting Self and Other: Trans Deliverance in Caribbean Texts.' *Callaloo* 31.2 (2008): 581–99.

Lazarus, Neil. 'The South African Ideology: The Myth of Exceptionalism, the Idea of Renaissance.' *South Atlantic Quarterly* 103.4 (2004): 607–28.

McClintock, Anne. *Imperial Leather: Race, Gender and Sexuality in the Colonial Contest.* London: Routledge, 1995.

McLeod, John. *Postcolonial London: Rewriting the Metropolis.* Abingdon: Routledge, 2004.

Memon, Muhammad Umar. 'Urdu Fiction from India.' *Annual of Urdu Studies* 26 (2011): 236–8.

Meyer, Stefan G. *The Experimental Arabic Novel: Postcolonial Literary Modernism in the Levant.* New York: SUNY Press, 2001.

O'Brien, Anthony. *Against Normalization: Writing Radical Democracy in South Africa.* Durham NC and London: Duke University Press, 2001.

Punter, David. *Postcolonial Imaginings: Fictions of a New World Order.* Edinburgh University Press, 2000.

Rajan, Gita and Radhika Mohanram, eds. *Postcolonial Discourse and Changing Cultural Contexts: Theory and Criticism.* Westport CT: Greenwood Press, 1995.
Rooney, Caroline, 'Egyptian Literary Culture and Egyptian Modernity: Introduction.' *Journal of Postcolonial Writing* 47.4 (2011): 369–76.
Rutherford, Jonathan, ed. *Identity: Community, Culture, Difference.* London: Lawrence and Wishart, 1990.
Said, Edward. *Culture and Imperialism.* London: Chatto & Windus, 1993.
Scheub, Harold. 'A Review of African Oral Traditions and Literature.' *African Studies Review* 28.2/3 (1985): 1–72.
Spencer, Robert. *Cosmopolitan Criticism and Postcolonial Literature.* Basingstoke: Palgrave Macmillan, 2011.
Suleri, Sara. *The Rhetoric of English India.* Chicago University Press, 1992.
Walkowitz, Rebecca L. *Cosmopolitan Style: Modernism beyond the Nation.* New York: Columbia University Press, 2006.
Williams, Emily Allen. *Beyond the Canebrakes: Caribbean Women Writers in Canada.* Trenton NJ: Africa World Press, 2008.
Woodall, Richardine. '(Re)Thinking my "-Ness": Diaspora Caribbean Blacks in the Canadian Context.' *Shibboleths: A Journal of Comparative Theory* 1.2 (2007): 120–6.
Yancy, George. *Black Bodies, White Gazes.* Lanham MD: Rowman and Littlefield, 2008.
Young, Robert. *White Mythologies: Writing History and the West.* London: Routledge, 1990.

On general theory and criticism

Adorno, Theodor W. *The Jargon of Authenticity.* Trans. Knut Tarnowski and Frederic Will. London: Routledge, 2003.
Adorno, Theodor W. and Walter Benjamin. *The Complete Correspondence, 1928–1940.* Trans. Nicholas Walker, ed. Henri Lonitz. Cambridge: Polity Press, 1999.
Anderson, Benedict R. *Imagined Communities: Reflections on the Origin and Spread of Nationalism.* 1983. London: Verso, 1991.
Bal, Mieke. *Narratology: Introduction to the Theory of Narrative.* Trans. Christine Van Boheemen. University of Toronto Press, 2009.
Beauvoir, Simone de. *The Second Sex.* Trans. and ed. H.M. Parshley. London: Vintage, 1997.
Belsey, Catherine. *Critical Practice.* London: Methuen, 1980.
Benjamin, Walter. *Illuminations.* Trans. Harry Zohn, ed. Hannah Arendt. London: Fontana, 1992.
Berger, John. *About Looking.* London: Writers and Readers, 1980.
Bogue, Ronald. *Deleuze and Guattari.* London: Routledge, 1989.
Callaghan, Karen, ed. *Ideals of Feminine Beauty: Philosophical, Social, and Cultural Dimensions.* Westport CT: Greenwood Press, 1994.
Caruth, Cathy. *Unclaimed Experience: Trauma, Narrative, and History.* Baltimore and London: Johns Hopkins University Press, 1996.

Certeau, Michel de. *The Practice of Everyday Life.* Trans. Steven Rendall. Berkeley: University of California Press, 1984.

Chancy, Myriam J.A. 'Subversive Sexualities Revolutionizing Gendered Identities.' *Frontiers: A Journal of Women Studies* 29.1 (2008): 51–74.

Deleuze, Gilles. *The Logic of Sense.* Ed. Constantin V. Boundas, trans. Mark Lester with Charles Stivale. London: Athlone Press, 1990.

Deleuze, Gilles and Félix Guattari. *Kafka: Toward a Minor Literature.* Trans. Dana Polan. Minneapolis: University of Minnesota Press, 1986.

—— *A Thousand Plateaus.* Trans. Brian Massumi. London: Continuum, 2004.

—— 'What is a Minor Literature?' *Poetry and Cultural Studies: A Reader.* Ed. Maria Damon and Ira Livingston. Chicago: University of Illinois Press, 2009. 56–60.

Derrida, Jacques. *Of Grammatology.* Baltimore: Johns Hopkins University Press, 1973.

Felman, Shoshana and Dori Laub. *Testimony: Crises of Witnessing in Literature, Psychoanalysis and History.* New York: Routledge, 1992.

Freud, Sigmund. *Pelican Freud Library, 14.* Trans. James Strachey. Harmondsworth: Penguin, 1985.

—— *The Standard Edition of the Complete Psychological Works of Sigmund Freud, Volume IX.* Trans. James Strachey. London: Hogarth Press, 1959.

Genette, Gérard. *Narrative Discourse: An Essay in Method.* Trans. Jane E. Lewin. Ithaca NY: Cornell University Press, 1980.

Gilman, Sander. *Making the Body Beautiful: A Cultural History of Aesthetic Surgery.* Princeton University Press, 1999.

JanMohamed, Abdul R. and David Lloyd. 'The Nature and Context of Minor Literature.' *Cultural Critique* 7 (1987): 5–19.

Knabb, Ken, ed. and trans. *Situationist International Anthology.* Berkeley: Bureau of Public Secrets, 1981.

Koskimaa, Raine. 'The Challenge of Cybertext: Teaching Literature in the Digital World.' *Uoc.edu. Papers: e-journal on the Knowledge Society.* March 2007. http://www.uoc.edu/uocpapers/4/dt/eng/koskimaa.html

Kristeva, Julia. *Powers of Horror: An Essay on Abjection.* Trans. Leon S. Roudiez. New York: Columbia University Press, 1982.

Lacan, Jacques. *Ecrits: A Selection.* Trans. Alan Sheridan. London: Tavistock, 1977.

Lefebvre, Henri. *The Production of Space.* Trans. Donald Nicholson-Smith. Oxford: Blackwell, 1991.

Mulvey, Laura. *Visual and Other Pleasures.* Basingstoke: Macmillan, 1989.

Nicholson, Geoff. *The Lost Art of Walking: The History, Science, Philosophy and Literature of Pedestrianism.* New York: Riverhead, 2008.

Royle, Nicholas. *The Uncanny.* Manchester University Press, 2003.

Scarry, Elaine. *The Body in Pain.* Oxford University Press, 1985.

Solnit, Rebecca. *Wanderlust: A History of Walking.* London: Verso, 2001.

Todorov, Tzvetan. *The Fantastic: A Structural Approach to a Literary Genre.* Trans. Richard Howard. Ithaca NY: Cornell University Press, 1976.

Warner, Michael, ed. *Fear of a Queer Planet: Queer Politics and Social Theory.* Minneapolis: University of Minnesota Press, 1993.

Wright, Patrick. *On Living in an Old Country: The National Past in Contemporary Britain.* London: Verso, 1985.

Žižek, Slavoj. 'Shoplifters of the World Unite.' *London Review of Books.* 19 August 2011. http://www.lrb.co.uk/2011/08/19/slavoj-zizek/shoplifters-of-the-world-unite

—— *Welcome to the Desert of the Real.* London: Verso, 2002.

Index